"This book will end free speech!"

Only one of the more unusual comments made by the
following thirty publishers who rejected *Steal This Book*:

Random House ❧ *Delta* ❧ *Macmillan* ❧ *Signet* ❧ *Dell*
McGraw-Hill ❧ *Lyle Stuart* ❧ *Vintage* ❧ *Simon & Schuster*
William Morrow ❧ *Dial* ❧ *Bobbs-Merrill* ❧ *Prentice-Hall*
Scribner ❧ *World Books* ❧ *Bantam* ❧ *Atheneum* ❧ *Knopf*
Viking ❧ *New American Library* ❧ *Pocket Books* ❧ *Avon*
Ballantine ❧ *Dutton* ❧ *Lancer* ❧ *Putnam* ❧ *Coward-McCann*
Pantheon ❧ *Harper & Row* ❧ *Doubleday*

ALSO BY ABBIE HOFFMAN

Fuck the System

Revolution for the Hell of It

Woodstock Nation

Vote!
(with Jerry Rubin and Ed Sanders)

To america with Love: Letters from the Underground
(with Anita Hoffman)

The Autobiography of Abbie Hoffman
(formerly *Soon To Be a Major Motion Picture*)

Square Dancing in the Ice Age: Underground Writings

Steal This Urine Test
(with Jonathan Silvers)

The Best of Abbie Hoffman

STEAL THIS BOOK

Abbie Hoffman

Co-conspirator: Izak Haber
Accessory after the fact: Bert Cohen

With a new foreword by Lisa Fithian
and a new introduction by Al Giordano

THUNDER'S MOUTH PRESS
NEW YORK

STEAL THIS BOOK

Published by
Thunder's Mouth Press
An Imprint of Avalon Publishing Group, Inc.
245 West 17th Street, 11th floor
New York, NY 10011
www.thundersmouth.com

AVALON
publishing group incorporated

Copyright © 1996 Johanna Lawrenson, the Estate of Abbie Hoffman

With special thanks to Eliot Katz

First printing, February 2002

Library of Congress Cataloging-in-Publication Data:
Hoffman, Abbie.
Steal this book / by Abbie Hoffman ; co-conspirator, Izak Haber ; accessor
after the fact, Bert Cohen.
p. cm.
Includes bibliographical references.
ISBN-10: 1-56858-217-X
ISBN-13: 978-1-56858-217-7
1. Anarchism—United States. 2. Radicalism—United States. I. Haber, Izak.
II. Cohen, Bert. III. Title.
HX843.7.H64A3 1971a
335'.83dc20   95-4840
CIP

ABOUT THE AUTHOR

One of the most influential and recognizable American activists of the twentieth century, Abbie Hoffman was born in 1936 in Worcester, Massachusetts. After graduating from Brandeis University in 1959 with a degree in psychology, Hoffman became active in the civil rights movement of the early 1960s. Along with many others determined to make a difference, he traveled to Mississippi to help register voters. In New York City, he founded Liberty House, a crafts store that sold goods made by cooperatives in Mississippi.

In the mid-1960s, Hoffman became an organizer in both the growing U.S. counterculture and the anti-Vietnam War movement. In his autobiography, Hoffman wrote: "A semi-structure freak among the love children, I was determined to bring the hippie movement into a broader protest." With his unique political wit and humor, and his knowledge of television's growing importance in shaping social awareness, Hoffman helped organize such memorable acts of 1960s protest as dropping dollar bills onto the New York Stock Exchange in April 1967, and "levitating" the Pentagon in October of that same year. In 1968, together with his then-wife Anita, Jerry Rubin, Nancy Kurshan, Paul Krassner, and others, Hoffman founded the Youth International Party ("Yippies!") and began organizing a Festival of Life outside the Democratic Party's 1968 national convention in Chicago. Following what investigators later called a "police riot," Hoffman and seven others (the "Chicago 8") were put on trial in what became known as the Chicago Conspiracy Trial–"the most important political trial of this century," according to the ACLU.

In 1973, Hoffman went underground, and using aliases like Barry Freed still managed to stay politically active, working successfully with his "running mate" Johanna Lawrenson on Save the River!—a campaign which stopped the Army Corps of Engineers from dredging the St. Lawrence River for winter navigation. He emerged from the underground on national television in September of 1980 and continued his work, in his own words, as "an American dissident and a community organizer" throughout the 1980s. His projects included working with environmental groups throughout the Great Lakes and the Northeast, taking delegations to Central America to question American policies in the region, and opposing workplace drug testing in the U.S.

Student activists gained much from Hoffman's experience—the veteran organizer dedicated considerable time and energy to passing along the skills he had developed. Arrested in 1986 with Amy Carter and other students at the University of Massachusetts while protesting CIA recruitment on campus, Hoffman yet again shaped a precedent-setting trial. Hoffman and the students successfully pleaded not guilty using the "necessity defense," convincing a jury that their minor crime of trespass was needed to stop larger crimes of CIA covert actions in Central America and elsewhere. In his closing argument, Hoffman told the jury: "I grew up with the idea that democracy is not something you believe in, or a place you hang your hat, but it's something you do. You participate. If you stop doing it, democracy crumbles and falls apart. . . . Young people, if you participate, the future is yours." Throughout the '80s, Hoffman traveled extensively across the country speaking on college campuses and was the major adviser for such activist groups as National Student Convention '88 (at Rutgers University) and Student Action Union—helping student activists learn tools and strategies for building effective, democratically structured movements for social change.

Hoffman married three times, to Sheila Karklin, Anita Kushner, and Johanna Lawrenson. He had three children: Andrew and Ilya (with Sheila), and america (with Anita). He wrote seven books, including several classics that have since helped to define the culture and politics of his times.

Abbie Hoffman will forever be remembered as an activist who inspired young people to question authority, as an American radical who introduced humor and theatre into political organizing, and as an embodiment of a hopeful era in which millions of people throughout the globe embraced their democratic potential to help create a better world.

Abbie and Johanna Lawrenson (back row), wife, co-organizer, and running mate, flying back from Nicaragua with young activists Lisa Fithian and Al Giordano in 1985. Abbie and Johanna got together in Mexico in the spring of 1974 while Abbie was underground. From 1974 until Abbie's death in 1989, they worked on numerous environmental projects, Central American anti-intervention issues, and CIA campus recruitment policies, as well as other student movements. Today, Johanna is president of the Abbie Hoffman Activist Foundation.

Lisa Fithian worked with Abbie throughout the 1980s at Save the River! and against the U.S. war in Central America. A union organizer with the Justice for Janitors campaign during the 1990s, she now organizes non-violent direct action in the growing global justice movement. In November 2001, Lisa was arrested, searched and detained while preparing protests for the G-20 summit in Ottawa. She was released after two days because authorities "didn't have a case" against the non-violent activist.

DEAR ABBIE
A foreword by Lisa Fithian

Dear Abbie,

The world is as crazy as ever. We need you, man. Your spirit is alive and well, but for your thoughts, we'll have to settle for your words. *Steal This Book* is timeless.

Today we are dropping bombs on Afghanistan, while "elite" U.S. ground forces make raids against terrorism. It's retaliation. America got hit hard. Beyond anyone's conceivable imagination. Planes turned into bombs. The Twin Towers collapsed. The Pentagon in flames. Two of the most powerful symbols of capitalism and militarism left gaping and destroyed in a matter of moments. The foundations of the old order were cracked open.

Unbelievable destruction and death. Over fifty countries lost people. New York City will never be the same again. The compassion and awakening that has resulted gives hope. More than ever in my lifetime, people are asking why. People are reaching out to understand. People are questioning. Why did this happen? What is it about who we are as a people, as a nation, that has left us open to such hatred? What can we do now, in terms of national policy, to stop this cycle of violence?

Meanwhile the Government Inc. propaganda machine is in full-tilt boogie and the right-wing is doing everything it can to consolidate its power. Our democratic system is a joke. Would you believe the Supreme Court actually chose the last President? You know when his wife's nickname for him is STUPID, we're in trouble. Yup, baby George W., son of the ex-CIA director drug dealer and oil man, George Bush, is now the Prez. He can barely articulate a coherent sentence. Just makes you sick. Now he gets to wage a war in the name of fighting terrorism.

In reality this war is just another front in the capitalists' efforts to expand and control world markets, keep the rich, white boys in charge and squash an intensely amazing, growing resistance movement. A movement that captured the attention of the world on your birthday! November 30, 1999, over fifty thousand people swarmed through the streets with song and dance to shut down the Millennial Rounds of the World Trade Organization in Seattle.

This movement arose from the fact that corporations with the support of elected officials are selling our water, endlessly polluting our air, genetically modifying our food, clear-cutting our forests. For them, "developing" means "destroying." Global sweatshops are on the rise as corporations move about seeking the cheapest, unregulated, non-union labor. They are privatizing public services including health care, education, electricity and prisons. The prison-industrial complex, as it is now called, has led to the criminalization of an entire generation of youth, immigrants and anyone else who speaks out. The police state is on the rise and has been awarded millions of dollars over the past few years to expand its arsenal, including more and more of the "non-lethal" weapons.

The bureaucrats and capitalists are trying to write a global corporate constitution, enabling the countries/corporations of the Global North to rule the world. They have created an enforcement body called the World Trade Organization (WTO) that allows them to gain access and control all the resources, labor and policies of developing nations and–can you believe it–they call it "free" trade. They wanted all of us to accept its inevitability, that there is nothing anyone can do to stop it. They thought: "We'll open all borders to capital and we'll close them to people. No problem."

Little did they know, the people would not stand for their crap. Every time they try to meet, we are there. Any time they try to legislate a new policy, we are there. Any time they kill or wound one of our brothers or sisters, we are there. People have been and are continuing to rise up all around the world in ways we have never seen before.

Over eight hundred farmers in India burned a whole crop of genetically modified food to the ground. The nations of Africa and South America said to hell with intellectual property rights, we will make generic AIDS drugs even if it is a violation of your new global set of rules. Korean workers have taken over the auto plants. The people of India have resisted displacement from their land as a result of a massive dam project. The people of Cochabamba, Boliva, stopped Bechtel Corporation from privatizing their water. Squatting is spreading like wildfire and people all over are reclaiming public and private space. Now hundreds of thousands of people all around the world are in the streets again and again saying "no" to this war.

Their plan is not inevitable. This new war will not stop us. Everything is still up for grabs. And we are winning. This new resurgence of activism has dramatically changed the political landscape. As both a participant and student of this work, I know that the roots of this work are varied.

We don't have the language quite right yet. Is this an anticorporate globalization movement? Is this a global justice movement? Is it a peace and justice movement? Is this a popular movement? Is it one movement or many?

Convergence says it best. It is a coming together of all the strands of reform and resistance. It's an emerging culture or "counter-culture" that has again taken hold. Anarchist in its foundation. Rejecting the material-laden, consumer-driven, antidemocratic multinational corporate planet fuck that permeates everything around us.

In truth, resistance to this system of oppression and exploitation has been going on well over five hundred years. And one of the most exciting things today is the growing awareness of indigenous models of social organization and what they offer the world as an alternative.

The most recent upsurge can be traced back to January 1, 1994, when the Zapatista movement in Mexico named neoliberalism as the enemy. This came on the heels of the work of Reclaim the Streets out of the UK, which took action—and land—on the day that NAFTA went into effect. They e-mailed their poetic wisdom all over the network, using the resources of organizations such as Carnivals Against Capitalism and Earth

First, radical direct action movements that advance a new set of creative tools and tactics. The People's Global Action grew out of this convergence of energies and launched a movement transcending North and South that aims for the heart of the beast–transnational/global capital.

Going a little further back, however, the influences of the movements from the '50s and '60s are so present. The civil rights movement, the women's movement, the anti-war movement and yes, the Yippie! movement is especially alive and well in today's people's uprising.

And yet, Abbie, from a quality-of-life perspective, very little has gotten better. Same shit, different generation, really. But like you, we have hope. We see the potential, we see the opportunities, we believe that Another World Is Possible!

It starts with us and grows. Abbie, we are still dealing with the same problems you faced. Racism, sexism, homophobia, transphobia and class divisions are rampant. We have our ideological divides. We have our tactical differences. We have our egos, our arrogance, and our righteousness. But despite all of this, we are moving to a higher level of engagement and solidarity. We recognize our diversity as our strength. We recognize the power of direct democracy and direct action. To sustain ourselves, we recognize the importance of humor, beauty and celebration and we aim to bring our joy into the work and into the streets. As Emma Goldman said, "If I can't dance I don't want to be a part of the revolution!" and as Gandhi said, "Be the change you want to be." We have been learning from you all . . . and especially from you!

Your work, especially *Steal This Book*, offers a basic orientation. It is a precursor to the emerging culture of today. We don't have to re-invent the wheel; we just have to keep it rolling. It'd be great to have you here, but we've got your stories and we know you are with us on the ride. . . . Abbie, thank you.

Lisa Fithian
Los Angeles
October 2001

STILL A STEAL
An introduction by Al Giordano

He just had the idea it would be a good little gag to liberate this book from the bookstores. And we put "STEAL THIS BOOK" on the back cover of Woodstock Nation *and the Random House sales manager went bananas. "We can't do this!" The crazier he went, the more Abbie loved it.*

At that point Abbie decided that his next book was going to be called Steal This Book *and that's at least part of the reason that Random House refused to publish it. Also, they had a few problems with instructions for how to blow up things. I don't know if they ever noticed that the little Random House logo on* Woodstock Nation *was the little Random House being blown up.*

Chris Cerf
Editor, Random House
From *Steal This Dream,* by Larry Sloman

Abbie Hoffman was one hundred percent into anything he did. There was no such thing as halfway with Abbie. A task was either something worth going to jail for, worth dying for, or it was not worth doing.

Abbie had the same approach to writing books.

He wrote the introduction to *Steal This Book* from the Cook County Jail in 1970, from where he boasted that he was learning "the only rehabilitation possible—hatred of oppression."

Of all his seven published works, *Steal This Book* is the most widely read, the most notorious.

Revolution for the Hell of It, Woodstock Nation, or *The Autobiography of Abbie Hoffman* may be better literature, but *Steal This Book* was, and remains, the most memorable of his written works for the scandals it caused. It was also probably his most effectively radical creation because it was, largely, a how-to book.

"The title is ninety percent of the work," lamented the late independent filmmaker Jack Smith, but Abbie would somehow find another 110 percent, and that's what he put into *Steal This Book*. It was a "survival guide," exhaustively researched, to finding "Free food . . . free clothing and furniture . . . free transportation . . . free land . . . free housing . . . free education . . . free medical care . . . free communication . . . free play . . . free money . . . free dope . . ." to list the opening chapter titles. A lot of *Steal This Book* seems today—three decades later—so basic. Today, any fifteen-year-old knows how to do a lot of these things. And part of why they know it is because Abbie didn't just push the envelope—he ripped it open, and declared everybody the winner of the treasures inside. I was one of many early teens who used that book to make free long-distance telephone calls, to set off firecrackers and M-80s as "time bombs" with a simple wind-up alarm clock and some wires, and to otherwise cause trouble. Above all, *Steal This Book* was utilitarian and working-class. It dealt with the basic necessities of life: how to eat, to find clothing and shelter, and (we accept this, as Abbie did, as a basic human instinct) to have fun.

The press usually refers to Abbie as a "sixties radical" (his most famous book came out in the seventies, and his masterpiece political organizing work occurred in the eighties). And it associates Abbie, accurately, with the best-known causes of that era: particularly civil rights, opposition to the Vietnam War and the defense of the youth counterculture that today is thoroughly marketed to death by the same forces that once opposed it. Less spoken of today is the economic theory he laid out with his first pamphlet—titled *Fuck the System*—and in his first book, *Revolution for the Hell of It*. There must be, said Abbie, "a better means of exchange than money."

And that's what *Steal This Book* focused on: How to live free. He found cracks in the system, and he spotlighted them. Some long-accepted "facts of life"—that teenagers must obey their parents or other authorities, for example—simply fell by the wayside. Other "cracks" discovered by Abbie and his pals were later sealed up by the system. (Techniques revealed here for hacking public telephones have long been technologically corrected and thus are obsolete.) For that reason, many—but not all—of the tips in *Steal This Book* are obsolete. Hitchhiking, anyone? Ripping off automats? (Anyone under thirty know what an automat is?) Draft dodging? Yes, there was a military draft to avoid back then; there's not one today. Thank you, Abbie.

So when you get to the points of the book that are merely pointing out the obvious and you proclaim, "Jesus! He's telling us how to make a bookcase out of cinder blocks and lumber? How lame is that?" that is the precise moment to pay attention. On those pages, we see just how far behind American society was only a few decades ago. Kids didn't have the internet then to seek out the information that their parents and the media didn't want them to have. They didn't even have a hundred cable TV channels. They had three television networks in the major markets, and maybe one or two in rural areas. It was an atmosphere of total control. There was no Bart Simpson. But there was Abbie Hoffman, without whom Bart would not have been possible. And he was a living, breathing person who got clubbed over the head, spied on, infiltrated, outlawed, imprisoned, exiled, forgotten, rediscovered, forgotten again, and then, as Artaud wrote about Van Gogh, he was suicided by society. And a whole hell of a lot of what we take for granted today as basic "rights" are here and present because real human beings fought for them, and were persecuted for waging that fight. His era was full of heroes. But none were as effectively heroic as Abbie.

To read *Steal This Book* in the twenty-first century is an historical adventure. Thus, a little historic context may be helpful. When he wrote *Steal This Book*, Abbie had been on trial in Chicago in a conspiracy case—stemming from demonstrations outside the 1968 Democratic National Convention—in what the American Civil Liberties Union later called "the political trial of the century." He was America's most widely recognized radical, a media personality, an emblem, a symbol, a myth, and still—I may be giving away his secret weapon here—a human being, obviously so, to anyone who encountered him. He wasn't bigger than life, or better than it. He was, in a word, alive. And this was better and more exciting than the walking death that most public figures offered then and now.

Abbie recounts a dialogue between him and Random House publisher Jason Epstein when he was preparing to write *Steal This Book*. He described it in the May 1974 issue of *Harper's* magazine, in an essay titled "Steal This Author: In which the master of the rip-off learns that anything he can do, big business can do better." Abbie recounted that Epstein "roared with laughter" at the idea of writing a book no one would publish. "He had studied society," Abbie wrote of Jason. "He knew how fame was bottled and that infamy was even more saleable in the fanciful world of pop politics." The dialogue part is repeated here:

Jason: "What book are you going to do next?"

Abbie: "Jason, I'm going to write a book no one will publish. . . . I'm going to call it *Steal This Book*, and it'll be a handbook for living free, stealing, and making violent revolution. I'm going to take on the entire publishing industry. I want to test the limits of free speech."

Jason: "You'll lose, Abbie; everybody does in the end."

Abbie: "We'll see."

The result is now legend. After being rejected by thirty publishers, the book finally made it into print when Barney Rosset's Grove Press agreed to publish *Steal This Book*, and it was one of the most smashing successes in publishing history. Abbie turned the publishing of *Steal This Book* into a public teach-in on the entire industry of bestsellers.

"Grove estimated that half the book sales were made in New York City," wrote Abbie in his *Harper's* piece. "In Pittsburgh no stores carried the book. In Philadelphia only one store did, and it charged a dollar more than the cover price. No books were to be found in Boston when I took reporters on a tour. None in the San Francisco Bay area either. The entire

Doubleday chain of bookstores was boycotting the book. Vice-president George Hecht stated, 'We don't want to tell people to steal. We object only to the title. If it was titled *How to Live for Free*, we'd sell it.'"

Dotson Rader then reviewed it for the *New York Times Book Review* during John Leonard's disobedient tenure as editor, even as the *Times* refused to accept advertising for *Steal This Book*. "I clipped the review, wrote a check, and sent the *Times* its own review for an ad," recalled Abbie. The ad was rejected by the *Times*, that self-defined cathedral of freedom of the press.

Today, the lid is back on the book publishing industry. I can hardly find a book worth shoplifting in the chain stores. It's all formula. But if you like books, or once liked them, even if you end up paying for the new edition of *Steal This Book*, you're getting an authentic book . . . and that, in this age of corporate tyranny, is a steal.

Al Giordano
Somewhere in Mexico
November 2001

Al Giordano worked with Abbie Hoffman as a young political organizer in the 1980s. Today he is publisher of The Narco News Bulletin–www.narconews.com–*reporting on the drug war from Latin America. He is a free speech defendant currently being sued by billionaires in the* Drug War on Trial *case in New York City.*

steal this book

BY ABBIE HOFFMAN

Co-conspirator: Izak Haber

Accessory after the Fact: Bert Cohen

INTRODUCTION

It's perhaps fitting that I write this introduction in jail--that graduate school of survival. Here you learn how to use toothpaste as glue, fashion a shiv out of a spoon and build intricate communication networks. Here too, you learn the only rehabilitation possible—hatred of oppression.

Steal This Book is, in a way, a manual of survival in the prison that is Amerika. It preaches jailbreak. It shows you where and exactly how to place the dynamite that will destroy the walls. The first section—SURVIVE!—lays out a potential action program for our new Nation. The chapter headings spell out the demands for a free society. A community where the technology produces goods and services for whoever needs them, come who may. It calls on the Robin Hoods of Santa Barbara Forest to steal from the robber barons who own the castles of capitalism. It implies that the reader already is "ideologically set," in that he understands corporate feudalism as the only robbery worthy of being called "crime," for it is committed against the people as a whole. Whether the ways it describes to rip-off shit are legal or illegal is irrelevant. The dictionary of law is written by the bosses of order. Our moral dictionary says no heisting from each other. To steal from a brother or sister is evil. To *not* steal from the institutions that are the pillars of the Pig Empire is equally immoral.

Community within our Nation, chaos in theirs; that is the message of SURVIVE!

We cannot survive without learning to fight and that is the lesson in the second section. FIGHT! separates revolutionaries from outlaws. The purpose of part two is not to fuck the system, but destroy it. The weapons are carefully chosen. They are "home-made," in that they are designed for use in our unique electronic jungle. Here the uptown reviewer will find ample proof of our "violent" nature. But again, the dictionary of law fails us. Murder in a uniform is heroic, in a costume it is a crime. False advertisements win awards, forgers end up in jail. Inflated prices guarantee large profits while shoplifters are punished. Politicians conspire to create police riots and the victims are convicted in the courts. Students are gunned down and then indicted by suburban grand juries as the trouble-makers. A modern, highly mechanized army travels 9,000 miles to commit genocide against a small nation of great vision and then accuses its people of aggression. Slumlords allow rats to maim children and then complain of violence in the streets. Everything is topsy-turvy. If we internalize the language and imagery of the pigs, we will forever be fucked. Let me illustrate the point. Amerika was built on the slaughter of a people. That is its history. For years we watched movie after movie that demonstrated the white man's benevolence. Jimmy Stewart, the epitome of fairness, puts his arm around Cochise and tells how the Indians and the whites can live in peace if only both sides will be reasonable, responsible and rational (the three R's imperialists always teach the "natives"). "You will find good grazing land on the other side of the mountain," drawls the public relations man. "Take your people and go in peace." Cochise, as well as millions of youngsters in the balcony of learning, were being dealt off the bottom of the deck. The Indians should have offed Jimmy Stewart in every picture and we should have cheered ourselves hoarse. Until we understand the nature of institutional violence and how it manipulates values and mores to maintain the power of the few, we will forever be imprisoned in the caves of ignorance. When we conclude that bank robbers rather than bankers should be the trustees of the universities, then we begin to think clearly. When we see the Army Mathematics Research and Development Center and the Bank of Amerika as cesspools of violence, filling the minds of our young with hatred, turning one against another, then we begin to think revolutionary.

Be clever using section two; clever as a snake. Dig the spirit of the struggle. Don't get hung up on a sacrifice trip. Revolution is not about suicide, it is about life. With your fingers probe the holiness of your body and see that it was meant to live. Your body is just one in a mass of cuddly humanity. Become an internationalist and learn to respect all life. Make war on machines, and in particular the sterile machines of corporate death and the robots that guard them. The duty of a revolutionary is to make love and that means staying alive and free. That doesn't allow for cop-outs. Smoking dope and hanging up Che's picture is no more a committment than drinking milk and collecting postage stamps. A revolution in consciousness is an empty high without a revolution in the distribution of power. We are not interested in the greening of Amerika except for the grass that will cover its grave.

Section three — LIBERATE! — concerns itself with efforts to free stuff (or at least make it cheap) in four cities. Sort of a quicky U.S. on no dollars a day. It begins to scratch the potential for a national effort in this area. Since we are a nation of gypsies, dope on how to move around and dig in anywhere is always needed. Together we can expand this section. It is far from complete, as is the entire project. Incomplete chapters on how to identify police agents, steal a car, run day-care centers, conduct your own trial, organize a G.I. coffee house, start a rock and roll band and make neat clothes, are scattered all over the floor of the cell. The book as it now stands was completed in the late summer of 1970. For three months manuscripts made the rounds of every major publisher. In all, over 30 rejections occurred before the decision to publish the book ourselves was made, or rather made for us. Perhaps no other book in modern times presented such a dilemma. Everyone agreed the book would be a commercial success. But even greed had its limits, and the IRS and FBI following the manuscript with their little jive rap had a telling effect. Thirty "yeses" become thirty "noes" after "thinking it over." Liberals, who supposedly led the fight against censorship, talked of how the book "will end free speech."

Finally the day we were bringing the proofs to the printer, Grove consented to act as distributor. To pull a total solo trip, including distribution, would have been neat, but such an effort would be doomed from the start. We had tried it before and blew it. In fact, if anyone is interested in 4,000 1969 Yippie calendars, they've got a deal. Even with a distributor joining the fight, the battle will only begin when the books come off the press. There is a saying that "Freedom of the press belongs to those who own one." In past eras, this was probably the case, but now, high speed methods of typesetting, offset printing and a host of other developments have made substantial reductions in printing costs. Literally anyone is free to print their own works. In even the most repressive society imaginable, you can get away with some form of private publishing. Because Amerika allows this, does not make it the democracy Jefferson envisioned. Repressive tolerance is a real phenomenon. To talk of true freedom of the press, we must talk of the availability of the channels of communication that are designed to reach the entire population, or at least that segment of the population that might participate in such a dialogue. Freedom of the press belongs to those that own the distribution system. Perhaps that has always been the case, but in a mass society where nearly everyone is instantaneously plugged into a variety of national communications systems, wide-spread dissemination of the information is the crux of the matter. To make the claim that the right to print your own book means freedom of the press is to completely misunderstand the nature of a mass society. It is like making the claim that anyone with a pushcart can challenge Safeway supermarkets, or that any child can grow up to be president.

State legislators, librarians, PTA members, FBI agents, church-goers, and parents: a veritable legion of decency and order already is on the march. To get the book to you might be the biggest challenge we face. The next few months should prove really exciting.

Obviously such a project as *Steal This Book* could not have been carried out alone. Izak Haber shared the vision from the beginning. He did months of valuable research and contributed many of the survival techniques. Carole Ramer and Gus Reichbach of the New York Law Commune guided the book through its many stages. Anna Kaufman Moon did almost all the photographs. The cartoonists who have made contributions include Skip Williamson and Gilbert Sheldon. Tom Forcade, of the UPS, patiently did the editing. Bert Cohen of Concert Hall did the book's graphic design. Amber and John Wilcox set the type. Anita Hoffman and Lynn Borman helped me rewrite a number of sections. There are others who participated in the testing of many of the techniques demonstrated in the following pages and for obvious reasons have to remain anonymous. There were perhaps over 50 brothers and sisters who played particularly vital roles in the grard conspiracy. Some of the many others are listed on the following page. We hope to keep the information up to date. If you have comments, law suits, suggestions or death threats, please send them to: Dear Abbie P.O. Box 213, Cooper Station, New York, NY 10003. Many of the tips might not work in your area, some might be obsolete by the time you get to try them out, and many addresses and phone numbers might be changed. If the reader becomes a paticipating researcher then we will have achieved our purpose.

Watch for a special edition called *Steal This White House*, complete with blueprints of underground passages, methods of jamming the communications network and a detailed map of the celebrated room where according to Tricia Nixon, "Daddy loves to listen to Mantovanni records, turn up the air conditioner full blast, sit by the fireplace, gaze out the window to the Washington Monument and meditate on those difficult problems that face all the peoples of this world."

December, 1970
Cook County Jail
Chicago

"FREE SPEECH IS THE RIGHT TO SHOUT 'THEATER' IN A CROWDED FIRE."

— A YIPPIE PROVERB

AIDING AND ABETTING

Tim Leary, Tom, Geronimo, Pearl Paperhanger, Sonny, Pat Solomon, Allan Katzman, Jacob Kohn, Nguyen Van Troi, Susan, Marty, Andy, Ami, Marshall Bloom, Viva, Ben, Oanh, Robin Palmer, Mom and Dad, Janie Fonda, Jerry, Denis, LNS, Bernadine Dohrn, a wall in Harvard Square, Nancy, an anonymous stewardess, Shirley Wonderful, Roz, Gumbo, Janis, Jimi, Dylan Liberation Front, Jeannie, God Slick, John, David, Rusty, Barney, Richard, Denny, Ron Cobb, the entire Viet Cong, Sam Shephard, Ma Bell, Eric, David, Joe, Kim Agnew, the Partridge Family, Carol, Alan Ginsburg, america, Vali, Julius Lester, Lenny Bruce, Hack, Billy, Paul, Willy, Colleen, Sid, Johnny Appleseed, the Rat, Craig, Che, Willie Sutton, Wanda, EVO, Jeff, Crazy Horse, Casey, Bobby, Alice, Mao, Rip, Ed, Bob, Gay Liberation Front, WPAX, Frank Dudock, Manny, Mungo, Lottie, Rosemary, Marshall, Rennie, Judy, Jennifer, Mr. Martin, Keith, Madame Binh, Mike, Eleanor, Dr. Spock, Afeni, Candice, the Tupamaros, Berkeley Tribe, Gilbert Sheldon, Stanley Kubrick, Sam, Anna, Skip Williamson, UPS, Andy Stapp, the Yippies, Richard Brautigan, Jano, Carlos Marighella, the Weathermen, Julius Jennings Hoffman, Quentin, the inmates of TIER A-1 Cook County Jail, Houdini, 37, Rosa Luxemberg, the Kent 25, the Chicago 15, the New York 21, the Motor City 3, the Indianapolis 500, Jack, Joan, Malcolm X, Mayakovsky, Dotson, R. Crumb, Daniel Clyne, Justin, The FBI Top 10 (now 16), Unis, Dana, Jim Morrison, Brian, John, Gus, Ruth, Nancy Unger, Pun, Jomo, Peter, Mark Rudd, Billy Kunstler, Genie, Ken, the Law Commune, Paula, Robby, Terry, Dianna, Angela, Ted, Phil, Jefferson Airplane, Len, Tricky Prickers, the Berrigans, Stu, Rayanne, J.B., Jonathan Jackson, the Armstrong Brothers, Homer, Sharon, Fred Hampton, Jean Jacques Lebel, A. H. Maslow, Hanoi Rose, Sylvia, Fellini, Amaru, Ann Fettamen, Artaud, Bert, Merrill, Lynne, Anita, and last but not least to Spiro what's his name who provided the incentive.

TABLE OF DISCONTENTS

SURVIVE!

FREE FOOD

RESTAURANTS

In a country such as Amerika, there is bound to be a hell-of-a-lot of food lying around just waiting to be ripped off. If you want to live high off the hog without having to do the dishes, restaurants are easy pickings. In general, many of these targets are easier marks if you are wearing the correct uniform. You should always have one suit or fashionable dress outfit hanging in the closet for the proper heists. Specialized uniforms, such as nun and priest garb, can be most helpful. Check out your local uniform store for a wide range of clothes that will get you in, and especially out, of all kinds of stores. Every movement organization should have a prop and costume department.

In every major city there are usually bars that cater to the Now Generation type riff-raff, trying to hustle their way up the escalator of Big Business. Many of these bars have a buffet or hors-d'oeuvres served free as a come-on to drink more mindless booze. Take a half-empty glass from a table and use it as a prop to ward off the anxious waitress. Walk around sampling the free food until you've had enough. Often, there are five or six such bars in close proximity, so moving around can produce a delightful "street smorgasbord." Dinner usually begins at 5:00 PM.

If you are really hungry, you can go into a self-service cafeteria and finish the meal of someone who left a lot on the plate. Self-service restaurants are usually good places to cop things like mustard, ketchup, salt, sugar, toilet paper, silverware and cups for home use. Bring an empty school bag and load up after you've cased the joint. Also, if you can stomach the food, you can use slugs at the automat. Finishing leftovers can be worked in even the fanciest of restaurants. When you are seated at a place where the dishes still remain, chow-down real quick. Then after the waitress hands you the menu, say you have to meet someone outside first, and leave.

There are still some places where you can get all you can eat for a fixed price. The best of these places are in Las Vegas. Sew a plastic bag onto your tee-shirt or belt and wear a loose-fitting jacket or coat to cover any noticeable bulge. Fried chicken is the best and the easiest to pocket, or should we say bag. Another trick is to pour your second free cup of hot coffee into the plastic bag sewed inside your pocket and take it with you.

At large take-out stands you can say you or your brother just picked up an order of fifteen hamburgers or a bucket of chicken, and got shorted. We have never seen or heard of anybody getting turned down using this method. If you want to get into a grand food heist from take-out stands, you can work the following nervy bit: from a pay phone, place an order from a large delivery restaurant. Have the order sent to a nearby apartment house. Wait a few minutes in the booth after you've hung up, as they sometimes call back to confirm the order. When the delivery man goes into the apartment house to deliver the order, you can swipe the remaining orders that are still in his truck.

In fancy sit-down restaurants, you can order a large meal and halfway through the main course, take a little dead cockroach or a piece of glass out of your pocket and place it deftly on the plate. Jump up astonished and summon the headwaiter. "Never have I been so insulted. I could have been poisoned" you scream, slapping down

3

the napkin. You can refuse to pay and leave, or let the waiter talk you into having a brand new meal on the house for this terrible inconvenience.

In restaurants where you pay at the door just before leaving, there are a number of free-loading tricks that can be utilized. After you've eaten a full meal and gotten the check, go into the restroom. When you come out go to the counter or another section of the restaurant and order coffee and pie. Now you have two bills. Simply pay the cheaper one when you leave the place. This can be worked with a friend in the following way. Sit next to each other at the counter. He should order a big meal and you a cup of coffee. Pretend you don't know each other. When he leaves, he takes your check and leaves the one for the large meal on the counter. After he has paid the cashier and left the restaurant, you pick up the large check, and then go into the astonishment routine, complaining that somebody took the wrong check. You end up only paying for your coffee. Later, meet your partner and reverse the roles in another place.

In all these methods, you should leave a good tip for the waiter or waitress, especially with the roach-in-the-plate gambit. You should try to avoid getting the employees in trouble or screwing them out of a tip.

One fantastic method of not only getting free food but getting the best available is the following technique that can be used in metropolitan areas. Look in a large magazine shop for gourmet digests and tourist manuals. Swipe one or two and copy down a good name from the masthead inside the cover. Making up a name can also work. Next invest $5.00 to print business cards with the

name of the magazine and the new "associate editor." Call or simply drop into a fancy restaurant, show a copy of the magazine and present the manager with your card. They will insist that the meal be on the house.

Great places to get fantastic meals are weddings, bar-mitzvahs, testimonials and the like. The newspaper society sections have lists of weddings and locations. If your city has a large Jewish population, subscribe to the newspaper that services the Jewish community. There are extensive lists in these papers of family occasions where tons of good food is served. Show up at the back of the synagogue a few hours after the affair has begun with a story of how you'd like to bring some leftovers of "good Jewish food" back to your fraternity or sorority. If you want to get the food served to you out front, you naturally have to disguise yourself to look straight. Remarks such as, "I'm Marvin's cousin," or learning the bride's name, "Gee, Dorothy looks marvelous" are great. Lines like "Betty doesn't look pregnant" are frowned upon. A man and woman team can work this free-load much better than a single person as they can chatter back and forth while stuffing themselves.

If you're really into a classy free meal, and you are in a city with a large harbor, check out the passenger ship section in the back pages of the newspaper. There you find the schedule of departures for ocean cruises. Most trips (these kind, anyway) begin with a fantastic bon voyage party on board ship. Just walk on a few hours before departure time and start swinging. Champagne, caviar, lobster, shrimp and more, all as free as the open seas. If you get really bombed and miss getting off, you can also wiggle a ride across the ocean. You get sent back as soon as you hit the other side, but it's a free ocean cruise. You should have a pretty good story ready to go, or you might end up rowing in the galley.

Another possibility for getting a free meal is to go down to the docks and get friendly with a sailor. He can often invite you for dinner on board ship. Foreign sailors are more than glad to meet friends and you can get great foreign dinners this way.

FOOD PROGRAMS

In Amerika, there is a national food stamp program that unfortunately is controlled by the states. Many states, for racist reasons, do not want to make it too available or to publicize the fact that it even exists. It is a much better deal than the food program connected with welfare, because you can use the stamps to buy any kind of food. The only items excluded are tobacco products and alcoholic beverages. In general, you can qualify if you earn less than $165 per month; the less you earn, the more stamps you can receive. There is minimal hassle involved once you get by the first hurdle. Show up at your local food stamp office, which can be found by calling the Welfare Department in your city. Make an appointment to see a representative for your area. They will tell you to bring all sorts of receipts, but the only thing you need are a few rent stubs for the most recent months. An array of various receipt books is a nice supplement to one's prop room. If the receipts are for a high rent, tell them you rent a room from a

group of people and eat separately. They really only want to prove that you have cooking facilities. Once you get the stamps, you can pick them up regularly. Some states even mail them to your pad. You can get up to a hundred dollars worth of free purchases a month per person in the most liberal states.

Large amounts of highly nutritional food can be gotten for as little as three cents per meal from a non-profit organization called Multi-Purpose Food for Millions Foundation, Inc., 1800 Olympic Ave., Santa Monica, California. Write and they will send you details.

SUPERMARKETS

Talking about food in Amerika means talking about supermarkets—mammoth neon lighted streets of food packaged to hoodwink the consumers. Many a Yippie can be found in the aisles, stuffing his pockets with assorted delicacies. We have been shoplifting from supermarkets on a regular basis without raising the slightest suspicion, ever since they began.

We are not alone, and the fact that so much stealing goes on and the supermarkets still bring in huge profits shows exactly how much overcharging has occurred in the first place. Supermarkets, like other businesses, refer to shoplifting as "inventory shrinkage." It's as if we thieves were helping Big Business reduce weight. So let's view our efforts as methods designed to trim the economy and push forward with a positive attitude.

Women should never go shopping without a large handbag. In those crowded aisles, especially the ones with piles of cases, all sorts of goodies can be transferred

Well, it's 2 for 39 cents and 1 for . . . .

from shopping cart to handbag. A drop bag can be sewn inside a trench coat, for more efficient thievery. Don't worry about the mirrors; attendants never look at them. Become a discriminating shopper and don't stuff any of the cheap shit in your pockets.

Small bottles and jars often have the same size cap as the larger expensive sizes. If they have the price stamped on the cap, switch caps, getting the larger size for the cheaper price. You can empty a pound box of margarine and fill it with sticks of butter. Small narrow items can be hidden in the middle of rolls of toilet paper. Larger supermarkets sell records. You can sneak two good LP's into one of those large frozen' pizza boxes. In the produce department, there are bags for fruit and vegetables. Slip a few steaks or some lamb chops into the bottom of a large brown bag and pile some potatoes on top. Have a little man in the white coat weigh the bag, staple it and mark the price. With a black crayon you can mark your own prices, or bring your own adhesive price tags.

It's best to work shoplifting in the supermarket with a partner who can act as look-out and shield you from the eyes of nosy employees, shoppers and other crooks trying to pick up some pointers. Work out a prearranged set of signals with your partner. Diversions, like knocking over displays, getting into fist fights with the manager, breaking plate glass windows and such are effective and even if you don't get anything they're fun. Haven't you always wanted to knock over those carefully constructed nine-foot pyramids of garbage?

You can walk into a supermarket, get a few items from the shelves, and walk around eating food in the aisles. Pick up some cherries and eat them. Have a spoon

Rice.

in your pocket and open some yogurt. Open a pickle or olive jar. Get some sliced meat or cheese from the delicatessen counter and eat it up, making sure to ditch the wrapper. The cart full of items, used as a decoy, can just be left in an aisle before you leave the store.

Case the joint before pulling a big rip-off. Know the least crowded hours, learn the best aisles to be busy in, and check out the store's security system. Once you get into shoplifting in supermarkets, you'll really dig it. You'll be surprised to learn that the food tastes better.

Large scale thievery can best be carried out with the help of an employee. Two ways we know of work best. A woman can get a job as a cashier and ring up a small bill as her brothers and sisters bring home tons of stuff.

The method for men involves getting a job loading and unloading trucks in the receiving department. Some accomplices dressed right can just pull in and, with your help, load up on a few cases. Infiltrating an employee into a store is probably the best way to steal. Cashiers, sales clerks, shippers, and the like are readily available jobs with such high turnover and low pay that little checking on your background goes on. Also, you can learn what you have to do in a few days. The rest of the week, you can work out ways to clean out the store. After a month or so of action you might want to move on to another store before things get heavy. We know one woman working as a cashier who swiped over $500 worth of food a week. She had to leave after a month because her boss thought she was such an efficient cashier that he insisted on promoting her to a job that didn't have as many fringe benefits for her and her friends.

Large chain stores like Safeway throw away day-old vegetables, the outer leaves of lettuce, celery and the like. This stuff is usually found in crates outside the back of the building. Tell them you're working with animals at the college labs, or that you raise guinea pigs. They might even get into saving them for you, but if they don't just show up before the garbage is collected, (generally early in the morning), and they'll let you cart away what you want.

Dented cans and fruit can often be gotten free, but certainly at a reduced rate. They are still as good as the undamaged ones. So be sure to dent all your cans before you go to the cashier.

Look up catering services and businesses that service factories and office buildings with ready-made sandwiches. Showing up at these places at the right times (catering services on late Sunday night and sandwich dealers at 5:00 PM on weekdays) will produce loads of good food. Legally, they have to dispose of the food that's left over. They would be more than happy to give it to you if you spin a good story.

Butchers can be hustled for meat scraps with a "for my dog" story, and bakeries can be asked for day-old rolls and bread.

WHOLESALE MARKETS

Large cities all have a wholesale fruit and vegetable area where often the workers will give you tons of free food just for the asking. Get a good story together. Get some church stationery and type a letter introducing yourself "to whom it may concern," or better still, wear some clerical garb. Orchards also make good pickings just after the harvest has been completed.

Factories often will give you a case or two of free merchandise for a "charitable" reason. Make some calls around town and then go pick up the stuff at the end of the week. A great idea is to get a good list of a few hundred large corporations around the country by looking up their addresses at the library. *Poor's Register of Companies, Directors and Executives* has the most complete list. Send them all letters complaining about how the last box of cereal was only half full, or you found a dead fly in the can of peaches. They often will send you an ample supply of items just to keep you from complaining to your friends or worse, taking them to court. Often you can get stuff sent to you by just telling them how good their product is compared to the trash you see nowadays. You know the type of letter — "Rice Krispies have had a fantastic effect on my sexual prowess," or "Your frozen asparagus has given a whole new meaning to my life." In general though, the nasties get the best results.

Slaughterhouses usually have meat they will give away. They are anxious to give to church children's programs and things like that. In most states, there is a law that if the slab of meat touches the ground, they have to throw it away. Drop around meat houses late in the day and trip a few trucks.

Fishermen always have hundreds of pounds of fish that have to be thrown out. You can have as much as you can cart away, generally just for the asking. Boats come in late in the afternoon and they'll give you some of the catch, or you can go to the markets early in the morning when the fishing is best.

These methods of getting food in large quantities can only be appreciated by those who have tried it. You will be totally baffled by the unbelievable quantities of food that will be laid on you and with the ease of panhandling.

Investing in a freezer will allow you to make bi-weekly or even monthly trips to the wholesale markets and you'll get the freshest foods to boot. Nothing can beat getting it wholesale for free. Or is it free for wholesale? In any event, "bon appetit."

FOOD CONSPIRACIES

Forming a food cooperative is one of the best ways to promote solidarity and get every kind of food you need to survive real cheap. It also provides a ready-made bridge for developing alliances with blacks, Puerto Ricans, chicanos and other groups fighting our common oppressor on a community level.

Call a meeting of about 20 communes, collectives or community organizations. Set up the ground rules. There should be a hard-core of really good hustlers that serve as the shopping or hunting party and another group of people who have their heads together enough to keep records and run the central distribution center. Two or three in each group should do it. They can get their food free for the effort. Another method is to rotate the activity among all members of the conspiracy. The method you choose depends upon your politics and whether you favor a division of labor or using the food conspiracy as a training for collective living. Probably a blend of the two is best, but you'll have to hassle that out for yourself. The next thing to agree upon is how the operation and all the shit you get will be paid for. This is dependent on a number of variables, so we'll map out one scheme and you can modify it to suit your particular situation. Each member of every commune could be assessed a fee for joining. You want to get together about $2,000, so at 200 members, this is ten bucks a piece. After the joining fee, each person or group has to pay only for the low budget food they order, but some loot is needed to get things rolling. The money goes to getting a store front or garage, a cheap truck, some scales, freezers, bags, shelving, chopping blocks, slicer and whatever else you need. You can get great deals by looking in the classified ads of the local overground newspaper and checking for restaurants or markets going out of business. Remember the idea of a conspiracy is to get tons of stuff at real low prices or free into a store front, and then break it down into smaller units for each group and eventually each member. The freezers allow you to store perishables for a longer time.

The hunting party should be well acquainted with how to rip off shit totally free and where all the best deals are to be found. They should know what food is seasonal and about nutritional diets. There is a lot to learn, such as where to get raw grains in 100 pound lots and how to cut up a side of beef. A good idea is to get a diet freak to give weekly talks in the store front. There can also be cooking lessons taught, especially to men, so women can get out of the kitchen.

Organizing a community around a basic issue of survival, such as food, makes a lot of nitty gritty sense. After your conspiracy gets off the ground and looks permanent, you should seek to expand it to include more members and an emergency food fund should be set up in case something happens in the community. There should also be a fund whereby the conspiracy can sponsor free community dinners tied into celebrations. Get it together and join the fight for a world-wide food conspiracy. Seize the steak!

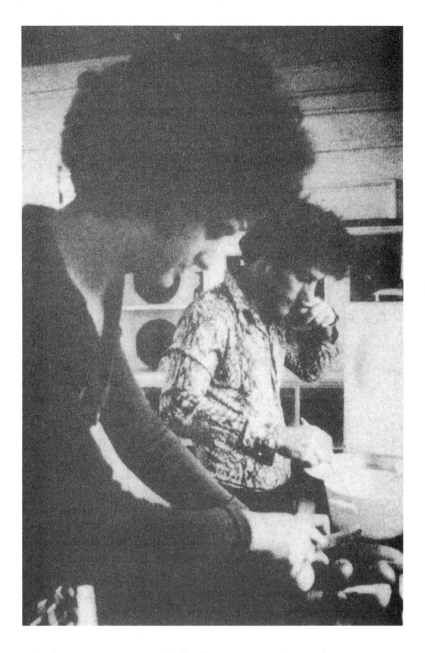

Let's see now, one middle finger, a teaspoon of snot and ....

CHEAP CHOW

There are hundreds of good paperback cook books with nutritional cheap recipes available in any bookstore. Cooking is a vastly overrated skill. The following are a few all-purpose dishes that are easy to make, nutritional and cheap as mud pies. You can add or subtract many of the ingredients for variety.

Road Hog Crispies

½ c millet	2 c raw oats
½ c cracked wheat	1 c rye flakes
½ c buckwheat groats	1 c wheat flakes
½ c wheat germ	1 c dried fruits and/or nuts
½c sunflower seeds	3 tbs soy oil
¼ c sesame seeds	1 c honey
2 tbs cornmeal	

Boil the millet in a double boiler for 1/2 hour. Mix in a large bowl all the ingredients including the millet. The soy oil and honey should be heated in a saucepan over a low flame until bubbles form. Spread the cereal in a baking pan and cover with the honey syrup. Toast in oven until brown. Stir once or twice so that all the cereal will be toasted. Serve plain or with milk. Refrigerate portion not used in a covered container. Enough for ten to twenty people. Make lots and store for later meals. All these ingredients can be purchased at any health store in a variety of quantities. You can also get natural sugar if you need a sweetener. If bought and made in quantity, this fantastically healthy breakfast food will be cheaper than the brand name cellophane that passes for cereal.

Whole Earth Bread

1 c oats, corn meal, or wheat germ	2 tsp salt
1½ c water (warm)	2 egg yolks
¼ c sugar (raw is best)	4 c flour
1 pkg active dry yeast	1/3 c corn oil
1 c dry milk	or butter

Stir lightly in a large bowl the oats, cornmeal or wheat germ (depending on the flavor bread you desire), the water and sugar. Sprinkle in the yeast and wait 10 minutes for the yeast to do its thing. Add salt, egg yolks, corn oil and dry milk. Mix with a fork. Blend in the flour. The dough should be dry and a little lumpy. Cover with a towel and leave in a warm place for a half hour. Now mash, punch, blend and kick the dough and return it covered to its warm place. The dough will double in size. When this happens, separate the dough into two even masses and mash each one into a greased bread (loaf) pan. Cover the pans and let sit until the dough rises to the top of the pans. Bake for 40-45 minutes in a 350 degree oven that has not been pre-heated. A shallow tray of water in the bottom of the oven will keep the bread nice and moist. When you remove the pans from the oven, turn out the bread into a rack and let it cool off. Once you get the hang of it, you'll never touch ready-made bread, and it's a gas seeing yeast work.

Street Salad

Salad can be made by chopping up almost any variety of vegetables, nuts and fruits including the stuff you panhandled at the back of supermarkets; dandelions, shav, and other wild vegetables; and goods you ripped off inside stores or from large farms. A neat fresh dressing consists of one part oil, two parts wine vinegar, 2 finely chopped garlic cloves, salt and pepper. Mix up the ingredients in a bottle and add to the salad as you serve it. Russian dressing is simply mayonnaise and ketchup mixed.

Yippie Yogurt

Yogurt is one of the most nutritional foods in the world. The stuff you buy in stores has preservatives added to it reducing its health properties and increasing the cost. Yogurt is a bacteria that spreads throughout a suitable culture at the correct temperature. Begin by going to a Turkish or Syrian restaurant and buying some yogurt to go. Some restaurants boast of yogurt that goes back over a hundred years. Put it in the refrigerator.

Now prepare the culture in which the yogurt will multiply. The consistency you want will determine what you use. A milk culture will produce thin yogurt, while sweet cream will make a thicker batch. It's the butter fat content that determines the consistency and also the number of calories. Half milk and half cream combines the best of both worlds. Heat a quart of half and half on a low flame until just before the boiling point and remove from the stove. This knocks out other bacteria that will compete with the yogurt. Now take a tablespoon of the yogurt you got from the restaurant and place it in the bottom of a bowl (not metal). Now add the warm liquid. Cover the bowl with a lid and wrap tightly with a heavy towel. Place the bowl in a warm spot such as on top of a radiator or in a sunny window. A turned-off oven with a tray of boiling water placed in it will do well. Just let the bowl sit for about 8 hours (overnight). The yogurt simply grows until the whole bowl is yogurt. Yippie! It will keep in the refrigerator for about two weeks before turning sour, but even then, the bacteria will produce a fresh batch of top quality. Remember when eating it to leave a little to start the next batch. For a neat treat add some honey and cinnamon and mix into the yogurt before serving. Chopped fruit and nuts are also good.

Rice and Cong Sauce

1 c brown rice	vegetables
2 c water	2½ tbs soy sauce
tsp salt	

Bring the water to a boil in a pot and add the salt and rice. Cover and reduce flame. Cooking time is about 40 minutes or until rice has absorbed all the water. Meanwhile, in a well-greased frying pan, saute a variety of chopped vegetables you enjoy. When they become soft and brownish, add salt and 2 cups of water. Cover with a lid and lower flame. Simmer for about 40 minutes, peeking to stir every once in a while. Then add 2 1/2 tbs of soy sauce, stir and cook another 10 minutes. The rice should be just cooling off now, so add the sauce to the top of it and serve. Great for those long guerrilla hikes. This literally makes up almost the entire diet of the National Liberation Front fighter.

Weatherbeans

1 lb red kidney beans	2 tbs parsley (chopped)
2 quarts water	½ lb pork, smoked sausage
1 onion (chopped)	or ham hock
1 tbs celery (chopped)	1 lg bay leaf
1 tsp garlic (minced)	salt to season

Rinse the beans, then place in covered pot and add water and salt. Cook over low flame. While cooking, chop up meat and brown in a frying pan. Add onion, celery, garlic and parsley and continue sauteing over low flame. Add the pieces of meat, vegetables and bay leaf to the beans and cook covered for 1 1/2 to 2 hours. It may be necessary to add more water if the beans get too dry. Fifteen minutes before beans are done, mash about a half cup of the stuff against the side of the pan to thicken the liquid. Pour the beans and liquid over some steaming rice that you've made by following the directions above. This should provide a cheap nutritional meal for about 6 people.

Hedonist's Deluxe

2 lobsters	2 qts water
seaweed	¼ lb butter

Steal two lobsters, watching out for the claw thingies. Beg some seaweed from any fish market. Cop the butter using the switcheroo method described in the Supermarket section above. When you get home, boil the water in a large covered pot and drop in the seaweed and then the lobsters. Put the cover back on and cook for about 20 minutes. Melt the butter in a sauce pan and dip the lobster pieces in it as you eat. With a booster box, described later, you'll be able to rip off a bottle of vintage Pouilly-Fuisse in a fancy liquor store. Really, rice is nice but . . .

At these prices who can afford not to

FREE CLOTHING & FURNITURE

FREE CLOTHING

If shoplifting food seems easy, it's nothing compared to the snatching of clothing. Shop only the better stores. Try things on in those neat little secluded stalls. The less bulky items, such as shirts, vests, belts and socks can be tied around your waist or leg with large rubber bands if needed. Just take a number of items in and come out with a few less.

In some cities there are still free stores left over from the flower power days. Churches often have give-away clothing programs. You can impersonate a clergyman and call one of the large clothing manufacturers in your area. They are usually willing to donate a case or two of shirts, trousers or underwear to your church raffle or drive to dress up skid row. Be sure to get your sizes. Tell them "your boy" will pick up the blessed donation and you'll mention his company in the evening prayers.

If you notice people moving from an apartment or house, ask them if they'll be leaving behind clothing. They usually abandon all sorts of items including food, furniture and books. Offer to help them carry out stuff if you can keep what they won't be taking.

Make the rounds of a fancy neighborhood with a truck and some friends. Ring doorbells and tell the person who answers that you are collecting wearable clothing for the "poor homeless victims of the recent tidal wave in Quianto, a small village in Saudi Arabia." You get the pitch. Make it food and clothing, and say you're with a group called *Heartline for Decency.* A phony letter from a church might help here.

The Salvation Army does this, and you can pick up

clothes from them at very cheap prices. You can get a pair of snappy casual shoes for 25 cents in many bowling alleys by walking out with them on your feet. If you have to leave your shoes as a deposit, leave the most beat-up pair you can find.

Notice if your friends have lost or gained weight. A big change means a lot of clothes doing nothing but taking up closet space. Show up at dormitories when college is over for the summer or winter season. Go to the train or bus stations and tell them you left your raincoat, gloves or umbrella when you came into town. They'll take you to a room with thousands of unclaimed items. Pick out what you like. While there, notice a neat suitcase or trunk and memorize the markings. Later a friend can claim the item. There will be loads of surprises in any suitcase. We have a close friend who inherited ten kilos of grass this way.

Large laundry and dry cleaning chains usually have thousands of items that have gone unclaimed. Manufacturers also have shirts, dresses and suits for rock-bottom prices because of a crooked seam or other fuck-up. Stores have reduced rates on display models. Mannequins are mostly all size 40 for men and 10 for women. Size 7 1/2 is the standard display size for men's shoes. If you are these sizes, you can get top styles for less than half price.

SANDALS

The Vietnamese and people throughout the Third World make a fantastically durable and comfortable pair of sandals out of rubber tires. They cut out a section of the outer tire (trace around the outside of the foot with a piece of chalk) which when trimmed forms the sole. Next 6 slits are made in the sole so the rubber straps can be criss-crossed and slid through the slits. The straps are made out of inner tubing. No nails are needed. If you have wide feet, use the new wide tread low profiles. For hard going, try radials. For best satisfaction and quality steal the tires off a pig car or a government limousine.

Let's face it, if you really are into beating the clothing problem, move to a warm climate and run around naked. Skin is absolutely free, and will always be in style. Speaking of style, the midi and the maxi have obvious advantages when it comes to shoplifting and transporting weapons or bombs.

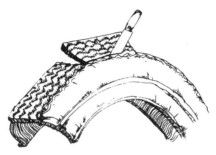

CUT A GOOD-SIZED HUNK OF TIRE

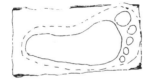

TRACE YOUR FOOT, LEAVING ABOUT ¼" EXTRA

STRAPS MADE FROM INNER TUBE

FREE FURNITURE

Apartment lobbies are good for all kinds of neat furniture. If you want to get fancy about it, rent a truck (not one that says U-HAUL-IT or other rental markings) and make the pick-up with moving-man-type uniforms. When schools are on strike and students hold seminars and debate into the night, Yippies can be found going through the dorm lobbies and storage closets hauling off couches, desks, printing supplies, typewriters, mimeos, etc. to store in secret underground nests. A nervy group of Yippies in the Midwest tried to swipe a giant IBM 360 computer while a school was in turmoil. All power to those that bring a wheelbarrow to sit-ins.

Check into a high-class hotel or motel remembering to dress like the wallpaper. Carry a large dummy suitcase with you and register under a phony name. Make sure you and not the bellboy carry this bag. Use others as a.decoy. When you get inside the room, grab everything you can stuff in the suitcase: radio, T.V. sets (even if it has a special plug you can cut it with a knife and replace the cord), blankets, toilet paper, glasses, towels, sheets, lamps, (forget the imitation Winslow Homer on the wall) a Bible, soap and toss rugs. Before you leave (odd hours are best) hang the DO NOT DISTURB sign on your doorknob. This will give you an extra few hours to beat it across the border or check into a new hotel.

Landlords renovating buildings throw out stoves, tables, lamps, refrigerators and carpeting. In most cities, each area has a day designated for discarding bulk objects. Call the Sanitation Department and say you live in that part of town which would be putting out the most expensive shit and find out the pick-up day. Fantastic buys can be found cruising the streets late at night. Check out the backs of large department stores for floor models, window displays and slightly damaged furniture being discarded.

Construction sites are a good source for building materials to construct furniture. (Not to mention explosives.) The large wooden cable spools make great tables. Cinderblocks, bricks and boards can quickly be turned into a sharp looking bookcase. Doors make tables. Nail kegs convert into stools or chairs. You can also always find a number of other supplies hanging around like wiring, pipes, lighting fixtures and hard hats. And don't forget those blinking signs and the red lanterns for your own light show. Those black oil-fed burners are O.K. for cooking, although smoky, and highway flares are swell for making fake dynamite bombs.

24

STEAL THIS ROOM!

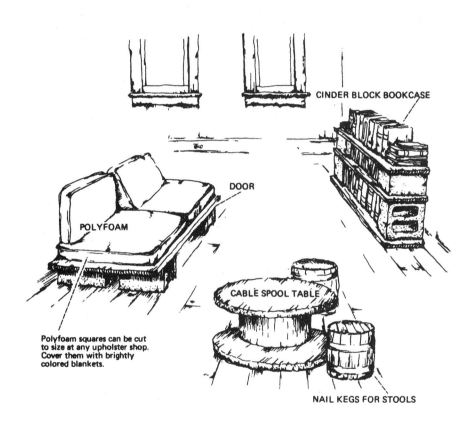

CINDER BLOCK BOOKCASE

DOOR

POLYFOAM

Polyfoam squares can be cut
to size at any upholster shop.
Cover them with brightly
colored blankets.

CABLE SPOOL TABLE

NAIL KEGS FOR STOOLS

FREE FURNITURE ROOM

Designed by OFFTHESTREETINI

25

Shit, I told you we should've taken the plane

FREE TRANSPORTATION

HITCH-HIKING

Certainly one of the neatest ways of getting where you want to go for nothing is to hitch. In the city it's a real snap. Just position yourself at a busy intersection and ask the drivers for a lift when they stop for the red light. If you're hitching on a road where the traffic zooms by pretty fast, be sure to stand where the car will have room to safely pull off the road. Traveling long distances, even cross-country, can be easy if you have some sense of what you are doing.

A lone hitch-hiker will do much better than two or more. A man and woman will do very well together. Single women are certain to get propositioned and possibly worse. Amerikan males have endless sexual fantasies about picking up a poor lonesome damsel in distress. Unless your karate and head are in top form, women should avoid hitching alone. Telling men you have V.D. might help in difficult situations.

New England and the entire West Coast are the best sections for easy hitches. The South and Midwest can sometimes be a real hassle. Easy Rider and all that. The best season to hitch is in the summer. Daytime is much better than night. If you have to hitch at night, get under some type of illumination where you'll be seen.

Hitch-hiking is legal in most states, but remember you always can get a "say-so" bust. A "say-so" arrest is to police what Catch-22 is to the Army. When you ask why you're under arrest, the pig answers, "cause I say-so." If you stand on the shoulder of the road, the pigs won't give you too bad a time. If you've got long hair, cops will often stop to play games. You can wear a hat with your hair tucked under to avoid hassles.

However this might hurt your ability to get rides, since many straights will pick up hippies out of curiosity who would not pick up a straight scruffy looking kid. Freak drivers usually only pick up other freaks.

Once in a while you hear stories of fines levied or even a few arrests for hitching (Flagstaff, Arizona is notorious), but even in the states where it is illegal, the law is rarely enforced. If you're stopped by the pigs, play dumb and they'll just tell you to move along. You can wait until they leave and then let your thumb hang out again.

Hitching on super highways is really far out. It's illegal but you won't get hassled if you hitch at the entrances. On a fucked-up exit, take your chances hitching right on the road, but keep a sharp eye out for porkers. When you get a ride be discriminating. Find out where the driver is headed. If you are at a good spot, don't take a ride under a hundred miles that won't end up in a location just as good. When the driver is headed to an out-of-the-way place, ask him to let you off where you can get the best rides. If he's going to a particularly small town, ask him to drive you to the other side of the town line. It's usually only a mile or two. Small towns often enforce all sorts of "say-so" ordinances. If you get stuck on the wrong side of town, it would be wise to even hoof it through the place. Getting to a point on the road where the cars are inter-city rather than local traffic is always preferable.

When you hit the road you should have a good idea of how to get where you are going. You can pick up a free map at any gas station. Long distance routes, road conditions, weather and all sorts of information can be gotten free by calling the *American Automobile Association* in any city. Say that you are a member driving to Phoenix, Arizona or wherever your destination is, and find out what you want to know. Always carry a sign indicating where you are going. If you get stranded on the road without one, ask in a diner or gas station for a piece of cardboard and a magic marker. Make the letters bold and fill them in so they can be seen by drivers from a distance. If your destination is a small town, the sign should indicate the state. For really long distances, EAST or WEST is best. Unless, of course, you're going north or south. A phony foreign flag sewed on your pack also helps.

Carrying dope is not advisable, and although searching you is illegal, few pigs can read the Constitution. If you are carrying when the patrol car pulls up, tell them you are Kanadian and hitching through Amerika. Highway patrols are very uptight about promoting incidents with foreigners. The foreign bit goes over especially well with small-town types, and is also amazingly good for avoiding hassles with greasers. If you can't hack this one, tell them you are a reporter for a newspaper writing a feature story on hitching around the country. This story has averted many a bust.

Don't be shy when you hitch. Go into diners and gas stations and ask people if they're heading East or to Texas. Sometimes gas station attendants will help. When in the car be friendly as hell. Offer to share the driving if you've got a license. If you're broke, you can usually bum a meal or a few bucks, maybe even a free night's lodging. Never be intimidated into giving money for a ride.

As for what to carry when hitching, the advice is to travel light. The rule is to make up a pack of the absolute minimum, then cut that in half. Hitching is an art form as is all survival. Master it and you'll travel on a free trip forever.

FREIGHTING

There is a way to hitch long distances that has certain advantages over letting your thumb hang out for hours on some deserted two-laner. Learn about riding the trains and you'll always have that alternative. Hitchhiking at night can be impossible, but hopping a freight is easier at night than by day. By hitchhiking days and hopping freights and sleeping on them at night, you can cover incredible distances rapidly and stay well rested. Every city and most large towns have a freight yard. You can find it by following the tracks or asking where the freight yard is located.

When you get to the yard, ask the workmen when the next train leaving in your direction will be pulling out. Unlike the phony Hollywood image, railroad men are nice to folks who drop by to grab a ride. Most yards don't have a guard or a "bull" as they are called. Even if they do, he is generally not around. If there is a bull around, the most he's going to do is tell you it's private property and ask you to leave. There are exceptions to this rule, such as the notorious Lincoln, Nebraska, and Las Vegas, Nevada, but by asking you can find out. Even if he asks you to leave or throws you out, sneak back when your train is pulling out and jump aboard.

After you've located the right train for your trip, hunt for an empty boxcar to ride. The men in the yards will generally point one out if you ask. Pig-sties, flat cars and coal cars are definitely third class due to exposure to the elements. Boxcars are by far the best. They are clean and the roof over your head helps in bad weather and cuts down the wind. Boxcars with a hydro-cushion suspension system used for carrying fragile cargo make for the smoothest ride. Unless you get one, you should be prepared for a pretty bumpy and noisy voyage.

You should avoid cars with only one door open, because the pin may break, locking you in. A car with both doors open gives you one free chance. Pig-backs (trailers on flatcars) are generally considered unsafe. Most trains make a number of short hops, so if time is an important factor try to get on a "hot shot" express. A hot shot travels faster and has priority over other trains in crowded yards. You should favor a hot shot even if you have to wait an extra hour or two or more to get one going your way.

If you're traveling at night, be sure to dress warmly. You can freeze your ass off. Trains might not offer the most comfortable ride, but they go through beautiful countryside that you'd never see from the highway or airway. There are no billboards, road signs, cops, Jack-in-the-Boxes, gas stations or other artifacts of honky culture. You'll get dirty on the trains so wear old clothes. Don't pass up this great way to travel 'cause some bullshit western scared you out of it.

CARS

If you know how to drive and want to travel long distances, the auto transportation agencies are a good deal. Look in the Yellow Pages under *Automobile*

Transportation and Trucking or *Driveaway*. Rules vary, but normally you must be over 21 and have a valid license. Call up and tell them when and where you want to go and they will let you know if they have a car available. They give you the car and a tank of gas free. You pay the rest. Go to pick up the car alone, then get some people to ride along and help with the driving and expenses. You can make New York to San Francisco for about eighty dollars in tolls and gas in four days without pushing. Usually you have the car for longer and can make a whole thing out of it. You must look straight when you go to the agency. This can simply be done by wetting down your hair and shoving it under a cap.

Another good way to travel cheaply is to find somebody who has a car and is going your way. Usually underground newspapers list people who either want rides or riders. Another excellent place to find information is your local campus. Every campus has a bulletin board for rides. Head shops and other community-minded stores have notices up on the wall.

Gas

If you have a car and need some gas late at night you can get a quart and then some by emptying the hoses from the pumps into your tank. There is always a fair amount of surplus gas left when the pumps are shut off.

If you're traveling in a car and don't have enough money for gas and tolls, stop at the bus station and see if anybody wants a lift. If you find someone, explain your money situation and make a deal with him. Hitch-hikers also can be asked to chip in on the gas.

You can carry a piece of tubing in the trunk of your car and when the gas indicator gets low, pull up to a nice looking Cadillac on some dark street and syphon off some of his gas. Just park your car so the gas tank is next to the Caddy's, or use a large can. Stick the hose into his tank, suck up enough to get things flowing, and stick the other end into your tank. Having a lower level of liquid, you tank will draw gas until you and the Caddy are equal. "To each according to his need, from each according to his ability," wrote Marx. Bet you hadn't realized until now that the law of gravity affects economics.

Another way is to park in a service station over their filler hole. Lift off one lid (like a small manhole cover), run down twenty feet of rubber tubing thru the hole you've cut in your floorboard, then turn on the electric pump which you have installed to feed into your gas tank. All they ever see is a parked car. This technique is especially rewarding when you have a bus.

BUSES

If you'd rather leave the driving and the paying to them, try swiping a ride on the bus. Here's a method that has worked well. Get a rough idea of where the bus has stopped before it arrived at your station. If you are not at the beginning or final stop on the route, wait until the bus you want pulls in and then out of the station. Make like the bus just pulled off without you while you went to the bathroom. If there is a station master, complain like crazy to him. Tell him you're going to sue the company if your luggage gets stolen. He'll put you on the next bus for free. If there is no station master, lay your sad tale on the next driver that comes along. If you know when the last bus left, just tell the driver you've been stranded there for eight hours and you left your kid sleeping on the other bus. Tell him you called ahead to the company and they said to grab the next bus and they would take care of it.

The next method isn't totally free but close enough. It's called the hopper-bopper. Find a bus that makes a few stops before it gets to where you want to go. The more stops with people getting in or out, the better. Buy a ticket for the short hop and stay on the bus until you end up at your destination. You must develop a whole style in order to pull this off because the driver has to forget you are connected with the ticket you gave him. Dress unobtrusively or make sure the driver hasn't seen your face. Pretend to be asleep when the short hop station is reached. If you get questioned, just act upset about sleeping through the stop you "really" want and ask if it's possible to get a ride back.

AIRLINES

Up and away, junior outlaws! If you really want to get where you're going in a hurry, don't forget skyjacker's paradise. Don't forget the airlines. They make an unbelievable amount of bread on their inflated prices, ruin the land with incredible amounts of polluting wastes and noise, and deliberately hold back aviation advances that would reduce prices and time of flight. We know two foolproof methods to fly free, but unfortunately we feel publishing them would cause the airlines to change their policy. The following methods have been talked about enough, so the time seems right to make them known to a larger circle of friends.

A word should be said right off about stolen tickets. Literally millions of dollars worth of airline tickets are stolen each year. If you have good underworld contacts, you can get a ticket to anywhere you want at one-fourth the regular price. If you are charged more, you are getting a slight rooking. In any case, you can get a ticket for any flight or date and just trade it in. They are actually as good as cash, except that it takes 30 days to get a refund, and by then they might have traced the stolen tickets. If you can get a stolen ticket, exchange or use it as soon as possible, and always fly under a phony name. A stolen ticket for a trip around the world currently goes for one hundred and fifty dollars in New York.

One successful scheme requires access to the mailbox of a person listed in the local phone book. Let's use the name Ron Davis as an example. A woman calls one of the airlines with a very efficient sounding rap such as: "Hello, this is Mr. Davis' secretary at Allied Chemical. He and his wife would like to fly to Chicago on Friday. Could you mail two first-class tickets to his home and bill us here at Allied?" Every major corporation probably has a Ron Davis, and the airlines rarely bother checking anyway. Order your tickets two days before you wish to travel, and pick them up at the mailbox or address you had them sent to. If you are uptight in the airport about the tickets, just go up to another airline and have the tickets exchanged.

One gutsy way to hitch a free ride is to board the plane without a ticket. This is how it works. Locate the flight you want and rummage through a wastebasket until you find an envelope for that particular airline. Shuffle by the counter men (which is fairly easy if it's busy). When the boarding call is made, stand in line and get on the plane. Flash the empty envelope at the stewardess as you board the plane. Carry a number of packages as a decoy, so the stewardess won't ask you to open the envelope. If she does, which is rare, and sees you have no ticket, act surprised. "Oh my gosh, it must have fallen out in the wash room," will do fine. Run back down the ramp as if you're going to retrieve the ticket. Disappear and try later on a different airline. Nine out of ten revolutionaries say it's the only way to fly. This trick works only on airlines that don't use the boarding pass system.

If you want to be covered completely, use the hopper-bopper method described in the section on Buses, with this added security precaution. Buy two tickets from different cashiers, or better still, one from an agent in town. Both will be on the same flight. Only one ticket will be under a phony name and for the short hop, while the ticket under your real name will be for your actual destination. At the boarding counter, present the short hop ticket. You will be given an envelope with a white receipt in it. Actually, the white receipt is the last leaf in your ticket. Once you are securely seated and aloft, take out the ticket with your name and final destination. Gently peel away everything but the white receipt. Place the still valid ticket back in your pocket. Now remove from the envelope and destroy the short hop receipt. In its place, put the receipt for the ticket you have in your pocket.

When you land at the short hop airport, stay on the plane. Usually the stewardesses just ask you if you are remaining on the flight. If you have to, you can actually show her your authentic receipt. When you get to your destination, you merely put the receipt back on the bonafide ticket that you still have in your pocket. It isn't necessary that they be glued together. Present the ticket for a refund or exchange it for another ticket. This method works well even in foreign countries. You can actually fly around the world for $88.00 using the hopper-bopper method and switching receipts.

If you can't hack these shucks, you should at least get a Youth Card and travel for half fare. If you are over twenty-two but still in your twenties, you can easily pass. Get a card from a friend who has similar color hair and eyes. Your friend can easily get one from another airline. You can master your friend's signature and get a supporting piece of identification from him to back up your youth card if you find it necessary. If you have a friend who works for an airline or travel agency, just get a card under your own name and an age below the limit. Your friend can validate the card. Flying youth fare is on stand-by, so it's always a good idea to call ahead and book a number of reservations under fictitious names on the flight you'll be taking. This will fuck up the booking of regular passengers and insure you a seat.

By the way, if you fly cross-country a number of times, swipe one of the plug-in head sets. Always remember to pack it in your traveling bag. This way you'll save a two dollar fee charged for the in-flight movie. The headsets are interchangeable on all airlines.

One way to fly free is to actually hitch a ride. Look for the private plane area located at every airport, usually in some remote part of the field. You can find it by noticing where the small planes without airline markings take off and land. Go over to the runways and ask around. Often the mechanics will let you know when someone is leaving for your destination and point out a pilot. Tell him you lost your ticket and have to get back to school. Single

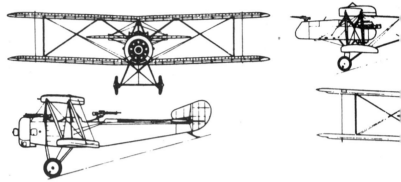

pilots often like to have a passenger along and it's a real gas flying in a small plane.

Some foreign countries have special arrangements for free air travel to visiting writers, artists or reporters. Brazil and Argentina are two we know of for sure. Call or write the embassy of the country you wish to visit in Washington or their mission to the United Nations in New York. Writing works best, especially if you can cop some stationery from a newspaper or publishing house. Tell them you will be writing a feature story for some magazine on the tourist spots or handcrafts of the country. The embassy will arrange for you to travel gratis aboard one of their air force planes. The planes leave only from Washington and New York at unscheduled times. Once you have the O.K. letter from the embassy you're all set. This is definitely worth checking out if you want to vacation in a foreign country with all sorts of free bonuses thrown in.

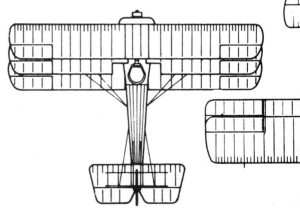

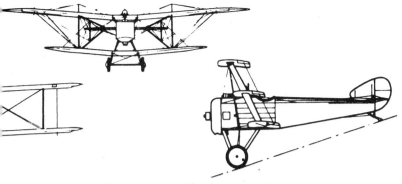

A one-way ride is easy if you want to get into skyjacking. Keep the piece or knife in your shoe to avoid possible detection with the "metal scanner," a long black tube that acts like a geiger counter. Or use a plastic knife or bomb. It's also advisable to wrap your dope in a non-metallic material. Avoid tinfoil.

The crews have instructions to take you wherever you want to go even if they have to refuel, but watch out for air marshals. To avoid air marshals and searches pick an airline which flies short domestic hops. You should plan to end up in a country hostile to the United States or you'll end up right back where you came from in some sturdy handcuffs. One dude wanted to travel in style so he demanded $100,000 as a going-away gift. The airlines quickly paid off. The guy then got greedy and demanded a hundred million dollars. When he returned to pick up the extra pocket money, he got nabbed. None the less, skyjacking appears to be the cheapest, fastest way to get away from it all.

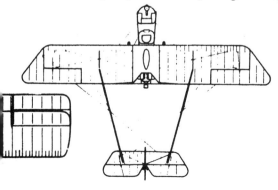

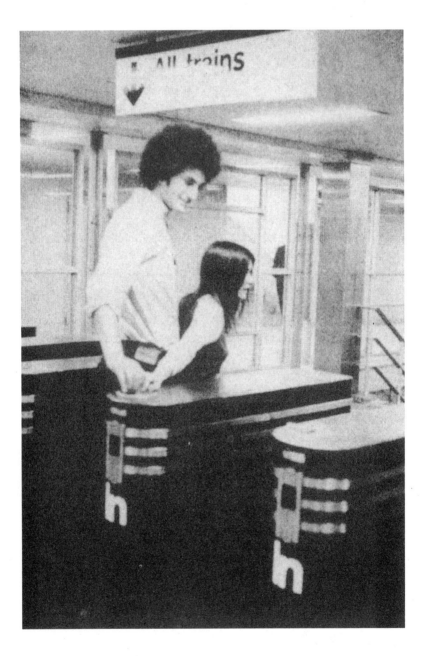

Come on, inhale and stop shoving

IN CITY TRAVEL

Any of the public means of transportation can be ripped off easily. Get on the bus with a large bill and present it after the bus has left the stop. If the bus is crowded, slip in the back door when it opens to dispatch passengers.

Two people can easily get through the turnstile in a subway on one token by doubling up. In some subway systems cards are given out to high school kids or senior citizens or employees of the city. The next time you are in a subway station notice people flashing cards to the man in the booth and entering through the "exit" door. Notice the color of the card used by people in your age group. Get a piece of colored paper in a stationery store or find some card of the same color you need. Put this "card" in a plastic window of your wallet and flash it in the same way those with a bona fide pass do.

Before entering a turnstile, always test the swing bar. If someone during the day put in an extra token, it's still in the machine waiting for you to enter free.

For every token and coin deposited in an automatic turnstile, there is a foreign coin the same size for much less that will work in the machine. (See the Yippie Currency Exchange, following, for more info.) Buy a cheap bag of assorted foreign coins from a dealer that you can locate in the Yellow Pages. Size up the coins with a token from your subway system. You can get any of these coins in bulk from a large dealer. Generally they are about 1,000 for five dollars. Tell him you make jewelry out of them if he gets suspicious. Giving what almost amounts to free subway rides away is a communal act of love. The best outlaws in the world rip-off shit for a lot more people than just themselves. Robin Hood lives!!

*

FREE LAND

Despite what you may have heard, there is still some rural land left in Amerika. The only really free land is available in Alaska and remote barren areas of the western states. The latest information in this area is found in a periodic publication called *Our Public Lands*, available from the Superintendent of Documents, Washington, D.C. 20402. It costs $1.00 for a subscription. Also contact the U.S. Department of the Interior, Bureau of Land Management, Washington, D.C. 20240 and ask for information on "homesteading." By the time this book is out though, the Secretary of the Interior's friends in the oil companies might have stolen all the available free land. Being an oil company is about the easiest way to steal millions. Never call it stealing though, always refer to it as "research and development."

Continental United States has no good free land that we know of, but there are some very low prices in areas suited for country communities. Write to School of Living, Freeland, Maryland, for their newspaper *Green Revolution* with the latest information in this area. Canada has free land available, and the Canadian government will send you a free list if you write to the Department of Land and Forests, Parliament Building, Quebec City, Canada. Also write to the Geographical Branch, Department of Mines and Technical Surveys, Parliament Building, Quebec City, Canada. Correspondence can be carried out with the Communications Group, 2630 Point Grey Road, Vancouver 8, British Columbia, Canada, for advice on establishing a community in Canada. The islands off the coast of British Columbia, its western region and the area along the Kootenai River are among the best locations.

If you just want to rip off some land, there are two ways to do it; openly or secretly. If you are going to do it out front, look around for a piece of land that's in dispute, which has its sovereignty in question—islands and deltas between the U.S. and Canada, or between the U.S. and Mexico, or any number of other borderline lands. You might even consider one of the abandoned oil-drilling platforms, which are fair game under high seas salvage laws. The possibilities are endless.

If you intend to do it quietly, you will want a completely different type of location. Find a rugged area with lots of elbow room and plenty of places to hide, like the Rocky Mountains, Florida swamps, Death Valley, or New York City. Put together a tight band of guerrillas and do your thing. With luck you will last forever.

If you just want to camp out or try some hermit living in the plushest surroundings available, you'll do best to head for one of the national parks. Since the parks are federal property, there's very little the local fuzz can do about you, and the forest rangers are generally the live-and-let-live types, although there have been increasing reports of long-hairs being vamped on by Smokey the Pig, as in Yosemite. You can get a complete list from National Park Service, Department of the Interior, Washington,

D.C. 20240. The following is a list of some good ones:

ALABAMA–Russell Cave National Monument, Bridgeport 35740

ARIZONA–Grand Canyon National Park, Box 129, Grand Canyon 86023

ARKANSAS–Hot Springs National Park, Box 1219, Hot Springs 71901

CALIFORNIA–Yosemite National Park, Box 577, Yosemite 95389*

COLORADO–Rocky Mountain National Park, Estes Park, 80517

FLORIDA–Everglades National Park, Box 279, Homestead 33030

IDAHO–Boise National Forest, 413 Idaho Street, Boise 83702

ILLINOIS–Shawnee National Forest, Harrisburg National Bank Building, Harrisburg 62946

KENTUCKY–Mammoth Cave National Park, Mammoth Cave 42259

LOUISIANA–Kisatchie National Forest, 2500 Shreveport Hwy., Pineville 71360

MAINE--Acadia National Park, Box 338, Bar Harbor 04609

MARYLAND–Assateague Island National Seashore, Rte. 2, Box 111, Berlin 21811

MASSACHUSETTS–Cape Cod National Seashore, South Wellfleet 02663

MICHIGAN–Hiawatha National Forest, Post Office Building, Escanaba 49829

MISSOURI–Mark Twain National Forest, 304 Pershing St., Springfield 65806

NEVADA–Lake Mead National Recreation Area, 601 Nevada Hwy, Boulder City 89005

NEW MEXICO–Aztec Ruins National Monument, Route 1, Box 101, Aztec 87410

*This summer Yosemite forest rangers tried to evict a group of Yippies from their encampment. The Yippies rioted in the valley, spooked the tourists, burned cars and fought for their right to stay.

NEW YORK—Fire Island National Seashore, c/o New York City National Park Service Group, 28 E. 20th St., New York, NY 10003

NORTH CAROLINA—Wright Brothers National Memorial, Box 457, Manteo 27954

OKLAHOMA—Platt National Park, Box 201, Sulphur 73086

OREGON—Crater Lake National Park, Box 7, Crater Lake 97604

UTAH—Bryce Canyon National Park, Bryce Canyon 84717

WYOMING—Yellowstone National Park, Yellowstone Park 83020

Earth People's Park is an endeavor to purchase land and allow people to come and live for free. They function as a clearing house for people that want to donate land and those who wish to settle. They own 600 acres in northern Vermont and are trying to raise money to buy more. Write to Earth People's Park, P.O. Box 313, 1230 Grant Ave., San Francisco, California 94133.

People's Parks are sprouting up all over as people reclaim the land being ripped off by universities, factories, and corrupt city planning agencies. The model is the People's Park struggle in Berkeley during the spring of 1969. The people fought to defend a barren parking lot they had turned into a community center with grass, swings, free-form sculpture and gardens. The University of California, with the aid of Ronald Reagan and the Berkeley storm troopers, fought with guns, clubs and tear gas to regain the land from the outlaw people. The pigs killed James Rector and won an empty victory. For now the park is fenced off, tarred over and converted into unused basketball courts and unused parking lots. Not one person has violated the oath never to set foot on the site. It stands, cold and empty, two blocks north of crowded Telegraph Avenue. If the revolution does not survive, all the land will perish under the steam roller of imperialism. People's Death Valley will happen in our lifetime.

FREE HOUSING

If you are in a city without a place to stay, ask the first group of hip-looking folks where you can crash. You might try the office of the local underground newspaper. In any hip community, the underground newspaper is generally the source of the best up-to-the-moment information. But remember that they are very busy, and don't impose on them. Many churches now have runaway houses. If you are under sixteen and can hack some bullshit jive about "adjusting," "opening a dialogue," and "things aren't that bad," then these are the best deals for free room and board. Check out the ground rules first, i.e., length of stay allowed, if they inform your parents or police, facilities and services available. Almost always they can be accepted at their word, which is something very sacred to missionaries. If they became known as double-crossers, their programs would be finished.

Some hip communities have crash pads set up, but these rarely last more than a few months. To give out the addresses we have would be quite impractical. We have never run across a crash pad that lasted more than a month or so. If in a city, try hustling a room at a college dorm. This is especially good in summer or on week-ends. If you have a sleeping bag, the parks are always good, as is "tar jungle" or sleeping on the roofs of tall buildings. Local folks will give you some good advice on what to watch out for and information on vagrancy laws which might help you avoid getting busted.

For more permanent needs, squatting is not only free, it's a revolutionary act. If you stay quiet you can stay indefinitely. If you have community support you may last forever.

COMMUNES

In the city or in the country, communes can be a cheap and enjoyable way of living. Although urban and rural communes face different physical environments, they share common group problems. The most important element in communal living is the people, for the commune will only make it if everyone is fairly compatible. A nucleus of 4 to 7 people is best and it is necessary that no member feels extremely hostile to any other member when the commune gets started. The idea that things will work out later is pigswill. More communes have busted up over incompatibility than any other single factor. People of similar interests and political philosophies should live together. One speed freak can wreck almost any group. There are just too many day-to-day hassles involved living in a commune to not start off compatible in as many ways as possible. The ideal arrangement is for the people to have known each other before they move in together.

Once you have made the opening moves, evening meetings will occasionally be necessary to divide up the responsibilities and work out the unique problems of a communal family. Basically, there are two areas that have to be pretty well agreed upon if the commune is to survive. People's attitudes toward Politics, Sex, Drugs and Decison-making have to be in fairly close agreement. Then the even more important decisions about raising the rent, cleaning, cooking and maintenance will have to be made. Ground rules for inviting non-members should be worked out before the first time it happens, as this is a common cause for friction. Another increasingly important issue involves defense. Communes have continually been targets of attack by the more Neanderthal elements of the surrounding community. In Minneapolis for example, "headhunts" as they are called are commonplace. You should have full knowledge of the local gun laws and a collective defense should be worked out.

Physical attacks are just one way of making war on communes and, hence, our Free Nation. Laws, cops, and courts are there to protect the power and the property of those that already got the shit. Police harassment, strict enforcement of health codes and fire regulations and the specially designed anti-commune laws being passed by town elders, should all be known and understood by the members of a commune before they even buy or rent property. On all these matters, you should seek out experienced members of communes already established in the vicinity you wish to settle. Work out mutual defense arrangements with nearby families—both legal and extralegal. Remember, not only do you have the right to self-defense, but it is your duty to our new Nation to erase the "Easy-Rider-take-any-shit" image which invites attack. Let them know you are willing to defend your way of living and your chances of survival will increase.

URBAN LIVING

If you're headed for city living, the first thing you'll have to do is locate an apartment or loft, an increasingly difficult task. At certain times of the year, notably June and September, the competition is fierce because of students leaving or entering school. If you can avoid these two months, you'll have a better selection. A knowledge of your plans in advance can aid a great deal in finding an apartment, for the area can be scouted before you move in. Often, if you know of people leaving a desirable apartment, you can make arrangements with the landlord, and a deposit will hold the place. If you let them know you're willing to buy their furniture, people will be more willing to give you information about when they plan to move. Watch out for getting screwed on exorbitant furniture swindles by the previous tenants and excessive demands on the part of the landlords. In most cities, the landlord is not legally allowed to ask for more than one month's rent as security. Often the monthly rent itself is regulated by a city agency. A little checking on the local laws and a visit to the housing agency might prove well worth it.

Don't go to a rental agency unless you are willing to pay an extra month's rent as a fee. Wanted ads in newspapers and bulletin boards located in community centers and supermarkets have some leads. Large universities have a service for finding good apartments for administrators, faculty and students, in that order. Call the university, say you have just been appointed to such-and-such position and you need housing in the area. They will want to know all your requirements and rent limitations, but often they have very good deals available, especially if you've appointed yourself to a high enough position.

Aside from these, the best way is to scout a desired area and inquire about future apartments. Often landlords or rental agencies have control over a number of buildings in a given area. You can generally find a nameplate inside the hall of the building. Calling them directly will let you know of any apartments available.

When you get an apartment, furnishing will be the next step. You can double your sleeping space by building bunk beds. Nail two by fours securely from ceiling to floor, about three feet from the walls, where the beds are desired. Then build a frame out of two by fours at a convenient height. Make sure you use nails or screws strong enough to support the weight of people sleeping or balling. Nail a sheet of 3/4 inch plywood on the frame. Mattresses and almost all furniture needed for your pad can be gotten free (see section on Free Furniture). Silverware can be copped at any self-service restaurant.

RURAL LIVING

If you are considering moving to the country, especially as a group, you are talking about farms and farmland. There are some farms for rent, and occasionally a family that has to be away for a year or two will let you live on their farm if you keep the place in repair. These can be found advertised in the back of various farming magazines and in the classified sections of newspapers, especially the Sunday editions. Generally speaking, however, if you're interested in a farm, you should be considering an outright purchase.

First, you have to determine in what part of the country you want to live in terms of the climate you prefer and how far away from the major cities you wish to locate. The least populated states, such as Utah, Idaho, the Dakotas, Montana and the like, have the cheapest prices and the lowest tax rates. The more populated a state, and in turn, the closer to a city, the higher the commercial value of the land.

There are hundreds of different types of farms, so the next set of questions you'll have to raise concerns the type of farm activity you'll want to engage in. Cattle farms are different than vegetable farms or orchards. Farms come in sizes: from half an acre to ranches larger than the state of Connecticut. They will run in price from $30 to $3000 an acre, with the most expensive being prime farmland in fertile river valleys located close to an urban area. The further away from the city and the further up a hill, the cheaper the land gets. It also gets woodier, rockier and steeper, which means less tillable land.

If you are talking of living in a farm house and maybe having a small garden and some livestock for your own use, with perhaps a pond on the property, you are looking for what is called a recreational farm.

When you buy a recreational farm, naturally you are interested in the house, barn, well, fences, chicken-coop, corrals, woodsheds and other physical structures on the property. Unless these are in unusually good condition or unique, they do not enter into the sale price as major factors. It is the land itself that is bought and sold.

Farmland is measured in acreage; an acre being slightly more than 43,560 square feet. The total area is measured in 40-acre plots. Thus, if a farmer or a real estate agent says he has a plot of land down the road, he means a 40-acre farm. Farms are generally measured this way, with an average recreational farm being 160 acres in size or an area covering about 1/2 square mile. A reasonable rate for recreational farmland 100 miles from a major city with good water and a livable house would be about $50 per acre. For a 160-acre farm, it would be $8,000, which is not an awful lot considering what you are getting. For an overall view, get the free catalogues and brochures provided by the United Farm Agency, 612 W. 47th St., Kansas City, Mo. 64112.

Now that you have a rough idea of where and what type of farm you want, you can begin to get more specific. Check out the classified section in the Sunday newspaper of the largest city near your desired location. Get the phone book and call or write to real estate agencies in the vicinity. Unlike the city, where there is a sellers' market, rural estate agents collect their fee from the seller of the property, so you won't have to worry about the agent's fee.

When you have narrowed down the choices, the next thing you'll want to look at is the plot book for the county. The plot book has all the farms in each township mapped out. It also shows terrain variations, type of housing on the land, location of rivers, roads and a host of other pertinent information. Road accessibility, especially in the winter, is an important factor. If the farms bordering the one you have selected are abandoned or not in full use, then for all intents and purposes, you have more land than you are buying.

After doing all this, you are prepared to go look at

the farm itself. Notice the condition of the auxiliary roads leading to the house. You'll want an idea of what sections of the land are tillable. Make note of how many boulders you'll have to clear to do some planting. Also note how many trees there are and to what extent the brush has to be cut down. Be sure and have a good idea of the insect problems you can expect. Mosquitoes or flies can bug the shit out of you. Feel the soil where you plan to have a garden and see how rich it is. If there are fruit trees, check their condition. Taste the water. Find out if hunters or tourists come through the land. Examine the house. The most important things are the basement and the roof. In the basement, examine the beams for dry rot and termites. See how long it will be before the roof must be replaced. Next check the heating system, the electrical wiring and the plumbing. Then you'll want to know about services such as schools, snow plowing, telephones, fire department and finally about your neighbors. If the house is beyond repair, you might still want the farm, especially if you are good at carpentry. Cabins, A-Frames, domes and tepees are all cheaply constructed with little experience. Get the materials from your nearest military installation.

Finally check out the secondary structures on the land to see how usable they are. If there is a pond, you'll want to see how deep it is for swimming. If there are streams, you'll want to know about the fishing possibilities; and if large wooded areas, the hunting.

In negotiating the final sales agreement, you should employ a lawyer. You'll also want to check out the possibility of negotiating a bank loan for the farm. Don't forget that you have to pay taxes on the land, so inquire from the previous owner or agent as to the tax bill. Usually, you can count on paying about $50 annually per 40-acre plot.

Finally, check out the federal programs available in the area. If you can learn the ins and outs of the government programs, you can rip off plenty. The Feed-Grain Program of the Department of Agriculture pays you not to grow grain. The Cotton Subsidy Program pays you not to grow cotton. Also look into the Soil Bank Program of the United States Development Association and various Department of Forestry programs which pay you to plant trees. Between not planting cotton and planting trees, you should be able to manage.

LIST OF COMMUNES

The most complete list of city and country communes is available for $1.00 from Alternatives Foundation, Modern Utopian, 1526 Gravenstein Highway North, Sebastopol, California 95427. The phone is (707) 823-6168. The list is kept up to date. For all communes, you must write in advance if you plan to visit. Almost every commune will give you information about the local conditions and the problems they face if you write them a letter. Here is a list of some you might like to write to for more information. Avoid becoming a free-loader on your sisters and brothers.

California
ALTERNATIVES FOUNDATION—Box 1264, Berkeley, California 94709. (Dick Fairfield) Communal living, total sexuality, peak experience training centers. Dedicated to the cybernated-tribal society.
BHODAN CENTER OF INQUIRY—Sierra Route, Oakhurst, California 93644. Phone (209) 683-4976. (Charles Davis) Seminars on Human Community, IC development on the land, founded 1934, 13 members. Trial period for new members. Visitors check in advance.
Colorado
DROP CITY—Rt. 1, Box 125, Trinidad, Colorado 81082. Founded 1965. New members must meet specific criteria. Anarchist, artist, dome houses.

New Mexico
LAMA FOUNDATION—Box 444, San Cristobal, N.M.
New York
CITY ISLAND COMMUNE—284 City Island Avenue, Bronx, NY. Visitors check in advance. Revolutionary.
ATLANTIS I—RFD 5, Box 22A, Saugerties, NY 12477. Visitors and new members welcome.
Oregon
FAMILY OF MYSTIC ARTS—Box 546, Sunny Valley, Oregon
Pennsylvania
TANGUY HOMESTEADS—West Chester, Pennsylvania. Suburban, non-sectarian, co-op housing and community fellowship.
Washington
MAGIC MOUNTAIN—52nd and 19th Streets, Seattle, Washington. (c/o Miriam Roder).

FREE EDUCATION

Usually when you ask somebody in college why they are there, they'll tell you it's to get an education. The truth of it is, they are there to get the degree so that they can get ahead in the rat race. Too many college radicals are two-timing punks. The only reason you should be in college is to destroy it. If there is stuff that you want to learn though, there is a way to get a college education absolutely free. Simply send away for the schedule of courses at the college of your choice. Make up the schedule you want and audit the classes. In smaller classes this might be a problem, but even then, if the teacher is worth anything at all, he'll let you stay. In large classes, no one will ever object.

If you need books for a course, write to the publisher claiming you are a lecturer at some school and considering using their book in your course. They will always send you free books.

There are Free Universities springing up all over our new Nation. Anybody can teach any course. People sign up for the courses and sometimes pay a token registration fee. This money is used to publish a catalogue and pay the rent. If you're on welfare you don't have to pay. You can take as many or as few courses as you want. Classes are held everywhere: in the instructor's house, in the park, on the beach, at one of the student's houses or in liberated buildings. Free Universities offer courses ranging from Astrology to the Use of Firearms. The teaching is usually of excellent quality and you'll learn in a community-type atmosphere.

LIST OF FREE UNIVERSITIES

Alternative University—69 W. 14th St., New York, NY 10011 (catalogue on request)

Baltimore Free U—c/o Harry, 233 E. 25th St., Baltimore, Maryland 21218

Berkeley Free U—1703 Grove St., Berkeley, California 94709

Bowling Green Free U—c/o Student Council, University of Bowling Green, Bowling Green, Ohio 43402

Colorado State Free U—Box 12—Fraisen, Colorado State College, Greeley, Colorado 80631

Detroit Area Free U—Student Union, 4001 W. McNichols Rd., University of Detroit, Detroit, Michigan 48221

Detroit Area Free U—343 University Center, Wayne State University, Detroit, Mich.

Georgetown Free U—Loyola Bldg., Rm. 28, Georgetown University, Washington, D.C. 20007

Golden Gate Free U—2120 Market St., Rm. 206, San Francisco, California 94114

Heliotrope—2201 Filbert, San Francisco, California 94118

Illinois Free U—298A Illini Union, University of Illinois, Champaign, Illinois 61820

Kansas Free U—107 W. 7th St., Lawrence, Kansas 66044

Knox College Free U—Galesburg, Illinois 60401

Madison Free U—c/o P. Carroll, 1205 Shorewood Blvd., Madison, Wisconsin 53705

Metropolitan State Free U—Associated Students, 1345 Banrock St., Denver, Colorado 80204

Michigan State Free U—Associated Students, Student Service Bldg., Michigan State College, East Lansing, Michigan 48823

Mid-Peninsula Free U—1060 El Camino Real, Menlo Park, California 94015

Minnesota Free U—1817 S. 3rd St., Minneapolis, Minnesota 55404

Monterey Peninsula Free U—2120 Etna Place, Monterey, California

New Free U—Box ALL 303, Santa Barbara, California 93107

Northwest Free U—Box 1255, Bellingham, Washington 98225

Ohio-Wesleyan Free U—Box 47—Welsh Hall, Ohio Wesleyan University, Delevan, Ohio 43015

Pittsburgh Free U—4401 Fifth Ave., Pittsburgh, Pennsylvania 15213

Rutgers Free U—Rutgers College, Student Center, 1 Lincoln Ave., Newark, NJ 07102

St. Louis Free U—c/o Student Congress, 3rd floor BMC, St. Louis University, St. Louis, Missouri 63103

San Luis Obispo Free U—Box 1305, San Luis Obispo, California 94301

Santa Cruz Free U–604 River St., Santa Cruz, California 95060

Seattle Free U–4144½ University Way NE, Seattle, Washington 98105

Southern Illinois Free U–Carbondale, Illinois 62901

Valley Free U–2045 N. Wishon Ave., Fresno, California 93704

Washington Area Free U–5519 Prospect Place, Chevy Chase, Maryland 20015 and 1854 Park Rd. NW, Washington, D.C. 20010

Wayne-Locke Free U–Student Congress, University of Texas, Arlington, Texas 76010

And a complete list of experimental schools, free universities, free schools, can be obtained by sending one dollar to ALTERNATIVES! 1526 Gravenstein Highway N., Sebastopol, California 97452, and requesting the *Directory of Free Schools.*

FREE MEDICAL CARE

Due to the efforts of the Medical Committee for Human Rights, the Student Health Organization and other progressive elements among younger doctors and nurses, Free People's Clinics have been happening in every major city. They usually operate out of store fronts and are staffed with volunteer help. An average clinic can handle about fifty patients a day.

If you've had an accident or have an acute illness, even a bad cold, check into the emergency room of any hospital. Given them a sob story complete with phony name and address. After treatment they present you with a slip and direct you to the cashier. Just walk on by, as the song suggests. A good decoy is to ask for the washroom. After waiting there a few moments, split. If you're caught sneaking out, tell them you ran out of the house without your wallet. Ask them to bill you at your phony address. This billing procedure works in both hospital emergency rooms and clinics. You can keep going back for repeated visits up to three months before the cashier's office tells the doctor about your fractured payments.

You can get speedy medical advice and avoid emergency room delays by calling the hospital, asking for the emergency unit and speaking directly to the doctor over the phone. Older doctors frown on this procedure since they cannot extort their usual exhorbitant fee over the phone. Younger ones generally do not share this hang-up.

Cities usually have free clinics for a variety of special ailments. Tuberculosis Clinics, Venereal Disease Clinics, and Free Shot Clinics (yellow fever, polio, tetanus, etc.) are some of the more common. A directory of these clinics and other free health services the local community provides can be obtained by writing your Chamber of Commerce or local Health Department.

Most universities have clinics connected with their dental, optometry or other specialized medical schools. If not for free, then certainly for very low rates, you can get dental work repaired, eyeglasses fitted and treatment of other specific health needs.

Free psychiatric treatment can often be gotten at the out-patient department of any mental hospital. Admission into these hospitals is free, but a real bummer. Use them as a last resort only. Some cities have a suicide prevention center and if you are desperate and need help, call them. Your best choice in a psychiatric emergency is to go to a large general hospital, find the emergency unit and ask to see the psychiatrist on duty.

BIRTH CONTROL CLINICS

Planned Parenthood and the Family Planning Association staff numerous free birth control clinics throughout the country. They provide such services as sex education, examinations, Pap smear and birth control information and devices. The devices include pills, a diaphram, or IUD (intra-uterine device) which they will insert. If you are unmarried and under 18, you might have to talk to a social worker, but it's no sweat because anybody gets contraceptive devices that wants them. Call up and ask them to send you their booklets on the different methods of birth control available.

If you would rather go to a private doctor, try to find out from a friend the name of a hip gynecologist, who is sympathetic to the fact that you're low on bread. Otherwise one visit could cost $25.00 or more.

Before deciding on a contraceptive, you should be hip to some general information. There has been much reasearch on the pill, and during the past 10 years it has proven its effectiveness, if not is safety. The two most famous name brands are Ortho-Novum and Envoid. They all require a doctor's prescription. Different type pills are accompanied by slightly different instructions, so read the directions carefully. In many women, the pills produce side effects such as weight increase, dizziness or nausea. Sometimes the pill affects your vision and more often your mood. Some women with specialized blood diseases are advised not to use them, but in general, women have little or no trouble. Different brand names have different hormonal balances (progesterone-estrogen). If you get uncomfortable side effects, insist that your doctor switch your brand. If you stop the pill method for any reason and don't want to get pregnant, be very careful to use another means right away.

Another contraceptive device becoming more popular is the IUD, or the loop. It is a small plastic or stainless steel irregularly-shaped spring that the doctor inserts inside the opening of the uterus. The insertion is not without pain, but it's safe if done by a physician, and it's second only to the pill in prevention of pregnancy. Once it's in place, you can forget about it for a few years or until you wish to get pregnant. Doctors are reluctant to prescribe them for women who have not borne children or had an abortion, because of the intense pain that accompanies insertion. But if you can stand the pain associated with three to four uterine contractions, you should push the doctor for this method. Inserting it during the last day of your period will make it easier.

The diaphram is a round piece of flexible rubber about 2 inches in diameter with a hard rubber rim on the outside. It used to be inserted just before the sex act, but hip doctors now recommend that it be worn continuously and taken out every few days for washing and also during the menstrual period. It is most effective when used with a sperm-killing jelly or cream. A doctor will fit you for a proper size diaphram.

The next best method is the foams that you insert twenty minutes before fucking. The best foams available are Delfen and Emko. They have the advantage of being nonprescription items so you can rush into any drug store and pick up a dispenser when the spirit moves you. Follow the directions carefully. Unfortunately, these foams taste terrible and are not available in flavors. It just shows you how far science has to go.

Another device is the prophylactic, or rubber as it is called. This is the *only* device available to men. It is a thin rubber sheath that fits over the penis. Because they are subject to breaking and sliding off, their effectiveness is not super great. If you are forced to use them, the best available are lubricated sheepskins with a reservoir tip.

The rhythm method or Vatican roulette as it is called by hip Catholics, is a waste unless you are ready to surround yourself with thermometers, graphs and charts. You also have to limit your fucking to prescribed days. Even with all these precautions, women have often gotten pregnant using the rhythm method.

The oldest and least effective method is simply for the male to pull out just before he comes. There are billions of sperm cells in each ejaculation, and only one is needed to fertilize the woman's egg and cause a pregnancy. Most of the sperm is in the first squirt, so you had better be quick if you employ this technique.

If the woman misses her period she shouldn't panic. It might be delayed because of emotional reasons. Just wait two weeks before going to a doctor or clinic for a pregnancy test. When you go, be sure to bring your first morning urine specimen.

ABORTIONS

The best way to find out about abortions is to contact your local woman's liberation organization through your underground newspaper or radio station, Some Family Planning Clinics and even some liberal churches set up abortions, but these might run as high as $700. Underground newspapers often have ads that read, "Any girl in trouble call − −," or something similar. The usual rate for an abortion is about $500 and it's awful hard to bargain when you need one badly. Only go to a physician who is practicing or might have just lost his license. Forget the stereotype image of these doctors as they are performing a vital service. Friends who have had an abortion can usually recommend a good doctor and fill you in on what's going to happen.

Abortions are very minor operations if done correctly. They can be done almost any time, but after three months, it's no longer so casual and more surgical skill is required. Start making plans as soon as you find out. The sooner the better, in terms of the operation.

Get a pregnancy test at a clinic. If it is positive and you want an abortion, start that day to make plans. If you get negative results from the test and still miss your period, have a gynecologist perform an examination if you are still worried.

If you cannot arrange an abortion through woman's liberation, Family Planning, a sympathetic clergyman or a friend who has had one, search out a liberal hospital and talk to one of their social workers. Almost all hospitals perform "therapeutic" abortions. Tell a sob story about the desertion of your boy friend or that you take LSD every day or that defects run in your family. Act mentally disturbed. If you qualify, you can get an abortion that will be free under Medicaid or other welfare medical plans. The safest form of abortion is the vacuum-curettage method, but not all doctors are hip to it. It is safer and quicker with less chance of complications than the old-fashioned scrape method.

Many states have recently passed liberalized abortion laws, such as New York* (by far the most extentive), Hawaii, and Maryland, due to the continuing pressure of radical women. The battle for abortion and certainly for free abortion is far from over even in the states with liberal laws. They are far too expensive for the ten to twenty minute minor operation involved and the red tape is horrendous. Free abortions must be look-on as a fundamental right, not a sneaky, messy trauma.

DISEASES TREATED FREE

Syph and Clap (syphillis and gonorrhea) are two diseases that are easy to pick up. They come from balling. Anyone who claims they got it from sitting on a toilet seat must have a fondness for weird positions.

Both men and women are subject to the diseases. Using a prophylactic usually will prevent the spreading of venereal disease, but you should really seek to have it cured. Syphillis usually begins with an infection which may look like a cold sore or pimple around the sex

*There is a residence requirement for New York, but using a friend's New York address at the hospital will be good enough. The procedure takes only a few days and costs between $200 and $500, depending on the place. The best advice is to call one of the New York Abortion Referral Services or Birth Control Groups listed in the New York Directory section.

organ. There is no pain associated with the lesions. Soon the sore disappears even without treatment. This is often followed by a period of rashes on the body (especially the palms of the hands) and inflammation of the mouth and throat. These symptoms also disappear without treatment. It must be understood, however, that even if these symptoms disappear, the disease still remains if left untreated. It can cause serious trouble such as heart disease, blindness, insanity and paralysis. Also, it can fuck up any kids you might produce and is easily passed on to anyone you ball.

Gonorrhea (clap) is more common than syphillis. Its first signs are a discharge from your sex organ that is painful. Like syphillis, it affects both men and women, but is often unnoticed in women. There is usually itching and burning associated with the affected area. It can leave you sterile if left untreated.

Both these venereal diseases can be treated in a short time with medical attention. Avail yourself of the free V.D. clinics in every town. Follow the doctor's instructions to the letter and try to let the other people you've had sexual contact with know you had V.D.

There are other fungus diseases that resemble

YIPPIE!

syphillis or gonorrhea, but are relatively harmless. Check out every infection in your crotch area, especially those with open sores or an unusual discharge and you'll be safe.

Crabs are not harmful, but they can make you scratch your crotch for hours on end. They are also highly transmittable by balling. Actually they are a form of body lice and easy to cure. Go to your local druggist and ask him for the best remedy available. He'll give you one of several lotions and instructions for proper use. We recommend Kwell.

A common disease in the hip community is hepatitis. There are two kinds. One you get from sticking dirty needles in your arm (serum hepatitis) and the other more common strain from eating infected food or having intimate contact with an infected carrier (infectious hepatitis). The symptoms for both are identical; yellowish skin and eyes, dark piss and light crap, loss of appetite and total listlessness. Hep is a very dangerous disease that can cause a number of permanent conditions, including death, which is extremely permanent. It should be treated by a doctor, often in a hospital.

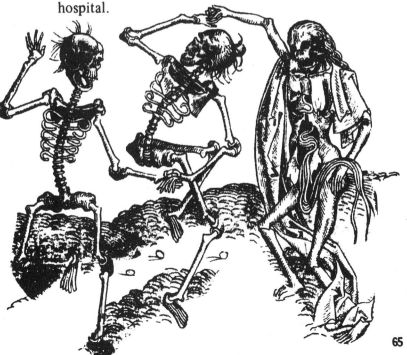

STRIKE! STRIKE! STRIKE!

FREE COMMUNICATION

If you don't like the news, why not go out and make your own? Creating free media depends to a large extent on your imagination and ability to follow through on ideas. The average Amerikan is exposed to over 1,600 commercials each day. Billboards, glossy ads and television spots make up much of the word environment they live in. To crack through the word mush means creating new forms of free communication. Advertisements for revolution are important in helping to educate and mold the milieu of people you wish to win over.

Guerrilla theater events are always good news items and if done right, people will remember them forever. Throwing out money at the Stock Exchange or dumping soot on executives at Con Edison or blowing up the policeman statue in Chicago immediately conveys an easily understood message by using the technique of creative disruption. Recently to dramatize the illegal invasion of Cambodia, 400 Yippies stormed across the Canadian border in an invasion of the United States. They threw paint on store windows and physically attacked residents of Blair, Washington. A group of Victnam veterans marched in battle gear from Trenton to Valley Forge. Along the way they performed mock attacks on civilians the way they were trained to do in Southeast Asia.

Dying all the outdoor fountains red and then sending a message to the newspaper explaining why you did it, dramatizes the idea that blood is being shed needlessly in imperialist wars. A special metallic bonding glue available from Eastman-Kodak will form a permanent bond in only 45 seconds. Gluing up locks of all the office buildings in your town is a great way to dramatize the fact that our brothers and sisters are being jailed all the time. Then, of course, there are always explosives which dramatically make your point and then some.

PRESS CONFERENCES

Another way of using the news to advertise the revolution and make propaganda is to call a press conference. Get an appropriate place that has some relationship to the content of your message. Send out announcements to as many members of the press as you can. If you do not have a press list, you can make one up by looking through the Yellow Pages under *Newspapers, Radio Stations, Television Stations, Magazines* and *Wire Services.* Check out your list with other groups and pick up names of reporters who attend movement press conferences. Address a special invitation to them as well as one to their newspaper.

Address the announcements to "City Desk" or "News Department." Schedule the press conference for about 11:00 A.M. as this allows the reporters to file the story in time for the evening newscast or papers. On the day of the scheduled conference, call the important city desks or reporters about 9:00 A.M. and remind them to come.

Everything about a successful press conference must be dramatic, from the announcements and phone calls to the statements themselves. Nothing creates a worse image than four or five men in business suits sitting behind a table and talking in a calm manner at a fashionable hotel. Constantly seek to have every detail of the press conference differ in style as well as content from the conferences of people in power. Make use of music and visual effects. Don't stiffen up before the press. Make the statement as short and to the point as possible. Don't read from notes, look directly into the camera. The usual television spot is one minute and twenty seconds. The cameras start buzzing on your opening statement and often run out of film before you finish. So make it brief and action packed. The question period should be even more dramatic. Use the questioner's first name when answering a question. This adds an air of informality and networks are more apt to use an answer directed personally to one of their newsmen. Express your emotional feelings. Be funny, get angry, be sad or ecstatic. If you cannot convey that you are deeply excited or troubled or outraged about what you are saying, how do you expect it of others who are watching a little image box in their living room? Remember, you are advertising a new way of life to people. Watch TV commercials. See how they are able to convey everything they need to be effective in such a short time and limited space. At the same time you're mocking the shit they are pushing, steal their techniques.

At rock concerts, during intermission or at the end of the performance, fight your way to the stage.

Announce that if the electricity is cut off the walls will be torn down. This galvanizes the audience and makes the owners of the hall the villains if they fuck around. Lay out a short exciting rap on what's coming down. Focus on a call around one action. Sometimes it might be good to engage rock groups in dialogues about their commitment to the revolution. Interrupting the concert is frowned upon since it is only spitting in the faces of the people you are trying to reach. Use the Culture as ocean to swim in. Treat it with care.

Sandwich boards and hand-carried signs are effective advertisements. You can stand on a busy corner and hold up a sign saying "Apartment Needed," "Free Angela," "Smash the State" or other slogans. They can be written on dollar bills, envelopes that are being mailed and other items that are passed from person to person.

Take a flashlight with a large face to movie theaters and other dark public gathering places. Cut the word "STRIKE" or "REVOLT" or "YIPPIE" out of dark cellophane. Paste the stencil over the flashlight, thus allowing you to project the word on a distant wall.

There are a number of all night call-in shows that have a huge audience. If you call with what the moderator considers "exciting controversy," he may give you a special number so you won't have to compete in the switchboard roller-derby. It often can take hours before you get through to these shows. Here's a trick that will help you out if the switchboard is jammed. The call-in shows have a series of phones so that when one is busy the next will take the call. Usually the numbers run in sequence. Say a station gives out PL 5-8640, as the number to call. That means it also uses PL 5-8641, PL 5-8642 and so on. If you get a busy signal, hang up and try calling PL 5-8647 say. This trick works in a variety of situations where you want to get a call through a busy switchboard. Remember it for airline and bus information.

WALL PAINTING

One of the best forms of free communication is painting messages on a blank wall. The message must be short and bold. You want to be able to paint it on before the pigs come and yet have it large enough so that people can see it at a distance. Cans of spray paint that you can pick up at any hardware store work best. Pick spots that have lot of traffic. Exclamation points are good for emphasis. If you are writing the same message, make a stencil. You can make a stencil that says WAR and spray it on with white paint under the word "STOP" on stop signs. You can stencil a five-pointed star and using yellow paint, spray it on the dividing line between the red and blue on all post office boxes. This simulates the flag of the National Liberation Front of Vietnam. You can stencil a marijuana leaf and using green paint, spray it over cigarette and whisky billboards on buses and subways. The women's liberation sign with red paint is good for sexist ads. Sometimes you will wish to exhibit great daring in your choice of locations. When the Vietnamese hero Nguyen Van Troi was executed, the Viet Cong put up a poster the next day on the exact spot inside the highest security prison in the country.

Wall postering allows you to get more information before the public than a quickly scribbled slogan. Make sure the surface is smooth or finely porous. Smear the back of the poster with condensed milk, spread on with a brush, sponge, rag or your hands. Condensed milk dries very fast and hard. Also smear some on the front once the poster is up to give protection against the weather and busy fingers that like to pull at corners. Wallpaper pastes also work quickly and efficiently. It's best to work both painting and postering at night with a look-out. This way you can work the best spots without being harrassed by the pig patrol, which is usually unappreciative of Great Art.

USE OF THE FLAG

The generally agreed upon flag of our nation is black with a red, five pointed star behind a green marijuana · leaf in the center. It is used by groups that understand the correct use of culture and symbolism in a revolutionary struggle. When displayed, it immediately increases the feelings of solidarity between our brothers and sisters. High school kids have had great fights over which flag to salute in school. A sign of any liberated zone is the flag being flown. Rock concerts and festivals have their generally apolitical character instantly changed when the flag is displayed. The political theoreticians who do not recognize the flag and the importance of the culture it represents are ostriches who are ignorant of basic human nature. Throughout history people have fought for religion, life-style, land, a flag (nation), because they were ordered to, for fortune, because they were attacked or for the hell of it. If you don't think the flag is important, ask the hardhats.

RADIO

Want to construct your own neighborhood radio station? You can get a carrier-current transmitter designed by a group of brothers and sisters called Radio Free People. No FCC license is required for the range is less than 1/2 mile. The small transistorized units plug into any wall outlet. Write Radio Free People, 133 Mercer St., New York, New York 10012 for more details. For further information see the chapter on Guerrilla Broadcasting later in the book.

Honest operator, I just put in 87 dollars in change and ....

74

FREE TELEPHONES

Ripping off the phone company is so common that Bell Telephone has a special security division that tries to stay just a little ahead of the average free-loader. Many great devices like the coat hanger release switch have been scrapped because of changes in the phone box. Even the credit card fake-out is doomed to oblivion as the company switches to more computerized techniques. In our opinion, as long as there is a phone company, and as long as there are outlaws, nobody need ever pay for a call. In 1969 alone the phone company estimated that over 10 million dollars worth of free calls were placed from New York City. Nothing, however, compares with the rip-off of the people by the phone company. In that same year, American Telephone and Telegraph made a profit of 8.6 billion dollars! AT&T, like all public utilities, passes itself off as a service owned by the people, while in actuality nothing could be further from the truth. Only a small percentage of the public owns stock in these companies and a tiny elite clique makes all the policy decisions. Ripping-off the phone company is an act of revolutionary love, so help spread the word.

PAY PHONES

You can make a local 10 cent call for 2 cents by spitting on the pennies and dropping them in the nickel slot. As soon as they are about to hit the trigger mechanism, bang the coin-return button. Another way is to spin the pennies counter-clockwise into the nickel slot. Hold the penny in the slot with your finger and snap it spinning with a key or other flat object. Both systems take a certain knack, but once you've perfected the technique, you'll always have it in your survival kit.

If two cents is too much, how about a call for 1 penny? Cut a 1/4 strip off the telephone book cover. Insert the cardboard strip into the dime slot as far as it will go. Drop a penny in the nickel slot until it catches in the mechanism (spinning will help). Then slowly pull the strip out until you hear the dial tone.

A number 14 brass washer with a small piece of scotch tape over one side of the hole will not only get a free call, but works in about any vending machine that takes dimes. You can get a box of thousands for about a dollar at any hardware store. You should always have a box around for phones, laundromats, parking meters and drink machines.

Bend a bobby pin after removing the plastic from the tips and jab it down into the transmitter (mouthpiece). When it presses against the metal diaphragm, rub it on a metal wall or pipe to ground it. When you've made contact you'll hear the dial tone. If the phone uses old-fashioned rubber black tubing to enclose the wires running from the headset to the box, you can insert a metal tack through the tubing, wiggle it around a little until it makes contact with the bare wires and touch the tack to a nearby metal object for grounding.

Put a dime in the phone, dial the operator and tell her you have ten cents credit. She'll return your dime and get your call for free. If she asks why, say you made a call on another pay phone, lost the money, and the operator told you to switch phones and call the credit operator.

This same method works for long distance calls. Call the operator and find out the rate for your call. Hang up and call another operator telling her you just dialed San Francisco direct, got a wrong number and lost $.95 or whatever it is. She will get your call free of charge.

If there are two pay phones next to each other, you can call long distance on one and put the coins in the other. When the operator cuts in and asks you to deposit money, drop the coins into the one you are not using, but hold the receiver up to slots so the operator can hear the bells ring. When you've finished, you can simply press the return button on the phone with the coins in it and out they come. If you have a good tape recorder you can record the sounds of a quarter, dime and nickel going into a pay phone and play them for the operator in various combinations when she asks for the money. Turn the volume up as loud as you can get it.

You can make a long distance call and charge it to a phone number. Simply tell the operator you want to bill the call to your home phone because you don't have the correct change. Tell her there is no one there now to verify the call, but you will be home in an hour and she can call you then if there is any question. Make sure the exchange goes with the area you say it does.

Always have a number of made-up credit card numbers. The code letter for 1970 is S, then seven digits of the phone number and a three digit district number (not the same as area code). The district number should be under 599. Example: S-573-2100-421 or S-537-3402-035. Look up the phone numbers for your area by simply requesting a credit card for your home phone which is very easy to get and then using the last three numbers with another phone number. Usually making up exotic numbers from far away places will work quite well as it would be impossible for an operator to spot a phony number in the short time she has to check her list.

We advise against making phony credit card calls on a home phone. We have seen a gadget that you install between the wall socket and the cord which not only allows you to receive all the calls you want for free, but eliminates the most common form of electronic bugging. They are being manufactured and sold for fifty dollars by a disgruntled telephone engineer in Massachusetts. Unfortunately you are going to have to find him on your own or duplicate his efforts, for he has sworn us to secrecy. If someone does, however, offer you such a device, it probably really does work. Test it by installing it and having someone call you from a pay phone. If it's working, the person should get their dime back at the end of the call.

Actually, if you know the slightest information about wiring, you can have your present phone

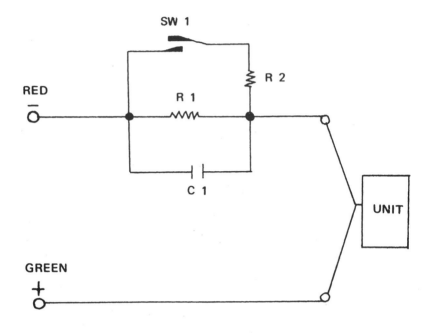

Key:

SW 1 — Single pole single throw switch
R 1 — 10 K Resistor 10% brown-black-orange 10,000 ½ watt
R 2 — 10 Resistor 10% brown-black-black ½ watt
C 1 — 100 Microfarad capacitor electrolytic @ 50 volts

SW 1 should be open for incoming and closed for outgoing

FLASH: the credit card system for 1971 has proven to be somewhat more complicated than past years. Here it is. The letter now
comes at the end of the number instead of the beginning, with
the sixth number being the Key. The code is as follows: 1—Q;
2—A; 3—E; 4—H; 5—J; 6—N; 7—R; 8—U; 9—W; 0—Z. The first
seven numbers make up the phone number and the last three are
the district numbers as before. Example: 759-5180-021 U would
work since 8 (the sixth number) goes with its code letter U. Also
759 is an actual exchange in the 021 district (Mid Manhattan).
We advise you not to use the number we've given as an example
but construct a few of your own.

disconnected on the excuse that you'll be leaving town for a few months and then connect the wires into the main trunk lines on your own. Extensions can easily be attached to your main line without the phone company knowing about it.

You can make all the free long distance calls you want by calling your party collect at a pay phone. Just have your friend go to a prearranged phone booth at a prearranged time. This can be done on the spot by having the friend call you person to person. Say you're not in, but ask for the number calling you since you'll be "back" in five minutes. Once you get the number simply hang up, wait a moment and call back your friend collect. The call has to be out of the state to work, since operators are familiar with the special extension numbers assigned to pay phones for her area and possibly for nearby areas as well. If she asks you if it is a pay phone say no. If she finds out during the call (which rarely happens) and informs you of this, simply say you didn't expect the party to have a pay phone in his house and accept the charges. We have never heard of this happening though. The trick of calling person-to-person collect should always be used when calling long distance on home-to-home phones also. You can hear the voice of your friend saying that he'll be back in a few minutes. Simply hang up, wait a moment and call station to station, thereby getting a person-to-person call without the extra charges which can be considerable on a long call during business hours.

If you plan to stay at your present address for only a few more months, stop paying the bill and call like crazy. After a month you get the regular bill which you avoid paying. Another month goes by and the next bill comes with last month's balance added to it. Shortly thereafter you get a note advising you that your service will be terminated in ten days if you don't pay the bill. Wait a few days and send them a five or ten dollar money order with a note saying you've had an accident and are pressed for funds because of large medical bills, but you'll send them the balance as soon as you are up and around again. That will hold them for another month. In all, you can stretch it out for four or five months with a variety of excuses and small payments. This also works with the gas and electric companies and with any department stores you conned into letting you charge.

You can get the service deposit reduced to half of the normal rate if you are a student or have other special qualifications. Surprisingly, these rates and discounts vary from area to area, so check around before you go into the business office for your phone. There is an incredible 50 cents charge per month for not having your phone listed. If you want an unlisted phone, you can avoid this fee by having the phone listed in a fictitious name, even if the bill is sent to you. Just say you want your roommate's name listed instead of your own.

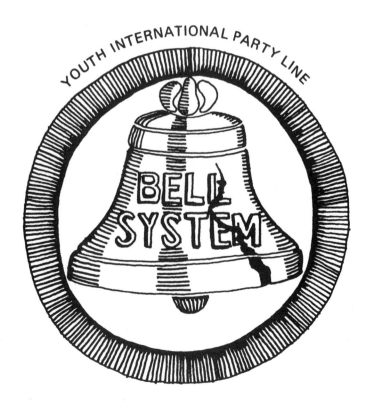

Fuck! I forgot my shirt ....

FREE PLAY

MOVIES AND CONCERTS

There are many ways to sneak into theaters, concerts, stadiums and other entertainment houses. All these places have numerous fire exits with push-bar doors that open easily from the inside. Arrive early with a group of friends, after casing the joint and selecting the most convenient exit. Pay for one person to get in. When he does he simply opens the designated exit door when the ushers are out of the area and everyone rushes inside.

For theatrical chains in large cities, call their home office and ask to speak to the vice-president in charge of publicity, sales, or personnel. Ask what his name is so you'll know who you're talking to. When you get the information you want, hang up. Now you have the name of a high official in the company. Compile a short list of officials in the various film, theater and sporting event companies. Next call the various theaters and do the same thing for the theater managers. Once you have the two lists you are ready to proceed. Call the theater you want to attend. When someone answers say you're Mr._____from the home office calling Mr._____ (manager's name) and you'd like to have two passes O.K'd for two important people from out of town. Invariably she'll just ask their names or tell them to mention your name at the box office. Not only will you get in free, but you can avoid waiting in line with this fake-out.

In Los Angeles and New York, the studios hold pre-release screenings for all movies. If you know roughly when a movie is about to come out, call the publicity department of the studio producing the film and say you're the critic for a newspaper or magazine (give the name) and ask them when you can screen the film. They'll give you the time and place of various screenings. When you go, ask them to put you on their list and you'll get notices of all future screenings.

One of our favorite ways to sneak into a theater with continuously running shows is the following. Arrive just as the show is emptying out and join the line leaving the theater. Exclaiming, "Oh, my gosh!" you slap your forehead, turn around and return, tell the usher you left your hat, pocketbook, etc. inside. Once you're inside the theater, just swipe some popcorn and wait for the next show.

RECORDS AND BOOKS

If you have access to a few addresses, you can get all kinds of records and books from clubs on introductory offers. Since the cards you mail back are not signed there is no legal way you can be held for the bill. You get all sorts of threatening mail, which, by the way, also comes free.

If you have a friend who is a member of a record club, ask him to submit your name as a free member. He gets 4 free records for getting you signed up. As soon as you get the letter saying how lucky you are to be a member, quit. Your friend's free records have already been shipped. We used to have at least 10 different names and addresses working on all the record and book companies. Every other day we would ride around collecting the big packages. To cap it off, we opened a credit account at a large department store and used to return most of the records and books to the store saying that they were gifts and we wanted something else. Since we had an account at the store, they always took the merchandise and gave credit for future purchases.

You can always use the public libraries. Find out when they do their yearly housecleaning. Every library discards thousands of books on this day. Just show up and ask if you can take some.

Almost anything you might want to know from plans for constructing a sundial to a complete blueprint for building a house may be obtained free from the Government Printing Office. Write: to Superintendent of Documents, Government Printing Office, Washington, D.C. 20402. Most publications are free. Those that are not are dirt cheap. Ask to be put on the list to receive the free biweekly list of *Selected U.S. Government Publications.*

One of the best ways to receive records and books free is to invest twenty dollars and print up some stationery with an artistic logo for some non-existent publication. Write to all the public relations departments of record companies, publishing houses, and movie studios. Say you are a newspaper with a large youth readership and have regular reviews of books, or records, or movies, and would like to be placed on their mailing list. Say that you would be glad to send them any reviews of their records that appear in the paper. That adds a note of authenticity to the letter. After a month or so you'll be receiving more records and books than you can use.

If you really want a book badly enough, follow the title of this one—Dig!

THIS NOTE ENTITLES THE
BEARER UPON DEMAND FREE
MUSIC, DOPE, AND GUNS

0176SNORT39157

Rusty Wagon
OLD PIONEER

FREE MONEY

No book on survival should fail to give you some good tips on how to rip-off bread. Really horning in on this chapter will put you on Free-loader Street for life, 'cause with all the money in Amerika, the only thing you'll have trouble getting is poor.

WELFARE

It's so easy to get on welfare that anyone who is broke and doesn't have a regular relief check coming in is nothing but a goddamn lazy bum! Each state has a different set up. The racist penny-pinchers of Mississippi dole out only $8.00 a month. New York dishes out the most with monthly payments up to $120.00. The Amerikan Public Welfare Association publishes a book called *The Public Welfare Directory* with information on

0176 SNORT 39157

DULUTH, MINNESOTA

7

ONE

D₁₁₉

WORLD SERIES *Hungry Chuck Biscuits* 7
WHOEVER HE IS

1

CATE
ATION

BUCK

1

—Daniel Clyne—

exactly what each welfare agency provides and how you go about qualifying. You can read the directory at any public library to find out all you can about how your local office operates.

When you've discovered everything you need to know, head on down to the Welfare Department in your grubbiest clothes. Not sleeping the night before helps. The receptionist will assign an "intaker" to interview you. After a long wait, you'll be directed to a desk. The intaker raps to you for a while, generally showing sympathy for your plight and turns you over to the caseworker who will make the final and ultimate assessment.

Have your heaviest story ready to ooze out. If you have no physical disabilities, lay down a "mentally deranged" rap. Getting medical papers saying you have any long-term illness or defect helps a lot. Tell the caseworker you get dizzy spells on the job and faint in the street. Keep bobbing your head, yawning, or scratching. Tell him that you have tried to commit suicide recently because you just can't make it in a world that has forgotten how to love. Don't lay it on too obviously. Wait till he "pries" some of the details from you. This makes the story even more convincing. Many welfare workers are young and hip. The image you are working on is that of a warm, sensitive kid victimized by brutal parents and a cold ruthless society. Tell them you held off coming for months because you wanted to maintain some self-respect even though you have been walking the streets broke and hungry. If you are a woman, tell him you were recently raped. In sexist Amerika, this will probably be true.

After about an hour or so of this soap-opera stuff, you'll be ready to get your first check. From then on it's a monthly check, complete medical care for free and all sorts of other outasight benefits. Occasionally the caseworker will drop by your pad or ask you down to the office to see how you're coming along, but with your condition, things don't look so good. Don't abandon hope though. Hope always helps fill in a caseworker's report.

The real trick is to parlay welfare payments in a few different states. Work out an exchange system with a buddy and mail each other the checks when they come in. If the caseworker comes by, your roommate can say you went to find a job or enrolled in a class. We know cats who have parlayed welfare payments up to six hundred dollars a month.

UNEMPLOYMENT

Every outlaw should learn everything there is to know about the rules governing unemployment insurance. As in the case of welfare, rules, eligibility, and the size of payments differ from state to state. In New York, you are eligible for payments equivalent to half your weekly salary before taxes up to $65 per week, on the condition that you have worked for a minimum of twenty weeks during the year. Payments are somewhat lower in most other states. In order to collect, you must show you are actively searching for a job and keep a record of employers you contact. This can easily be fudged. Every time you're questioned about it, mention one or two companies. If your hair is long, you'll have no problem. Just say they won't hire you until you get a haircut. When this is the case, the unemployment office canot cut off your payments or your hair. They also cannot make you accept a job you do not want. Tell them any job offer you get is not challenging enough for your talents. Unemployment can be collected for six months before payments are terminated. Twenty more weeks of slavery and you can go back to maintaining your dignity in the unemployment line. These job insurance payments cannot be taxed and since you are working so few weeks out of each year, your taxable income is at a minimum. Read all the fine print for tax form 1040 and discover all the deductible loopholes available to you. You should wind up paying no taxes at all or having all the taxes that were deducted from your pay reimbursed. Never turn over to the pig government any funds you can rip off. Remember, it isn't your government, so why submit to its taxation if you feel you do not have representation.

PANHANDLING

The practice of going up to folks and bumming money is a basic hustling art. If you are successful at panhandling, you'll be able to master all the skills in the book and then some. To be good at it requires a complete knowledge of what motivates people. Even if we don't need the bread, we panhandle on the streets in the same way doctors go back to medical school. It helps us stay in shape. Panhandling is illegal throughout Pig Empire, but it's one of those laws that is rarely enforced unless they want to "clean the area" of hippies. If you're in a strange locale, ask a fellow panhandler what the best places to work are without risking a bust. Do it in front of supermarkets, theaters, sporting events, hip dress shops and restaurants. College cafeterias are very good hunting grounds.

When you're hustling, be assertive. Don't lean against the wall with your palm out mumbling "Spare some change?" Go up to people and stand directly in front of them so they have to look you in the eye and say no. Bum from guys with dates. Bum from motherly looking types. After a while you'll get a sense of the type of people you get results with.

Theater can be real handy. The best actors get the most bread. Devising a street theater skit can help. A good prop is a charity cannister. You can get them by going to the offices of a mainstream charity and signing up as a collector. Don't feel bad about ripping them off. Charities are the biggest swindle around. 80% or more of the funds raised by honky charities go to the organization itself. New fancy cars for the Red Cross, inflated salaries for the executives of the Cancer Fund, tax write-offs for Jerry Lewis. You get the picture. A good way to work this and keep your karma in shape is to turn over half to a revolutionary group such as your local underground. Remember, fugitives from injustice depend on you to survive. Be a responsible member of our nation. Support the only war we have going!

RIP-OFFS

If you are closing out your checking account, overdraw your account by $10.00. The bank won't bother chasing you down for a lousy 10 bucks.

Call the telephone operator from time to time and tell her you lost some change in a pay phone. They will mail you the cash.

You can get $150 to $600 in advance by willing your body to a University medical school. They have you sign a lot of papers and put a tattoo on your foot. You can get the tattoo removed and sell your body to the folks across the street. The universities can be ripped off by enrolling, applying for a loan and bugging out after the loan comes through. This is a lot easier than you might imagine and you can hit them for up to $2,500 with a good enough story.

Put a number 14 brass washer in a newspaper vending machine and take out all the papers. Stand around the corner or go into the local bar and sell them. You often get tipped. Don't do this with underground papers. Remember they're your brothers and sisters.

The airlines will give you $250 for each piece of luggage you lose when flying. The following is a good way to lose your luggage. When you get off a plane, have a friend meet you at the gate. Give him your luggage claim stubs and arrange to meet at a washroom or restaurant. Your friend picks up the bags and takes them out of the baggage room. Before he leaves the airport, he turns over the stubs to you at your prearranged rendezvous. You casually wander over to the baggage department and search for your elusive luggage. When all the baggage has been claimed, file a complaint with the lost and found department. They'll have you fill out a form, explain that it probably got misplaced on another carrier and promise to send it to you as soon as it is located. In a month you'll receive a check for $250 per bag. Enjoy your flight.

THE INTERNATIONAL
YIPPIE CURRENCY EXCHANGE

Every time you drop a coin into a slot, you are losing money needlessly. There is at least one foreign coin that is the same size or close enough that will do the trick for less than a penny. The following are some of the foreign currencies that will get you that Coke, call or subway ride.

Quarter Size Coins

URUGUAYAN 10 CENTISIMO PIECE—works in many soda and candy machines, older telephones (3 slot types), toll machines, laundromats, parking meters, stamp machines, and restroom novelty machines. Works also in some electric cancerette machines but not most mechanical machines.

DANISH 5 ORE PIECE —works in 3 slot telephones, toll machines,laundromats,automats, some stamp machines, most novelty machines, and the Boston Subway. Does not work in soda or cancerette machines.

PERUVIAN 20 CENTAVO PIECE —generally similar to Danish 5 Ore Piece.

MEXICAN 10 CENTAVO PIECE —works in new (one slot) telephones and some electric cancerette machines, but does not work as many places as the Uruguay, Danish and Peruvian coins.

ICELANDIC 5 AURAN PIECE —most effective quarter in the world, even works in change machines. Unfortunately, this coin is practically impossible to get outside of Iceland and even there, it is becoming difficult since the government is attempting to remove it from circulation.

Dime Size Coins

MALASIAN PENNY —generally works in all dime slots, including old and new telephones, candy machines, soda machines, electric machines, stamp machines, parking meters, photocopy machines, and pay toilets. Does not work in some newer stamp dispensers, and some mechanical cancerette machines.

TRINIDAD PENNY —generally works the same as Malaysian Penny.

New York Subway Tokens

DANISH 25 ORE PIECE —works in 95% of all subway turnstiles. A very safe coin to use since it will not jam the turnstile. It is 5/1000th of an inch bigger than a token.

PORTUGUESE 50 CENTAVO PIECE —the average Portuguese Centavo Piece is 2/1000th of an inch smaller than a token.

JAMAICAN HALF PENNY, BAHAMA PENNY and *AUSTRALIAN SCHILLING* —these coins are

12/1000th to 15/1000th of an inch smaller than a token. They work in about 80% of all turnstiles. We have also had good success with *FRENCH 1 FRANC PIECE* (WW II issue), *SPANISH 10 CENTAVO PIECE, NICARAGUAN 25 CENTAVO PIECE.*

All of the coins listed have a currency value of a few cents, with most less than one penny. Foreign coins work more regularly than slugs and are non-magnetic, hence cannot be detected by "slug detector machines." Also unlike slugs, although they are illegal to use in machines, they are perfectly legal to possess and exchange.

Large coin dealers and currency exchanges are generally uptight about handling cheap foreign coins in quantity since they don't make much profit and are subject to certain pressures in selling coins that are the same size as Amerikan coins or tokens.

People planning trips to European or South American countries should bring back rolls of coins as souvenirs or for use in "coin jewelry."

If you do not plan to travel, a small coin store which is cool about selling to the public is located on the Lower East Side at 191 East Third Street, New York City. When their phone works, the number is 475-9897.

Washers are the most popular types of slugs. You can go to any hardware store and match them up with various coins. Sometimes you might have to put a small piece of scotch tape over one side of the hole to make it more effective. Each washer is identified by its material and a number, i.e. No. 14 brass washer with scotch tape on one side is a perfect dime. When you get the ones you want, you can buy thousands for next to nothing (especially at industrial supply stores) and pass them out to your friends.

Xerox copies of both sides of a dollar bill, carefully glued together, work in most machines that give you change for a dollar. Excuse us, there is a knock at the door . . . Fancy that! It's the Treasury Department. Wonder what they want?

94

FREE DOPE

BUYING, SELLING AND GIVING IT AWAY

As you probably know, most dope is illegal, therefore some risks are always involved in buying and selling. "Eternal vigilance and constant mobility are the passwords of survival," said Che Guevara, and nowhere do they apply more than in the world of dope. If you ever have the slightest doubt about the person with whom you're dealing—DON'T.

Buying

In the purchasing of dope, arrests are not a problem unless you're the fall guy for a bust on the dealer. The major hazard is getting burned. Buy from a friend or a reputable dealer. If you have to do business with a stranger, be extra careful. Never front money. One of the burn artist's tricks is to take your money, tell you to wait and split with your dough. There are various side show gimmicks each burn artist works. The most common is to ask you to walk with them a few blocks and then stop in front of an apartment building. He then tells you the dope is upstairs and asks you to hand over the money in advance. He explains that his partner is real uptight 'cause they were raided once and won't let anybody in the pad. He takes your dough and disappears inside the building, out the back door or up to the roof and into his getaway helicopter. You are left on the sidewalk with anxious eyes and that "can this really be happening to me" feeling.

Another burn method is to substitute oregano, parsley or catnip for pot, camel shit for hash, saccharin or plain pills for acid. If you got burned for heroin or speed, you're better off being taken, because these are body-fuck drugs that can mess you up badly. The people that deal them are total pigs and should be regarded as such. When you're buying from strangers, you have a right to sample the merchandise free unless it's coke. Check the weight of the grass with a small pocket scale. Feel the texture and check out how well it has been cleaned of seeds and twigs. Smoke a joint that is rolled from the stuff you get. Don't accept the dealer's sample that he pulled out of his pocket. When you are buying a large amount of acid, pick a sample. You should never buy acid from a stranger as it is too easy a burn.

If you buy cocaine, bring along a black light. Only the impurities glow under its florescence, thus giving you an idea of the quality of the coke. Make sure it's the real thing. Sniffing coke can perforate your nasal passages, so be super moderate. Too much will kill you. A little bit goes a long way.

Selling

Dealing, although dangerous, is a tax-free way of surviving even though it borders on work. The best way to start is to save up a little bread and buy a larger quantity than you usually get. Then deal out smaller amounts to your friends. The fewer strangers you deal with, the safer you are. The price of dope varies with the amount of stuff on the market in your area, the heat the narks are bringing down and the connections you have. A rough scale, say, for pot is $20 an ounce, $125 a pound and $230 a kilo (2.2 pounds). The price per ounce decreases depending on the amount you get. It's true you make more profit selling by the ounces, but the hassle is greater and the more contacts you must make increases the risk. Screwing your customers will prove to be bad karma (unless you consider dying groovy), so stick to honest dealing. Never deal from your pad and avoid keeping your stash there. Get into searching out the best markets which are generally in California, given its close proximity to good ol' Mexico. Kansas is a big distribution center for Mexican grass, too. You can ship the stuff (safer than carrying) via air freight anywhere in the country for about $30 a trunk. Keep the sending and receiving end looking straight. We have one friend who wears a priest's outfit to ship and receive dope. In fact, every time we see nuns or priests on the street, we assume they're outlaws just on their way to the next deal or bombing. For all we know, the church actually is nothing but a huge dope ring in drag. Anybody gotten high off communion wafers lately?

When you talk about deals on the phone, be cool. Make references to theater tickets or subscriptions. Don't keep extensive notes on your activities and contacts. Use code names where you can. Never deal with two other people present. Only you and the buyer should be in the immediate vicinity. Narks make busts in pairs so one can be the arresting officer and the other can be a court witness. Dealing is a paradox of unloading a good amount of shit but not trying to move too fast; of making new contacts but being careful of strangers; of dealing high quality and low prices; and of being simultaneously bold and cautious. If you get nabbed, get the best lawyer who specializes in dope busts. First offenders rarely end up serving time, but it's a different story for repeaters. Know how punitive the courts are and which judges and prosecutors can be bought off. Never deal in the month before an election. For complete information on how to avoid getting busted and what to do if busted, read *The Drug Bust* (listed in appendix).

Giving It Away

Giving dope away can be a real mind-blower. Every dealer should submit to voluntary taxation by the new Nation. If you are a conscientious dealer, you should be willing and eager to give a good hunk of your stash away at special events or to groups into free distribution. You should also be willing to give bread to bust trusts set up to bail out heads unable to get up the ransom money the whisky lush courts demand. Many groups have done huge mailings of joints to all sorts of people. A group in New York mailed 30,000 to people in the phone book on one Valentine's Day. A group in Los Angeles placed over 2,000 joints in library books and then advised kids

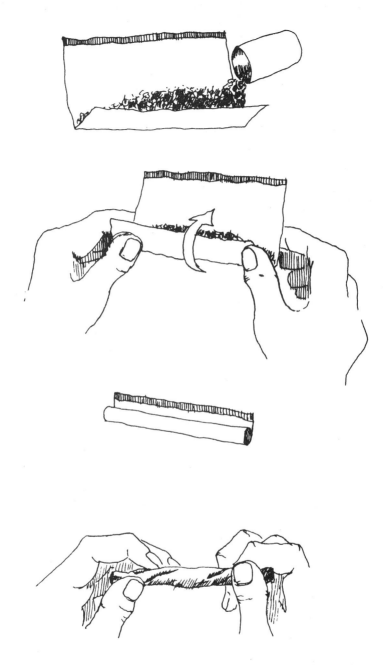

Avoid all needle drugs – the only dope worth shooting is
Richard Nixon

to smoke a book during National Library Week. Be cool about even giving stuff away since that counts as dealing in most states. John Sinclair, Chairman of the White Panther Party, is serving 9½ to 10 years for giving away two joints.

GROW YOUR OWN

Pot is a weed and as such grows in all climates under every kind of soil condition. We have seen acres and acres of grass growing in Kansas, Iowa and New Jersey. If you're not located next door to a large pot field growing in the wild, maybe you would have some success in growing your own. It's well worth it to try your potluck!

The first thing is to start with a bunch of good-quality seeds from grass that you really dig. Select the largest seeds and place them between two heavy-duty napkins or ink blotters in a pan. Soak the napkins with water until completely saturated. Cover the top of the pan or place it in a dark closet for three days or until a sprout about a half inch long appears from most of the seeds.

During this incubation period, you can prepare the seedling bed. Use a low wooden box such as a tomato flat and fill it with an inch of gravel. Fill the rest of the box with some soil mixed with a small amount of fertilizer. Moisten the soil until water seeps out the bottom of the box, then level the soil making a flat surface. With a pencil, punch holes two inches apart in straight rows. You can get about 2 dozen in a tomato flat.

When the incubation period is over, take those seeds that have an adequate sprout and plant one in each hole. The sprout goes down and the seed part should be a little above ground. Tamp the soil firmly (do not pack) around each plant as you insert the sprouts.

The seedlings should remain in their boxes in a sunny window until about mid-May. They should receive enough water during this period to keep the soil moist.

My, won't the folks at the Horticultural Show be amazed

By the time they are ready to go into the ground, the green plants should be about six to eight inches tall.

If it is late winter or early spring and you have a plot of land that gets enough sun and is sheltered from nosy neighbors, you should definitely grow grass in the great outdoors.

One idea is to plant sunflowers in your garden as these grow taller than the pot plants and camouflage them from view. The best idea is to find some little-used field and plant a section of it.

Prepare the land the way you would for any garden vegetable. Dig up the ground with a pitchfork or heavy duty rake, removing rocks. Rake the plot level and punch holes in the soil about three inches deep and about two feet apart in the same way you did in the seedling boxes. Remove the young plants from the box, being careful not to disturb the roots and keeping as much soil intact as possible. Transplant each plant into one of the punched-out holes and firmly press the soil to hold it in place. When all the plants are in the ground, water the entire area. Tend them the way you would any other garden. They should reach a height of about six feet by the end of the summer and be ready to harvest.

If you don't have access to a field, you can grow good stuff right in your own closet or garage using artificial lighting. Transplant the plants into larger wooden boxes or flower boxes. Be sure and cover the bottom of each box with a few inches of pebbles or broken pottery before you add the soil. This will insure proper drainage. Fertilize the soil according to the instructions on the box and punch out holes in much the same way you would do if you were growing outside. After the young plants have been transplanted and watered thoroughly, you will have to rig up a lighting system. Use blue light bulbs, which are available at hardware stores, for the first thirty days. These insure a shorter, sturdier stalk. Leave the lights on 24 hours a day and place them about a foot above the tops of the plants. If the plants begin to feel brittle or turn yellow at the edges, then the temperature is too hot. Use less illumination or raise the height of the lamp if this occurs.

After the first thirty days, change to red bulbs and cut down the lighting time to 16 hours a day. After a week, reduce the time to 14 hours and then on the third week to 12 hours. Maintain this lighting period until the plants flower. The female plants have a larger and heavier flower structure and the males are somewhat skimpy. The female plant produces the stronger grass and the choicest parts are the top leaves including the flowers.

Inside or outside, the plants will be best if allowed to reach maturity, although they are smokeable at any point along the way. When you want to harvest the crop, wet the soil and pull out the entire plant. If you want to separate the top leaves from the rest, you can do so and make two qualities of grass. In any event, let the plants dry in the sun for two weeks until they are thoroughly dried out. If you want to hurry the drying process, you can do it in an oven using a very low heat for about twenty minutes. After you've completed the drying, you can "cure" the grass by putting the plants in plastic bags and sprinkling drops of wine, rum or plain booze on them. This greatly increases the potency.

There are two other ways that we know work to increase the potency of grass you grow or buy. One consists of digging a hole and burying a stash of grass wrapped in a plastic bag. A few months in the ground will produce a mouldy grass that is far fuckin' out. A quick method is to get a hunk of dry ice, put it in a metal container or box with a tight lid (taping the lid airtight helps), and sprinkling the grass on top. Allow it to sit tightly covered for about three days until all the dry ice evaporates.

ASSORTED FREEBIES

LAUNDRY

Wait in a laundromat. Tell someone with a light load that you'll watch the machine for them if you can stick your clothes in with theirs.

PETS

Your local ASPCA will give you a free dog, cat, bird or other pet. Have them inspect and innoculate the animal which they will do free of charge. You can get free or very cheap medical care for your pet at a school for veterinary medicine.

Underground newspapers often carry a free-pets column in the back pages. Snakes can be caught in any wooded area and they make great pets. You can collect insects pretty easy. Ants are unbelievable to watch. You can make a simple 3/4 inch wide glass case about a foot high, fill it with sand and start an ant colony. A library book will tell you how to care for them.

Every year the National Park Service gives away surplus elks in order to keep the herds under its jurisdiction from outgrowing the amount of available land for grazing. Write to: Superintendent, Yellowstone National Park, Yellowstone, Wyoming 83020. You must be prepared to pay the freight charges for shipping the animal and guarantee that you can provide enough grazing land to keep the big fellow happy.

Under the same arrangement the government will send you a Free Buffalo. Write to: Office of Information, Department of the Interior, Washington, D.C. 20420. So many people have written them recently demanding their Free Buffalo, that they called a press conference to publicly attack the Yippies for creating chaos in the government. Don't take any buffalo shit from these petty bureaucrats, demand the real thing. Demand your Free Buffalo.

Oh wow! Where'd you get that cute little free buffalo?

You can get a free 16mm movie about parakeets called *"More Fun with Parakeets,"* by writing to: R.T. French Co., 9068 Mustard St., Rochester, New York 14609. This great film won an Academy Award for best picture of 1793.

POSTERS

Beautiful wall posters are available by writing to the National Tourist Agencies of various countries. Most are located between 42nd and 59th Streets on Fifth Ave. in New York City. You can find their addresses in the New York Yellow Pages under both National Tourist Agencies and Travel Agencies. There are over fifty of them. Prepare a form letter saying you are a high school geography teacher and would like some posters of the country to decorate your classroom. In a month you'll be flooded with them. Airline companies also have colorful wall posters they send out free.

SECURITY

For this trick you need some money to begin with. Deposit it in a bank and return in a few weeks telling them you lost your bank book. They give you a card to fill out and sign and in a week you will receive another book. Now withdraw your money, leaving you with your original money and a bank book showing a balance. You can use this as identification to prevent vagrancy busts when traveling, as collateral for bail, or for opening a charge account at a store.

Another trick is to buy some American Travelers Checks. Wait a week and report your checks lost. They'll give you new ones to replace the missing ones. You spend your new checks and keep the ones you reported lost as security. This security is great for international travel especially at border crossings. If you want, you can spend the Travelers Checks by giving them to a friend to forge your name. Before you call the office to report the loss, call the police station and say you were mugged and your wallet was stolen. The agency always asks if you have reported the lost checks to the police, so you can safely answer yes. Never do this for more than five hundred dollars and never more than once with any one company.

POSTAGE

When mailing to the same city, address the envelope or package to yourself and put the name of the person you are sending it to where the return address generally goes. Mail it without postage and it will be "returned" to the sender. Because almost all letters are machine processed, any stamp that is the correct size will pass. Easter Seals and a variety of other type stamps usually get by the electronic scanner. If you put the stamp on a spot other than the far upper right corner, it will not be cancelled and can be used again by the person who gets your letter. If you have a friend working in a large corporation, you can run your organization's mail through their postage meter.

Those ridiculous free introductory or subscription type letters that you get in the mail often have a postage-guaranteed return postcard for your convenience. The next one you get, paste it on a brick and drop it in the mailbox. The company is required by law to pay the postage. You can also get rid of all your garbage this way.

MAPS

You can get a free full-color World Atlas by writing to Hammond, Inc. Maplewood, New Jersey 07040.

MINISTRY

Unquestionably one of the best deals going is becoming a minister in the Universal Life Church. They will send you absolutely free, bona fide ordination papers. These entitle you to all sorts of discounts and tax exemptions. Right now, sit down and write to Universal Life Church Inc., 601 3rd St., Modesto, California 95351. Try cutting out the card on the following page and laminate it. Let us know how it works out.

```
┌ ─ ─ ─ ─ ─ ─ ─ ─ ─ ─ ─ ─ ─ ─ ─ ─ ─ ─ ┐
│          THE UNIVERSAL BAPTIST CHURCH          │
│                                                │
│                  Box 1776                      │
│                                                │
│            MIRACLE VALLEY, ARIZONA             │
│                                                │
│   Reverend ...........................................   │
│                          Ministry to the World   │
│                                                │
│   This is to certify that              is a    │
│   fully ordained minister in the Universal Baptist │
│   Church and entitled to the rights and privileges │
│   thereof.                                     │
│                                                │
│            "GOD IS COMING BACK"                │
└ ─ ─ ─ ─ ─ ─ ─ ─ ─ ─ ─ ─ ─ ─ ─ ─ ─ ─ ┘
```

cut me out.... cut me out.... cut me out.... cut me out.

ATROCITIES

Join the Army!

VETERAN'S BENEFITS

Write to the Veteran's Administration Information Service, Washington, D.C. 20420 asking them for the free services they provide for veterans. Send fifteen cents to the Government Printing Office for their booklet *Federal Benefits Available to Veterans and Their Dependents.*

WATCH

A $330 Bulova sport timer accurate to 1/10 of a second will be lent free to judges and referees to time any amateur sporting event. Call your local authorized Bulova dealer and get one lent to you under a phony name. Tell them you want to time an orgy.

VACATIONS

There are many ways to take a free vacation, but here's one you might not have considered. It's an all-expenses paid trip to Las Vegas for absolutely nothing. Call a travel agent and request information about Las Vegas gambling junkets (you'll probably have to hunt around because this practice is being curtailed). Different hotels have different deals, but the average one runs something like this: If you agree to buy $500 worth of chips that can only be spent on the gambling tables of the host hotel, they will fly you round trip, pay all hotel and food bills and provide you with a rented car. Go with a close friend and check into the hotel. Once at the routlette or craps table, you and your friend bet the same amount of chips against each other on even-paying chances. For example, he would bet on red and you on black. When either of you wins, you keep the house chips; when you lose, turn in the specially marked chips that cannot be cashed in. What you are doing is simply exchanging the chips you came with for house chips that you can cash in for real dough. Theoretically your two vacations should cost $23.00 if you do the betting at the crap table and $52.00 if you bet even chances at roulette. That is because the house wins if 0 or 00 comes up in roulette and if 12 comes up on the first roll of the dice, but it sure is a hell of a vacation for two for $23.00, and you get free champagne on some flights.

You can get half a vacation free by going to the Amerikan Embassy or Consulate in the country you find yourself in and claim that you're destitute. There is a law on the books that says they have to send you home. They might try to send you away, but be persistent. Make up a story about how your parents are away from home traveling. Say you got mugged or something and you are about to go to the newspapers with your story. Eventually they'll get you a free plane ticket. They stamp your passport invalid though, and you have to pay the government back before you can use it again.

DRINKS

When hitching, it's a good idea to carry a bottle opener and a straw. You take the caps off soda bottles while they're still in the machine and drink them dry without ever touching the bottle.

BURIALS

For ways to avoid the high cost of dying in Amerika, write to: Continental Association, 39 East Van Buren St., Chicago, Ill. 60605. Send them $1.00 for the Manual of Simple Burial and 25¢ for a list of Memorial Associates.

ASTRODOME PICTURES

Don't you just have to have a huge, glossy color photo of Houston's famed Astrodome to show all your friends? Use the teacher bit and write to: Greater Houston Convention and Visitors Council, 1006 Main St., Houston, Texas 77002.

DIPLOMA

Above the paper towel dispenser in a service station restroom was written: "San Francisco State Diplomas." If you really need a college or a high school diploma, send $2.00 to Glenco, Box 834, Warren, Michigan 48090. They send you one that looks real authentic. It ain't Harvard, but it looks good enough to frame and put on your wall.

TOILETS

SNEAK UNDER!

Candid shot of entire Daily News staff meeting a deadline.

Tell It All, Brothers and Sisters

STARTING A PRINTING WORKSHOP

Leaflets, posters, newsletters, pamphlets and other printed matter are important to any revolution. A printing workshop is a definite need in all communities, regardless of size. It can vary from a garage with a mimeograph machine to a mammoth operation complete with printing presses and fancy photo equipment. With less than a hundred dollars and some space, you can begin this vital service. It'll take a while before you get into printing greenbacks, phony identification papers and credit cards like the big boys, but to walk a mile you must start with one step as Gutenberg once said.

Paper

The standard size for paper is 8½" x 11". It comes 500 sheets to a "ream" and 10 reams to a case. You want a 16-20 bond weight sheet. The higher weights are better if you are printing on both sides. You can purchase what are termed "odd lots" from most paper companies. This means that the colors will be assorted and some sheets will be frayed at the edges or wrinkled. Odd lots can be purchased at great discounts. Some places sell paper this way for 10% of the original price and for leaflets, different colors help. Check this out with paper suppliers in your area.

Ink

Inks come in pastes and liquids and are available in stationary stores and office supply houses. Each machine requires its own type ink, so learn what works best with the one you have. Colored ink is slightly more expensive but available for most machines.

Stencils

Each machine uses a particular size and style stencil. If you get stuck with the wrong kind and can't get out to correct the mistake, you can punch extra holes in the top, trim them with a scissors if they are too big or add strips of tape to the sides if too narrow.

Be sure and use only the area that will fit on the paper you are using. Most stencils can be used for paper larger than standard size. Stencils will "cut" a lot neater if an electric typewriter is used. If you only have access to a manual machine, remove the ribbon so the keys will strike the stencil directly. A plastic sheet, provided by the supplier, can be inserted between the stencil and its backing to provide sharper cuts by the keys. If you hold the stencil up to a light, you should be able to clearly see the typing. If you can't, you'll have to apply more pressure.

Sketches can be done with a ball point pen or special stylus directly on the stencil. If you're really rushed, or there isn't that much info to get on the leaflet, you can hand-print the text using these instruments. Take care not to tear the stencil.

Mimeograph Machines

The price of a new mimeograph runs from $200 to $1200, depending on how sophisticated a machine you need and can afford. A.B. Dick and Gestetner are the most popular brands. Many supply houses have used machines for sale. Check the classified section for bargains. See if any large corporations are moving, going out of business or have just had a fire. Chances are they'll be unloading printing equipment at cheap prices. Campaign offices of losing candidates often have mimeos to unload in November. Many supply houses have renting and leasing terms that you might be interested in considering. Have an idea of the work load and type of printing you'll be handling before you go hunting. Talk to someone who knows what they're doing before you lay down a lot of cash cn a machine.

Duplicators

We prefer duplicators to mimeos even though the price is a little higher. They work faster, are easier to operate and print clearer leaflets. The Gestetner Silk Screen Duplicator is the best bet. It turns out stuff almost as good as offset printing. You can do 10 thousand sheets an hour in an assortment of colors.

Electronic Stencils

If you use electronic stencils you can do solid lettering, line drawings, cartoons and black and white pictures with good contrast. To make an electronic stencil, you map out on a sheet of paper everything you want printed. This is a photo process, so make sure only what you want printed shows up on the sheet. You can use a light blue pencil for guide lines as it won't photograph, but be neat anyway. Printing shops will cut a stencil on a special machine for about $3.00.

The Gestefax Electronic Stencil Cutter can be leased or rented in the same way as the duplicator. If you are doing a lot of printing for a number of different groups, this machine will eliminate plenty of hassle. The stencils cost about 20c each and take about fifteen minutes to make.

If you have an electronic stencil cutter, duplicator, electric typewriter and a cheap source of paper, you can do almost any printing job imaginable. Have a dual rate system: one for community groups and another for regular business orders. You can use the profits to go towards the purchasing of more equipment and to build toward the day when you can get your own offset press.

Silk Screening

Posters, banners and shirts that are unbelievable can be printed by this exciting method. The process is easy to learn and teach. You'll need a fairly large area to work in since the posters have to be hung up to dry.

Pick up any inexpensive paperback book on silk screening. The equipment costs less than $50.00 to begin. Once you get good at it, you can print complicated designs in a number of different colors, including portraits.

UNDERGROUND NEWSPAPERS

Food conspiracies, bust trusts, people's clinics and demonstrations are all part of the new Nation, but if asked to name the most important institution in our lives, one would have to say the underground newspaper. It keeps tuned in on what's going on in the community and around the world. Values, myths, symbols, and all the trappings of our culture are determined to a large extent by the underground press. Each office serves as a welcome mat for strangers, a meeting place for community organizers and a rallying force to fight pig repression. There are probably over 500 regularly publishing with readerships running from a few hundred to over 500,000. Most were started in the last three years. If your scene doesn't have a paper, you probably don't have a scene together. A firmly established paper can be started on about $2,500. Plan to begin with eight pages in black and white with a 5,000 copy run. Each such issue will cost about $300 to print. You should have six issues covered when you start. Another $700 will do for equipment. Offset printing is what you'll want to get from a commercial printing establishment.

You need some space to start, but don't rush into setting up a storefront office until you feel the paper's going to be successful. A garage, barn or spare apartment room will do just fine. Good overhead fluorescent lighting, a few long tables, a bookcase, desk, chairs, possibly a phone and you are ready to start.

Any typewriter will work, but you can rent an IBM Selectric typewriter with a deposit of $120.00 and payments of $20.00 per month. Leasing costs twice as much, but you'll own the machine when the payments are finished. The Selectric has interchangeable type that works on a ball system rather than the old-fashion keys. Each ball costs $18.00, so by getting a few you can vary the type the way a printer does.

A light-table can make things a lot easier when it comes to layout. Simply build a box (3' x 4' is a good size, but the larger the better) out of ½" plywood. The back should be higher than the front to provide a sloping effect. The top should consist of a shelf of frosted glass. Get one strong enough to lean on. Inside the box, attach two fluorescent light fixtures to the walls or base. The whole light table should cost less than $25.00. That really is about all you need, except someone with a camera, a few good writers who will serve as reporters, an artistic person to take care of layout, and someone to hassle printing deals, advertising and distribution. Most people start by having everyone do everything.

Layout

A tabloid size paper is 9 7/8" x 14 5/8" with an inch left over on each side for margins. Columns typically are 3 1/4" allowing for three per page. Experience has found that this size is easy to lay out and more importantly, easy to read. There is an indirect ratio between readability and academic snobbishness. Avoid the textbook look. Remember, the New York Times in its low form represents the Death Kulture.

Start off with a huge collection of old magazines and newspapers. You can cut up all sorts of letters, borders, designs and sketches and paste them together to make eye-catching headlines. Sheets of headline type are available in different styles from art stores for $1.25 a sheet. Buy one of each type and then photograph several copies of each, bringing the price way down. The basic content in the prescribed column size should be banged out on the IBM. The columns can be clipped together with a clothespin to avoid confusion. Use a good heavy bond white opaque paper.

All black and white photographs from newpapers and magazines can be used directly. Color pictures can also be used but it's tricky and you'll have to experiment a little to get an understanding of what colors photograph poorly. Glossy black and white photographs must be shot in half tones to keep the grey areas. You can have them processed at any photo lab. You might also need the photo lab for enlargements or reductions, so make contact and establish a good working relationship.

An Exacto knife is available for 29¢ and you can get a package of 100 blades for $10.00. A few metal rulers, a good pair of scissors, some spray adhesive or rubber cement and you're ready to paste the pages that will make up the "dummy" that goes to the printer. Each page is laid out on special layout sheets with faint blue guide lines that don't photograph. Any large art supply store sells these sheets and all the other supplies.

By working over a light-table, the paste-up can be done more professionally. Experiment with many different layouts for each page before finally pasting up the paper. Use artistic judgement. Don't have a picture in the corner and the rest solid columns. Print can be run over pictures and sketches by preparing two sheets for that page and shooting the background in half-tones. The columns don't have to be run straight up and down, but can run at different angles. The most newsworthy articles should be towards the front of the paper. The centerfold can be treated in an exciting manner. A good idea is to do the centerfold so that it can be used as a poster to put on a wall after the paper is read. If you have ads, they should be kept near the back. The masthead, which gives the staff, mailing address, and similar info, goes near the front. Your focus should be on local activities. A section should be reserved for a directory of local services and events. People giving things away should have a section. The rest really depends on the life style and politics of the staff.

National stories can be supplied by one or more of the news services. Nothing in the underground press is copyrighted, so you can reprint an interesting article from another paper. It's customary to indicate what paper printed it first, or news service it was sent out by. Any underground paper has permission to reprint hunks of this book.

Ads

Most papers find it necessary to get some advertising to help defray the production costs. Some rely totally on subscription; some are outgrowths of organizations and still others are printed up and just handed out free. The ones with ads seem to have the longest life. Make up an ad rate before you put out the first issue. Ads are measured in inches of length. The width is understood by everyone to be the width of the column. If you use the 3¼'' column, however, you'll want to let potential advertisers know you have wide columns.

The way to arrive at a reasonable rate is to estimate the total budget for each issue (adding some for overhead and labor), then each page and finally each column inch. After a little arithmetic you can get a good estimate of your printing cost per inch. Using our figures throughout this section, it should come to about $2.00 per inch. Double this figure and you'll arrive at the correct rate per advertising inch—$4.00. There should be special lower rates for large ads, such as half or full pages. There should also be a special arrangement for a continuous subscriber. If you have a classified section, another rate based on number of words or lines is constructed. A service charge is fixed if you make up the ad layout rather than the advertiser. The whole formula should be worked out and printed up before you lay out the first issue.

The best place to get advertising is locally. Theaters, hip clothing stores, ice cream parlors, and record stores are among the type of advertisers you should approach. After you build up a circulation, you might want to seek out national advertisers. The Underground Press Syndicate, Box 26, Village Station, New York, NY 10014, can be joined for $25.00, no dues thereafter. They try to get national ads for you in addition to sending out a newsletter, a news service, and making sure you get free subscriptions to the other underground papers. The U.P.S. can also do many other things for you, like list you in their directory, obtain legal advice, and bring you together with other underground papers for mutual benefit and defense. Another way to get national advertising is to see who tends to advertise in other underground papers. Send the publicity department of these companies letters and samples of your paper. Never let ads make up more than half the paper.

Distribution

At the beginning you should aim for a bi-weekly paper with a gradual increase in the number of pages. The price should be about 25¢. Check out the local laws about selling papers on the street. It's probably allowed and is a neat way to get the paper around. Give half to the street hawkers. Representatives at high schools and colleges should be sought out. Bookstores and newsstands are good places to distribute. After your paper gets going well, you might try for national distribution. The *Cosmep Newsletter* is put out by the Committee of Small Magazines, Editors and Publishers, PO Box 1425, Buffalo, NY 14214. In addition to good tips if you want to start a small literary magazine or publish your own book, they provide an up-to-date list of small stores around the country that would be likely to carry your paper. Subscriptions should be sought in the paper itself. If you get a lot, check out second class mailing privileges. UPS can help with out-of-city distribution.

If you're in a smaller town, you might have to shop

around or go to another city to get printing done. Many printers print only pigswill, which brings up the point of getting busted for obscenity which can be pretty common. You probably should incorporate, but contact a sympathetic lawyer before you put out your first issue. During the summer there are usually a few alternative media conferences organized by one group or another. You can pick up valuable information and exchange ideas at these gatherings. UPS and and the news services will keep you posted. Good luck and write on!

HIGH SCHOOL PAPERS

The usual high school paper is run by puppet lackeys of the administration. It avoids controversy, naughty language, and a host of other things foreign to the 4-H Club members the school is determined to mass produce. The only thing the staff is good at is kissing the principal's ass. Let's face it, the aim of a good high school newspaper should be to destroy the high school. Publishing and distributing a heavy paper isn't going to earn you the Junior Chamber of Commerce good citizenship award. You might have to be a little mysterious about who the staff is until you understand the ground rules and who controls the ballpark—the people or the principal.

Many schools do not allow papers to be handed out on the school premises. These cases are generally won by the newspapers that take the school to court. You can challenge the rule and make the administration look like the dinosaurs they are by distributing sheets of paper with only your logo and the school rule printed. By gaining outside publicity for the first distribution of the paper, you might put the administration up tight about clamping down on you. It might be difficult to explain in civics class when they get to the freedom of the press stuff. Your paper should have one purpose in mind—to piss off the principal and radicalize the

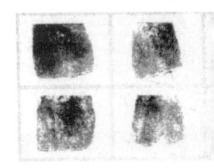

Photographs taken 1970

Nixon is wanted for conspiring to murder tens of thousands of
in connection with the murders of twenty-eight Black Panthe

IF YOU HAVE INFORMATION CONCERNING THIS PERS
PLEASE HELP TO BRING HIM TO JUSTICE.

students. If you run into problems, seek out a sympathetic lawyer. You can get a helpful pamphlet from the ACLU, 156 5th Ave., New York NY 10010, called "Academic Freedom in the Secondary Schools" for 25¢.

Tell your lawyer about the most recent (July 10, 1970) decision of the United States District Court in Connecticut which ruled that the high school students of Rippowan High School in Stamford can publish independent newspapers without having the contents screened in advance by school officials.

ONSPIRACY
ED
US NIXON

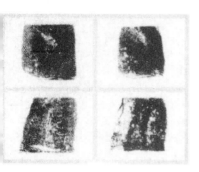

Richard Nixon [signature]

DESCRIPTION
AGE: 57, born January 9, 1913, Yorba Linda, Calif.
HEIGHT: 5' 11½"
WEIGHT: 170 pounds
BUILD: medium
HAIR: black
EYES: brown
COMPLEXION: mottled
RACE: white
NATIONALITY: American
LAST KNOWN ADDRESS: 1600 Pennsylvania Ave,
Washington, D.C.

CAUTION
NIXON REPORTEDLY HAS BEEN ASSOCIATED
WITH PERSONS WHO ADVOCATE THE USE OF
EXPLOSIVES AND MAY HAVE ACQUIRED FIRE-
ARMS. CONSIDER DANGEROUS.

east one million Vietnamese. He is also wanted
, and two Jackson State students.

The same info for underground papers applies to high school rags, only the price should be much less if not free. To begin with, you might just mimeograph the first few issues before trying photo-offset printing. It is very important to get the readers behind you in case you have to go to war with the administration in order to survive. Maintain friendships with above ground reporters, the local underground paper and radical community groups for alliances.

G.I. PAPERS

A heavier scene than even the high schools exists in the No-No Land of the military. None-the-less, against incredible odds, courageous G.I.'s both here and overseas have managed to put out a number of undergound newspapers. If you are a G.I. interested in starting a paper, the first thing to do is seek out a few buddies who share your views on the military and arrange a meeting, preferably off the base. Once you have your group together, getting the paper published will be no problem. Keeping your staff secret, you can have one member contact with someone from a G.I. coffee house, anti-war organization or nearby underground newspaper. This civilian contact person will be in a position to raise the bread and arrange the printing and distribution of the paper. You can write one of the national G.I. newspaper organizations listed at the end of this section if you are unable to find help locally. The paper should be printed off the base. Government equipment should be avoided.

Correspondence and subscriptions can be solicited through the use of a post office box. Such a box is inexpensive and secret (at least that's what the G.I. papers now publishing report) from military snoopers up tight about bad publicity if they get caught spying. If you are mailing the paper to other G.I.'s use first class mail and a plain envelope. This is advice to anybody sending stuff to a G.I. The mail is handled by "lifers" who will report troublemakers to their C.O. (Commanding Officer) if they notice anti-war slogans on envelopes or dirty commie rags coming their way.

You'll want to publish stuff relevant to the lives of the G.I.'s on your base. News of demonstrations, articles on the war, racism, counter-culture, and vital info on how to bug the higher-ups and get out of the military service are all good. Get samples of other newspapers already in operation to get the flavor of writing that has become popular.

Distributing the paper is really more of a problem than the publishing. Here you run smack into Catch 22, which says, "no printed matter may be distributed on a military base without prior written permission of the commanding officer." No such permit has been granted in military history. A few court battles have had limited success and you should go through the formality of obtaining a permit. Send the first issue of the paper to your C.O. with a cover letter stating where and when you intend to distribute the paper on the base. In no part of the application should you list your names. Have a civilian, preferably a civil liberties lawyer, sign the declaration of intent. If more info is requested, go over it with the lawyer before responding, Natch, they're going to want to know who you are and where you get your bread, but fuck 'em. Whether or not you get a permit or have a successful court battle is pretty academic. If the military pigs catch you handing out an underground paper on the base, you're headed for trouble. Use civilian volunteers from your local peace group in as many public roles as possible. They'll be glad to help out.

Print and distribute as many copies as you can rather than concentrating on an expensively printed paper with numerous pages. The very existence of the paper around the base is the most important info the paper can offer. Leave some in mess halls, theaters, benches, washrooms, and other suitable spots. Off base get the paper to sympathetic reporters, coffee houses, colleges and the like. Outside U.S.O. centers and bus terminals are a good place to get the paper out. Rely on donations, so you can make the paper free. Get it together. Demand the right to join the army of your choice. The People's Army! As Joe Hill said in one of his songs, "Yes, I'll pick up a gun but I won't guarantee which way I'll point it."

NEWS SERVICES

Aside from UPS, which is the association of papers, there are five news services that we know of that you might be interested in subscribing to for national stories, photos, production ideas, news of other papers and general movement dope. LNS is the best known. It sends out packets once a week that include about thirty pages with original articles, eye-witness reports, reprints from foreign papers and photographs. They tend to be heavily political rather than cultural and view themselves as molders of ideology rather than strictly a service organization of the underground papers. A subscription costs $15.00 per month, but if you're just starting out they're good about slow payments and such.

You should get in the habit of sending special articles, in particular eye-witness accounts of events that other papers might use, to one or more of the news services for distribution. If you hear of an important event that you would like to cover in your newspaper, call the paper in that area for a quick report. They might send you photos if you agree to reciprocate.

LIBERATION NEWS SERVICE– 160 Claremont Ave., New York, N.Y. 10027 (212) 749-2200
COLLEGE PRESS SERVICE–1779 Church St., NW, Washington, D. C. 20036 (202) 387-7575
CHICANO PRESS ASSOCIATION–La Raza, Box 31004, Los Angeles, California 90031
G.I. PRESS SERVICE–Rm 907, 1029 Vermont Ave., NW, Washington, D.C. 20005
FREE RANGER INTERTRIBAL NEWS SERVICE–Box 26, Village Station, N.Y., N.Y. 10014 (212) 691-6973

A complete and up-to-date list of G.I. underground papers can be obtained by writing to G.I. Press Service, 1029 Vermont Ave., NW, Rm 907, Washington, D.C. 20005. G.I. Alliance provides excellent national newsletters with all sorts of ways to fuck up the Army. Write G.I. Alliance, PO Box 9087, Washington, D.C. 20003. The phone is (202) 544-1654. American Serviceman's Union, 156 5th Avenue, New York, N.Y., 10010 will also help, as well as provide legal and medical aid to G.I.'s.

A complete and up to date list of Chicano underground papers can be obtained by writing to Chicano Press Association, La Raza, Box 31004, Los Angeles, California 90031.

The Young Lords Organization paper *Palante* can be obtained by writing to Young Lords Party, Ministry of Finance, 1678 Madison Ave., New York, N.Y. 10029. It's $5.75 for 24 issues.

The Black Panther Party paper can be obtained by writing to Black Panther Party, Ministry of Information, Box 2967, Custom House, San Francisco, Calif. 94126. It's $7.50 for 52 issues.

THE UNDERGROUND PRESS

ALBION'S VOICE, Box 9033, Savannah, Ga. 31401 $4/yr.

AMAZING GRACE, 212 W. College Ave. Tallahassee, Fla. $6/26 issues.

ANGRY CITY PRESS, 14016 Orinoco Ave., E. Cleveland, Ohio 44112

ANN ARBOR ARGUS, 708 Arch St., Ann Arbor, Mich. 48104 $3/yr.

AQUARIAN ORACLE, 8003 Santa Monica Blvd., L.A., Calif. .50/iss.

AQUARIAN TIMES, 331 Forest Acres Shipping Ctr., Easley, S.C. 29640

AQUARIAN WEEKLY, 292 Main St., Hackensack, N.J.

ASTRAL PROJECTION, Box 4383, Albuquerque, N. Mex. 87106

AUGUR, 207 Ransom Bldg., 115 E. 11th Ave., Eugene, Ore. 97401

BARD OBSERVER, Box 76, Bard College, Annandale-on-the Hudson, N.Y. 12504

BERKELEY BARB, Box 1247, Berkeley, Calif. 94715 $6/yr.

BERKELEY TRIBE, Box 9043, Berkeley, Calif. 94709 $8/

BOTH SIDES NOW, 10370 St. Augustine Rd., Jacksonville, Fla. 32217 $2/12 iss.

BROADSIDE/FREE PRESS, Box 65, Cambridge, Mass. 02139 $4.50/yr.

BURNING RIVER NEWS, 12027 Euclid Ave., Cleveland, Ohio 44112 $5/yr.

CHINOOK, 1452 Pennsylvania St., Denver, Col., 80203 $6/50 iss.

THE CLAM COMMUNITY LIBERATOR, Box 13101, St. Petersburg, Fla. 33733

COME OUT, Box 92, Village Station, New York, N.Y. 10014, $6.50/12 iss.

COUNTRY SENSES, Box 465, Woodbury, Conn. 06798 $5/yr.

CREEM, 3729 Cass Ave., Detroit, Mich. 48201 $5/24 iss.

DAILY PLANET, Suite 2-3514 S. Dixie Hwy., Coconut Grove, Fla. 33133 $5/yr.

DALLAS NOTES, Box 7140, Dallas, Texas 75209 $5/yr.

DIFFERENT DRUMMER, Box 2638, Little Rock, Ark. 72203 $2/14 iss.

DISTANT DRUMMER, 420 South St., Philadelphia, Pa. 19147 $7/yr.

DOOR TO LIBERATION, Box 2022, San Diego, Calif. 92112 $4/26 iss.

DWARFF, Box 26, Village Station, N.Y., N.Y. 10014

EAST VILLAGE OTHER, 20 E. 12 St., N.Y., N.Y. 10003 $6/yr.

EL GRITO DEL NORTE, Box 466, Fairview Station, Espanola N. M. $4/yr.

EYE OF THE BEAST, Box 9218, Tampa, Fla. 33604

FERAFERIA, Box 691, Altadena, Calif. 91001 $4/13 iss.

FIFTH ESTATE, 1107 W. Warren, Detroit, Mich. 48201 $3.75/yr.

FILMMAKERS NEWSLETTER, 80 Wooster St., N.Y., N.Y. 10012

FREEDOM NEWS, Box 1087, Richmond, Calif. 94801 $2.50/12 iss.

FREE SPAGHETTI DINNER, Box 984, Santa Cruz, Calif. 95060 $4/yr.

FREE YOU, 117 University Ave., Palo Alto, Calif. 94301 $6/yr.

FUSION, 909 Beacon St., Boston, Mass. 02215 $5/yr.

GEST, Box 1079, Northland Center, Southfield, Mich. 48075 $2/yr.

GREAT SPECKLED BIRD, Box 54495, Atlanta, Ga. 30308 $6/yr.

GREENFEEL, Jms Madison Law Inst., 4 Patchin Pl., N.Y., N.Y. 10011

GUARDIAN, 32 W. 22 St., N.Y., N.Y. 10010

HAIGHT-ASHBURY TRIBUNE, 1778 Haight St., San Francisco, Calif. 94117 $10/yr.

HARRY, 233 East 25th St., Baltimore, Md., 21218 $4/yr.

INDIANAPOLIS FREE PRESS Box 225, Indianapolis, Ind. 46206 $5/26 iss.

INQUISITION, Box 3882, Charlotte, N.C. 28203 $2/6 iss.

KALEIDOSCOPE, Box 5457, Milwaukee, Wisc. 53211 $5/26 iss.

KUDZU, Box 22502, Jackson, Miss. 39205 $4/yr.

LAS VEGAS FREE PRESS, Box 14096, Las Vegas, Nev. 89114
$7/yr.

LEFT FACE, Box 1595, Anniston, Ala. 36201

LIBERATION, 339 Lafayette St., N.Y. 10012

LIBERATION NEWS SERVICE, 160 Claremont Ave., N.Y. 10027
$15/mth.

LIBERATOR, Box 1147, Morgantown, W. Virginia 26505

LONGBEACH FREE PRESS, 1255 E. 10, Long Beach, Ca. 90813
$6/25 iss.

LOS ANGELES FREE PRESS, 7813 Beverly Blvd., Los Angeles, Ca.
90036 $6/yr.

MADISON KALEIDOSCOPE, Box 881, Madison, Wisc. 53701
$5/yr.

MARIJUANA REVIEW, Calif. Instit. of Arts, 7500 Glenoaks
Blvd., Burbank, Calif. 91504

MEMPHIS ROOT, Box 4747, Memphis, Tenn. 38104 $3.50/yr.

METRO, 906 W. Forest, Detroit, Mich. 48202 $4/yr.

MODERN UTOPIAN, P.O. Drawer A; Diamond Hts. Sta., S.F., Ca.
94131 $4/yr.

MOTHER EARTH NEWS, Box 38, Madison, Ohio 44057 $5/yr.

NEWS FROM NOWHERE, Box 501, Dekalb, Ill. 60115 $5/yr.

NEW PRAIRIE PRIMER, Box 726, Cedar Falls, Iowa 50613
$4/20 iss.

NEW YORK HERALD TRIBUNE, 110 St. Marks Place, N.Y.
$5/lifetime

NOLA EXPRESS, Box 2342, New Orleans, La. 70116 $3/yr.

NORTH CAROLINA ANVIL, Box 1148, Durham, N.C. 27702
$7.50/yr.

NORTHWEST PASSAGE, Box 105, Fairhaven Sta., Bellingham,
Wash. 98225 $5/yr.

OLD MOLE, 2 Brookline St., Cambridge, Mass. 02139 $5/20 iss.

ORACLE OF SAN FRANCISCO, 1764 Haight St., San Francisco,
Ca. 94117

OTHER SCENES, Box 8, Village Station, N.Y. 10014 $6/yr.

OTHER VOICE, c/o Why Not Inc., Box 3175, Shreveport, La.
71103 $5/yr.

PAPER WORKSHOP, 6 Helena Ave., Larchmont, N.Y. 10538 $4/yr.

PEOPLES DREADNAUGHT, Box 1071, Beloit, Wisc.

PHILADELPHIA FREE PRESS, Box 1986, Philadelphia, Pa. 19105

PROTEAN RADISH, Box 202, Chapel Hill, N.C. 27514 $8/yr.

PROVINCIAL PRESS, Madala Print Shop, Box 1276, Spokane,
Wash. 99210 $5/yr.

QUICKSILVER TIMES, 1736 R St., N.W., Wash., D.C. 20009 $8/yr.

RAG, 2330 Guadalupe, Austin, Tex. 78705 $7.50/yr.

RAT, 241 E. 14 St., N.Y. 10009 $6/yr.

REBIRTH, Box 729, Phoenix, Ariz. 85001

RISING UP ANGRY, Box 3746, Merchandise Mart, Chicago, Ill. 60654 $5/yr.

ROOSEVELT TORCH, 430 S. Michigan Ave., Chicago, Ill. 60605

SAN DIEGO STREET JOURNAL, Box 1332, San Diego, Calif. 92112

SECOND CITY, c/o The Guild, 2136 N. Halsted, Chicago, Ill. 60614 $6/26 iss.

SECOND COMING, Box 491, Ypsilanti, Mich. 48197

SEED, 950 W. Wrightwood, Chicago, Ill. 60614 $6/yr.

SPACE CITY, 1217 Wichita, Houston, Tex. 77004

SPECTATOR, c/o S. Indiana Media Corp., Box 1216, Bloomington, Ind. 47401

SUNDANCE, 1520 Hill, Ann Arbor, Mich. 48104 $3.50/yr.

UPROAR, 44 Wimbleton Lane, Great Neck, N.Y. 11023

VIEW FROM THE BOTTOM, 532 State St., New Haven, Conn. 06510 $5/20 iss.

VORTEX, 706 Mass St., Lawrence, Kansas 66044 $5/24 iss.

WALRUS, Box 2307 Sta. A, Champaign, Ill. 61820

WATER TUNNEL, Box 136, State College, Pa. 16801 $3/yr.

WILLIAMETTE BRIDGE, 6 SW 6th, Portland, Ore. 97209 $5/26 iss.

WIN, 339 Lafayette St., N.Y. 10012 $5/yr.

WORKER'S POWER, 14131 Woodward Ave., Highland Park, Mich. 48203 $3.50/yr.

USA/UPS ASSOCIATE MEMBERS

AKWESASNE NOTES, Roosevelton, N.Y. 13683 .50/iss.

ALESTLE, c/o Paul Gorden, 7404 Tower Lake Apt. 1D, Edwardsville, Ill. 62025

ALLIANCE MAGAZINE, Box 229, Athens, Ohio 45701

ALL YOU CAN EAT', R.P.O. 4949, New Brunswick, N.J. 08903 $3/yr.

ALLTOGETHER, 44208 Montgomery-33 Palm Desert, Calif. $10/yr.

ALBION'S VOICE, P.O. Box 9033, Savannah, Ga. 31401 $4/yr.

AQUARIAN HERALD, Box 83, Virginia Beach, Va. 23458

ATLANTIS, 204 Oxford, Dayton, Ohio

BOTH SIDES NOW, 10370 St. Augustine Rd., Jacksonville, Fla. 32217 $2/12 iss.

COLLECTIVE, 614 Clark St., Evanston, Ill. 60201

COME TOGETHER, P.O. Box 163, Encino, Calif. 91316

CROSSROADS, Hill School, Pottstown, Pa. 19464

DALLAS NEWS (CORP), P.O. Box 7013, Dallas, Texas 75209 $4/24 iss.

THE D.C. GAZETTE, 109 8th N.E., Washington, D.C. 20002 $5/yr.

EDGE CITY, 116 Standart St., Syracuse, N.Y. 13201 $3/yr.

EVERYWOMAN, 6516 W. 83 St., Los Angeles, Calif. 90045 $2.50/10 iss.

FAIR WITNESS, P.O. Box 7165, Oakland Sta., Pittsburgh, Pa. 15213

FOX VALLEY KALEIDOSCOPE, Box 252, Oshkosh, Wisc. 54901

FREE PRESS OF LOUISVILLE, 1438 S. First St., Louisville, Ky. 40208 $6/yr.

HIGH GAUGE, Box 4491, University, Ala. 35486 $5/yr.

THE HIPS VOICE, P.O. Box 5132, Santa Fe, N. Mexico 87501 $5/24 iss.

HOME NEWS CO., P.O. Box 5263, Grand Central Station, N.Y. 10017

HUNDRED FLOWERS, Box 7152, Minneapolis, Minn. 55407 $9/yr.

IT AIN'T ME BABE, c/o W.L. Office Box 6323, Albany, Calif. 94706 $6/yr.

LIBERATED GUARDIAN, 14 Cooper Sq., New York, N.Y. 10003 $10/yr.

THE LONG ISLAND FREE PRESS, P.O. Box 162, Westbury, N.Y. 11590 $6/2 yrs.

NEW TIMES, Box J, Temple, Ariz. 85281 $10/52 iss.

NOTES FROM UNDERGROUND, P.O. Box 15081, San Francisco, Calif. 94115

OUR TOWN (COLLECTIVE), Box 611, Eau Claire, Wisc.

PALANTE YLP, 1678 Madison Ave., New York, N.Y.

PROTOS, 1110 N. Edgemont St., Los Angeles, Calif. 90029 $3/yr.

PURPLE BERRIES, 449 West Seventh Ave., Columbus, Ohio

REARGUARD, P.O. Box 8115, Mobile, Ala. 36608 $4/yr.

THE S.S.PENTANGLE, Box 4429, New Orleans, La. 70118 $4/20 iss.

ST. LOUIS OUTLAW, Box 9501, Cabanne Sta., St. Louis, Mo. 63161

SUSQUEHANNA BUGLER, 700 Market St., Williamsport, Pa. 17701 .25/iss.

TASTY COMIX, Box 21101, Wash., D.C. 20009

THE TIMES NOW, Box 676, Coconut Grove, Fla. 33133

TUSCON FREE PRESS, Box 3403, College Sta., Tuscon, Ariz. 85716

CANADA/UPS

ALTERNATE SOCIETY, 10 Thomas St., St. Catharines, Ont. $3.50/12 iss.

CARILLON, Univ. of Sask. Regina Campus, Regina, Saskatchewan

CHEVRON, University of Waterloo, Waterloo, Ontario $8/yr.

DIME BAG, 3592 University St., Montreal 130, Que.

FOURTH ESTATE, 24 Brighton Ct., Fredericton, N.B.

GEORGIA STRAIGHT, 56A Powell St., Vancouver, 4, B.C. $9/52 iss.

HARBINGER, Box 751, Stn F, Toronto 285, Ontario $4/26 iss.

OCTOPUS, Box 1259, Station B, Ottawa , 4 $4.50/26 iss.

OMPHALOS, 279½ Fort St. No. 4, Winnipeg 1, Manitoba $5/26 iss.

PRAIRIE FIRE; FOURTH ESTATE, Regina Community Media Project, 210 Northern Crown Bldg. Regina, Sask.

SWEENEY, 119 Thomas St., Oakville, Ontario $2.50/12 iss.

UPS/Europe, Box 304, 8025, Zurich, Switzerland

FIFTH COLUMN, 100 New Cavendish Street, London W1, England
FRIENDS, 305 Portobello Rd., London W10, England
HAPT, Flat L, 42 Moore Ave., W. Howe, Bournemouth, Hampshire, England
HOLLAND HAPT, Keigersstraat 2a, Amsterdam, Holland
HOTCHA! Postfach 304-CH 8025, Zurich 25, Switz. $5/yr.
INTERNATIONAL TIMES, 27 Endell St., London, WC2, Eng. $5/yr.
KARGADOOR, Oude Gracht 36 bis. Utrecht, Holland
OEUF, 14 Ch de la Mogeonne, 1293 Bellevue, Geneva, Switzerland
OM, Kaizerstraat 2A, 11et, Amsterdam, Holland, Neth.
OPS VEDA, 16 Woodholm Rd., Sheffield 11, England
OZ, 52 Princedale Rd., London W11, England $6/yr.
PEACE NEWS, 5 Caledonian Rd., Kings Cross, London W1, Eng. $8.50/yr.
PIANETA FRESCA, 14 Via Manzoni, Milano, Italy 20121 $1/iss.
QUINTO LICEO, c/o Tommasco Bruccoleri, 3, Meadow Place, London, England
REAL FREE PRESS, Runstraat 31, Amsterdam, Netherlands $1/2 iss.
RED MOLE, 182 Pentonville Rd., London N1 Eng. $5.50/yr.
ROTTEN, Huset, Raadhusstraede 13, 1466 Copenhagen K. Denmark

EUROPEAN ASSOCIATE MEMBERS

CYCLOPS, 32. St. Petersburg Place, London, W2, Eng. (Comix)
GRASS EYE, 71 Osbourne Rd., Levenshulme, Manchester 19, Eng.
MOLE EXPRESS, 19 New Brown St., Manchester 4, Eng.
PANGGG, Upn-Sippenpresse, d-8500, Nurnberg Kopernikusstr. 4, Germany
PARIA, c/o Poretti, Viavalle Maggia 41, 6600 Locarno, Switz.
ZIGZAG, Yeoman Cottage, N. Marston, Bucks, England

LATIN AMERICA/UPS

ECO CONTEMPORANEO, C. Correo Central 1933, Buenos Aires, Argentina
...Membership list temporarily unavailable.

SWITCHBOARDS

A good way to quickly communicate what's coming down in the community is to build a telephone tree. It works on a pyramid system. A small core of people are responsible for placing five calls each. Each person on the line in turn calls five people and so on. If the system is prearranged correctly with adjustments made if some people don't answer the phone, you can have info transmitted to about a thousand people in less than an hour. A slower but more permanent method is to start a Switchboard. Basically, a Switchboard is a central telephone number or numbers that anybody can call night or day to get information. It can be as sophisticated as the community can support. The people that agree to answer the phone should have a complete knowledge of places, services and events happening in the community. Keep a complete updated file. The San Francisco Switchboard (see below) puts out an operator's manual explaining the organization and operation of a successful switchboard. They will send it out for 12¢ postage. San Francisco has the longest and most extensive Switchboard operation. From time to time there are national conferences with local switchboards sending a rep.

San Francisco

THE SWITCHBOARD — 1830 Fell St., San Francisco, Calif. 94117 (415) 387-3575

MUSIC SWITCHBOARD — 1826 Fell St., San Francisco, Calif. 94117 (415) 387-8008

MISSION SWITCHBOARD — 848 14th St., San Francisco, Calif. 94110 (415) 863-3040

CHINATOWN EXCHANGE — 1042 Grant Ave., San Francisco, Calif. 94108 (415) 421-0943

THE HELP UNIT — 86 3rd St., San Francisco, Calif. 94103 (415) 421-9850

WESTERN ADDITION SWITCHBOARD — Fell & Fillmore, San Francisco, Calif. (415) 626-8524

California

CHICO SWITCHBOARD – 120 W. 2nd St., Chico, Calif. (916) 342-7546

EAST OAKLAND SWITCHBOARD – 2812 73rd Ave., Oakland, Calif. (415) 569-6369

MARIN MUSIC SWITCHBOARD – 1017 "D" St., San Rafael, Calif. (415) 457-2104

WEST OAKLAND LEGAL SWITCHBOARD – 2713 San Pablo, Oakland, Calif. (415) 836-3013

SWITCHBOARD OF MARIN – 1017 "D" St., San Rafael, Calif. (415) 456-5300

BERKELEY SWITCHBOARD – 2389 Oregon, Berkeley, Calif. (415) 549-0649

SANTA CRUZ SWITCHBOARD – 604 River St., Santa Cruz, Calif. (408) 426-8500

PALO ALTO XCHANGE – 457 Kingsley Ave., Palo Alto, Calif. (415) 327-9008

SAN JOSE SWITCHBOARD – 50 S. 4th St., San Jose, Calif. (408) 295-2938

SANTA BARBARA SWITCHBOARD – 6575 Seville, Isla Vista, Calif. (805) 968-3564

EUREKA SWITCHBOARD – 1427 California, Eureka, Calif. (707) 443-8901 & 443-8311

Other Western States

TURNSTILE – 1900 Emerson, Denver, Colorado (303) 623-3445

BLACKHAWK INFORMATION CENTER –628 Walnut St., Waterloo, Iowa (319) 234-9965

TAOS SWITCHBOARD – c/o Gen. Del., Taos, New Mexico (505) 758-4288

PORTLAND SWITCHBOARD – 1216 SW Salmon, Portland, Oregon (503) 224-0313

HOUSTON SWITCHBOARD – 108 San Jacinto, Houston, Texas (713) 228-6072

YOUTH EMERGENCY SERVICE – 623 Cedar Ave. So., Minneapolis, Minn. (612) 338-7588

POWELTON TROUBLE CENTER – 222 N. 35th St., Phila.,Penna. (215) 382-6472

WASHINGTON D.C. SWITCHBOARD – 2201 P St. NW, Washington, D.C. (202) 667-4684

MIAMI CENTER FOR DIALOG – 2175 NW 26th St., Miami, Fla. (305) 634-7741

CANTERBURY HOUSE – 330 Maynard S, Ann Arbor, Michigan (313) 665-0606

THE LISTENING EAR – 547 E. Grand River, East Lansing, Michigan (517) 337-1717

THE ECSTATIC UMBRELLA – 3800 McGee, Kansas City, Missouri (816) 561-4524

OPEN CITY – 4726 3rd St., Detroit, Michigan (313) 831-2770

SWITCHBOARD INC. – 1722 Summit St., Number 6, Columbus, Ohio (614) 294-6378

HELP – c/o Marby Beil, 1708 E. Lafayette, Number 5, Milwaukee, Wisconsin (414) 273-5959

UNITED CHURCH PRESBYTERIAN – 181 Mount Horeb Rd., Warren, N.J. (201) 469-5044

BOSTON SWITCHBOARD – 45 Bowdoin St., Boston, Mass. (617) 246-4255

PROJECT PLACE – 37 Rutland St., Boston, Mass. (617) 267-5280

BEVERLY SWITCHBOARD – Beverly Hospital, Beverly, Mass. (617) 922-0000

FIRST CONGREGATIONAL CHURCH OF ACTON – 8 Concord Rd., Acton, Mass. (617) 263-3940

HALF WAY HOUSE – 20 Linwood Sq., Roxbury, Mass. (617) 442-7591

ACID – 13 Linden Ave., Malden, Mass. (617) 342-2218

PROJECT ASSIST – 945 Great Plain Ave., Needham, Mass. (617) 444-1902 & 3

LEXINGTON – ARLINGTON HOT LINE – 1912 Mass. Ave., Lexington, Mass. (617) 862-8130 & 1

COMMUNITY YOUTH COMMISSION – 945 Great Plain Ave., Needham, Mass. (617) 444-1795

HOT LINE – 429 Cherry St., West Newton, Mass. (617) 969-5906

UC DAVIS SWITCHBOARD – (on campus), UC Davis, Calif. (916) 752-3495

Other Countries

BINARY INFORMATION TRANSFER – 141 Westbourne Park Rd., London W2, England. Ask overseas operator for London 222-8219
CANADIAN SWITCHBOARD – 282 Rue Ste. Catherine, West, Montreal, Quebec, Canada (514) 866-2672

For a complete and up-to-date list of switchboards and similar projects around the country, write to San Francisco Switchboard. They need 25 cents to cover postage costs.

Guerrilla Broadcasting

GUERRILLA RADIO

Under FCC Low Power Transmission Regulations, it is legal to broadcast on the AM band without even obtaining a license, if you transmit with 100 milliwatts of power or less on a free band space that doesn't interfere with a licensed station. You are further allowed up to a 12-foot antenna or the use of carrier-current transmission (regular electric wall outlets). Using this legal set-up, you can broadcast from a 2 to 20 block radius depending on how high up you locate your antenna and the density of tall buildings in the area.

Carrier-current broadcasting consists of plugging the transmitter into a regular wall socket. It draws power in the same way as any other electrical appliance, and feeds its signal into the power line allowing the broadcast to be heard on any AM radio tuned into the ' operating frequency. The transmitter can be adjusted to different frequencies until a clear band is located. The signal will travel over the electrical wiring until it hits a transformer where it will be erased. The trouble with this method is that in large cities, almost every large office or apartment building has a transformer. You should experiment with this method first, but if you are in a city, chances are you'll need an antenna rigged up on the roof. Anything over twelve feet is illegal, but practice has shown that the FCC won't hassle you if you don't have commercials and refrain from interfering with licensed broadcasts. There are some cats in Connecticut broadcasting illegally with a 100-foot antenna over a thirty mile radius for hours on end and nobody gives them any trouble. Naturally if you insist upon using dirty language, issuing calls to revolution, broadcasting bombing information, interfering with above ground stations and becoming too well known, the FCC is going to try and knock you out. There are penalties that have never been handed out of up to a year in jail. It's possible you could get hit with a conspiracy rap, which could make it a felony, but the opinion of movement lawyers now is a warning if you're caught once, and a possible fine with stiffer penalties possible for repeaters that are caught.

If it gets really heavy, you could still broadcast for up to 15 minutes without being pin-pointed by the FCC sleuths. By locating your equipment in a panel truck and broadcasting from a fixed roof antenna, you can make it almost impossible for them to catch you by changing positions.

There has been a variety of transmitting equipment used, and the most effective has been found to be an AM transmitter manufactured by Low Power Broadcasting Co., 520 Lincoln Highway, Frazer, Penn. 19355. Call Dick Crompton at (215) NI 4-4096. The right transmitter will run about $200. If you plan to use carrier-current transmission you'll also need a capacitor that sells for $30. An antenna can be made out of aluminum tubing and antenna wiring available at any TV radio supply store (see diagram). You'll also need a good microphone that you can get for about $10. Naturally, equipment for heavier broadcasting is available if a member of your group has a license or good connections with someone who works in a large electronics supply house. Also with a good knowledge in the area you can build a transmitter for a fraction of the purchase price. You can always employ tape recorders, turntables and other broadcasting hardware depending on how much bread you have, how much stuff you have to hide (i.e., how legal your operation is) and the type of broadcasting you want to do.

It is possible to extend your range by sending a signal over the telephone lines to other transmitters which will immediately rebroadcast. Several areas in a city could be linked together and even from one city to another. Theoretically, if enough people rig up transmitters and antennas at proper locations and everyone operates on the same band, it is possible to build a nation-wide people's network that is equally theoretically legal.

Broadcasting, it should be remembered, is a one-way transmission of information. Communications which allow you to transmit and receive are illegal without a license (ham radio).

GUERRILLA TELEVISION

There are a number of outlaw radio projects going on around the country. Less frequent, but just as feasible, is a people's television network. Presently there are three basic types of TV systems: Broadcast, which is the sending of signals directly from a station's transmitter to home receiver sets; Cable, where the cable company employs extremely sensitive antenna to pick up broadcast transmissions and relay them and/or they originate and send them; and thirdly, Closed Circuit TV, such as the surveillance cameras in supermarkets, banks and apartment house lobbies.

The third system as used by the pigs is of little concern, unless we are interested in not being photographed. The cameras can be temporarily knocked out of commission by flashing a bright light (flashbulb, cigarette lighter, etc.) directly in front of its lens. For our own purposes, closed-circuit TV can be employed for broadcasting rallies, rock concerts or teach-ins to other locations. The equipment is not that expensive to rent and easy to operate. Just contact the largest television or electronics store in your area and ask about it. There are also closed-circuit and cable systems that work in harmony to broadcast special shows to campuses and other institutions. Many new systems are being developed and will be in operation soon.

Cable systems as such are in use only in a relatively few areas. They can be tapped either at the source or at any point along the cable by an engineer freak who knows what to do. The source is the best spot, since all the amplification and distribution equipment of the system is available at that point. Tapping along the cable itself can be a lot hairier, but more frustrating for the company when they try to trace you down.

Standard broadcasting that is received on almost all living room sets works on an RF (radio frequency) signal sent out on various frequencies which correspond to the channels on the tuner. In no area of the country are all these channels used. This raises important political questions as to why people do not have the right to broadcast on unused channels. By getting hold of a TV camera (Sony and Panasonic are the best for the price) that has an RF output, you can send pictures to a TV set simply by placing the camera cable on or near the antenna of the receiver set. When the set is operating on the same channel as the camera, it will show what the camera sees. Used video tape recorders such as the Sony CV series that record and play back audio and video information are becoming more available. These too can be easily adapted to send RF signals the same as a live camera.

Whether or not the program to be broadcasted is live or on tape, there are three steps to be taken in order to establish a people's TV network. First, you must convert the video and audio signals to an RF frequency-modulated (FM) signal corresponding to the desired broadcast channel. We suggest for political and technical reasons that you pick one of the unused channels in your area to begin experimenting. The commercial stations have an extremely powerful signal and can usually override your small output. Given time and experience you might want to go into direct competition with the big boys on their own channel. It is entirely possible, say in a 10 to 20 block radius, to interrupt a presidential press-conference with more important news. Electronic companies, such as Jerrold Electronics Corp., 4th and Walnut Sts., Philadelphia, Pa., make equipment that can RF both video and audio existing antenna of a commercial network. This requires a full knowledge of broadcasting; however, any amateur can rig up an antenna, attach it to a helium balloon and get it plenty high. For most, the roof of a tall building will suffice. If you're really uptight about your operation, the antenna can be hidden with a fake cardboard chimney.

We realize becoming TV guerrillas is not everyone's trip, but a small band with a few grand can indeed pull it off. There are a lot of technical freaks hanging around recording studios, guitar shops, hi-fi stores and engineering schools that can be turned on to the project. By showing them the guidelines laid out here, they can help you assemble and build various components that are difficult to purchase (i.e., the linear amplifier). Naturally, by building some of the components, the cost of the operation is kept way down. Equipment can be purchased in selective electronics stores. You'll need a camera, VTR, RF modulator, linear amplifier and antenna. Also a generator, voltage regulator and an alternator if you want the station to be mobile. One of the best sources of information on both television and radio broadcasting is the *Radio Amateur's Handbook* published by the American Radio Relay League, Newington, Conn. 06611 and available for $4.50. The handbook gives a complete course in electronics and the latest information on all techniques and equipment related to broadcasting. Back issues have easy to read do-it-yourself TV transmitter diagrams and instructions. Also available is a publication called *Radical Software*, put out by Raindance Corp., 24 E. 22nd St., New York, N.Y., with the latest info on all types of alternative communications.

Guerrilla TV is the vanguard of the communications revolution, rather than the avant-garde cellophane light shows and the weekend conferences. One pirate picture on the sets in Amerika's living rooms is worth a thousand wasted words.

With the fundamentals in this field mastered, you can rig up all sorts of shit. Cheap twenty-dollar tape recorders can be purchased and outfitted with a series of

144

information onto specific channels. The device y
interested in is called a cable driver or RF modula

When the signal is in the RF state, it is
possible to broadcast very short distances. The
step is to amplify the signal so it will reach as
possible. A linear amplifier of the proper frequ
required for this job. The stronger the amplifi
farther and more powerful the signal. A 10-watt j
cover approximately 5 miles (line of sight) in
Linear amplifiers are not that easily available, bu
can be constructed with some electrical engin
knowledge.

The third step is the antenna, which if the whole
is to be mobile to avoid detection, is going to i
some experimentation and possible camouflage
things to keep in mind about an antenna are
should be what is technically referred to as a "di
antenna (see diagram) and since TV signals travel c

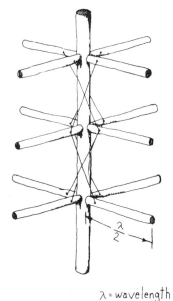

$\lambda = $ wavelength

of sight, it is important to place the antenna as hig
possible. Although it hasn't been done in practic
certainly is possible to reflect pirate signals off

small loud-speakers. Concealed in a school auditorium or other large hall, such a system can blast out any message or music you wish to play. The administration will go insane trying to locate the operation if it is well hidden. We know two cats who rigged a church with this type of setup and a timing device. Right in the middle of the sermon, on came Radio Heaven and said stuff like "Come on preacher, this is God, you don't believe all that crap now, do you?" It made for an exciting Sunday service .all right. You can build a miniature transmitter and with a small magnet attach it to the underbelly of a police car to keep track of where it's going. This would only be practical in a small town or on a campus where there are only a few security guards or patrol vehicles. If you rigged a small tape recorder to the transmitter and tuned it to a popular AM band, the patrol car as it rode around could actually broadcast the guerrilla message you prerecorded. Wouldn't they be surprised when they found out how you did it? You can get a "Bumper Beeper" and receiver that are constructed by professionals for use by private detectives. The dual unit costs close to $400. If you've got that kind of bread, you can write John Bomar, 6838 No. 3rd Ave., Phoenix, Arizona 85013 for a catalogue and literature.

Even though there are laws governing this area of sneaky surveillance, telephone taps, tracking devices and the like, a number of enterprising firms produce an unbelievable array of electronic hardware that allows you to match Big Brother's ears and eyes. Sugar cube transmitters, tie clasp microphones, phone taps, tape recorders that work in a hollowed-out book and other Brave New World equipment is available from the following places. Send for their catalogues just to marvel at the level of technology. R. B. Clifton, 11500 NW 7th Ave., Miami, Fla. 33168; Electrolab Corp., Bank of Stateboro Building, Stateboro, Ga. 30458; or Tracer Investigative Products, Inc., 256 Worth Ave., Palm Beach, Fla. 33482.

By the way, you can pick up Radio Hanoi on a short wave radio every day from 3:00 to 3:30 PM at 15013 kilocycles on the 19 meter band.

Negotiating a permit with city officials

Demonstrations

Demonstrations always will be an important form of protest. The structure can vary from a rally or teach-in to a massive civil disobedience such as the confronting of the warmakers at the Pentagon or a smoke-in. A demonstration is different from other forms of warfare because it invites people other than those planning the action via publicity to participate. It also is basically non-violent in nature. A complete understanding of the use of media is necessary to create the publicity needed to get the word out. Numbers of people are only one of the many factors in an effective demonstration. The timing, choice of target and tactics to be employed are equally important. There have been demonstrations of 400,000 that are hardly remembered and demonstrations of a few dozen that were remarkably effective. Often the critical element involved is the theater. Those who say a demonstration should be concerned with education rather than theater don't understand either and will never organize a successful demonstration, or for that matter, a successful revolution. Publicity includes everything from buttons and leaflets to press conferences. You should be in touch with the best artists you can locate to design the visual props. Posters can be silk screened very cheaply and people can be taught to do it in a very short time. Buttons have to be purchased. The cheapest are those printed directly on the metal. The paint rubs off after a while, but they are ideal for mass demonstrations. You can print 10,000 for about $250.00. Leaflets, like posters, should be well designed.

One way of getting publicity is to negotiate with the city for permits. Again, this raises political questions, but there is no doubt one reason for engaging in permit discussions is for added publicity.

The date, time and place of the demonstration all have to be chosen with skill. Know the projected weather reports. Pick a time and day of the week that are convenient to most people. Make sure the place itself adds some meaning to the message. Don't have a demonstration just because that's the way it's always been done. It is only one type of weapon and should be used as such. On the other hand, don't dismiss demonstrations because they have always turned out boring. You and your group can plan a demonstration within the demonstration that will play up your style or politics more accurately. Also don't tend to dismiss demonstrations outright because the repression is too great. During World War II, the Danes held street demonstrations against the Nazis who occupied their country. Even today there are public demonstrations against the Vietnam War in downtown Saigon. Repression is there, but overestimating it is more a tactical blunder than the reverse. None the less, it's wise to go to all demonstrations prepared for a vamping by the pigs.

DRESS

Most vamping is accompanied by clubbing, rough shoving and dragging, gassing and occasional buckshot or rifle fire. The clothing you wear should offer you the best protection possible, yet be light weight enough to allow you to be highly mobile. CS and CN are by far the most commonly employed tear gas dispersibles. Occasionally they are combined with pepper gas to give better results. Pepper gas is a nerve irritant that affects exposed areas of the skin. Clothing that is tight fitting and covers as much of the body surface as possible is advisable. This also offers some protection if you are dragged along the ground. Gloves come in handy as protection and if you want to pick up gas cannisters and throw them back at the pigs or chuck them through a store window.

Your shoes should be high sneakers for running or boots for kicking. Hiking boots sold in army surplus stores serve both purposes and are your best selection for street action. Men should wear a jock strap or protective cup. Rib guards can be purchased for about $6.00 at any sporting goods store. Shoulder pads and leg pads are also available, but unless you expect heavy fighting and are used to wearing this clumsy street armor, you'll be better off without it.

HELMETS

Everyone should have a helmet. Your head sticks out above the swarming crowd and dents like a tin can. Protect it! The type of helmet you get depends on what you can afford and how often you'll be using it. The

148

The latest in fall wear

cheapest helmet available is a heavy steel tank model. This one is good because it offers ear protection and has a built-in suspension system to absorb the blow. It is also bullet proof. It's disadvantages are that it only comes in large sizes and is the heaviest thing you'll ever have on your head. It costs about $3.00. For $5.00 you can get a Civil Defense helmet made for officers. It's much lighter, but doesn't offer protection for the ears. It has a good suspension system. If you get this model, paint it a dark color before using it and you'll be less conspicuous. Our fashion consultants suggest anarchy black.

Construction helmets or "hard hats" run between $8.00 and $10.00, depending on the type of suspension system and material used. They are good for women because they are extremely lightweight. The aluminum ones dent if struck repeatedly and the fiberglass type can crack. Also they offer no ear protection. If you prefer one of these you should find a way to attach a chin or neck strap so you won't lose it while you run. If you get a hard hat, make sure you remove the hard head before you take it home.

Probably the all-around good deal for the money is the standard M-1 Army issue helmet. These vary in quality and price, depending on age and condition. They run from $2.00 to $10.00. Make sure the one you get has a liner with webbing that fits well or is adjustable and has a chin strap. Their main disadvantage is that they are bulky and heavy.

The snappiest demonstrators use the familiar motorcycle crash helmet. They are the highest in price, running from $10.00 to as high as $40.00. Being made of fiberglass, they are extremely lightweight. They have a heavy-duty strap built in and they can be gotten to fit quite snugly around the head. They offer excellent ear protection. The foam rubber insulation is better than a webbing system, and will certainly cushion most blows. Being made of fiberglass, a few have been known to crack under repeated blows, but that is extremely rare. Most come with plastic face guards that offer a little added protection. Get only those with removable ones since you might want to make use of a gas mask.

GAS MASKS

Ski goggles or the face visor on a crash helmet will protect against Mace but will offer no protection against the chemical warfare gasses being increasingly used by pigs to disperse crowds. For this protection you'll need a gas mask. All the masks discussed give ideal protection against the gasses mentioned in the chart if used properly. If you do not have a gas mask, you should at least get a supply of surgical masks from a hospital supply store and a plastic bag filled with water and a cloth.

The familiar World War II Army gas mask with the filter in a long nose unit sells new (which is the only way gas masks can be sold) for about $5.00. Its disadvantages are that it doesn't cover the whole face, is easy to grab and pull off and the awkwardly placed filter makes running difficult. The Officer Civil Defense unit sells for the same price and overcomes the disadvantages of the World War II Army model. Most National Guard units use this type of mask. It offers full face protection, is lightweight and the filter cannister is conveniently located. Also the adjustable straps make for a nice tight fit. The U.S.A. Protective Field Combat Mask M9A1 offers the same type protection as the OCD, but costs twice as much. Its advantage is that you can get new filter cannisters when the chemicals in the one you are using become ineffective. New filters cost about $1.50. When you buy a mask, be sure and inquire if the filter has replacements. To get maximum efficiency out of a mask it needs an active chemical filter.

The U.S. Navy ND Mark IV Mask is the most effective gas mask available. It has replaceable filter cannisters and fits snugly to the head. It costs about $12.00. Its disadvantage is its dual tube filter system, which is somewhat bulky. Fix it so the cannister rests on the back of your neck. It's more difficult to grab and

GAS CHART

GAS	PROPERTIES	EFFECTS
CS (tear gas)	A fat-soluble gas with peppery smell and tear and nausea agents.	Copious flow of tears, burning sensation around the eyes, coughing, difficulty breathing, nausea, harassing sting and reddening of exposed areas. Stinging can last up to 2 hours.
CN (tear gas)	Milder than CS, smells like apple blossoms. Water soluble.	Same as CS minus nausea and stinging.
HC (smoke)	Heavy dense smoke, camphor-like smell.	Slightly irritating to eyes and nose. Mostly used to scare crowd.
Nausea Gas	Clear, colorless, odorless, cannisters look like duds when they go off but don't be fooled.	Nausea followed by projective vomiting. Instant diarrhea, severe stomach cramps. Pain and heat sensation in lungs.
Blister gas	Fat-soluble, fine white powder.	Skin blistering to exposed areas - instant or within 48 hours.
Mace	Liquid composed of CN, kerosene, general propellant and oxidizing agents.	Sharp pain if hit in the eyes. Burning sensation of other area hit. Nausea and possible vomiting if swallowed.

*Grenades unlike cannisters explode. If they do so near your face, they can cause very serious burns. Protect your eyes. They can be hand-thrown or fired from a rifle or grenade launcher.

152

GAS CHART

PROTECTION	FIRST AID	DISPENSED
Remove yourself from affected area. DO NOT RUB eyes, wash out with a dilute boric acid solution or eye drops such as Murine. If none, use water. Wipe exposed areas with mineral oil, if not available, use water then alcohol.	Gas mask, wet towels or handkerchief, surgical mask and tight-fitting clothing.**	Cannisters, plastic grenades* fog machines, Helicopter and spray truck devices.
Remove yourself from affected area and wash with water.	Same as CS, but you can stay in affected areas much longer without protection.	Same as CS
None needed.	Goggles good enough.	Grenades, pots, fog machines
Symptoms generally clear up in a few hours. See physician if they don't	Masks are not effective as you could choke on the vomit. Therefore it is not used very often. Run upwind.	Cannisters
Wash off with gauze pad saturated with mineral oil (salad oil or margerine will do). Treat as if 2nd degree burn.	Gas mask, gloves, long sleeves, towel around neck.	Cannisters
Wash out eyes with boric acid solution (see CS) or water if not available. Other area should be washed with alcohol to reduce burning.	Goggles, vaseline can be applied to exposed skin areas beforehand. If you use vaseline and get sprayed, wipe off vaseline with a rag and wash your face.	Propellant cannisters for person-to-person combat.

**A super deluxe antidote for both CS and CN gases has been developed by a biochemist brother in Berkeley named John McWhorter. Mix 8-10 eggs, 1 cup water and a teaspoon of baking soda in a bowl. Beat mixture well. Keep refrigerated in small plastic bottles until a demonstration. Wipe the stuff on your face before a gassing occurs.

easier to run.

When you get your gas mask home, try it out to get the feeling of using it. Make sure the fit is good and snug. Purchase an anti-fog cloth for 25 cents where you got the mask. Wipe the inside of the eye pieces before wearing to prevent the glasses from clouding. Another good reason for wearing a mask is that it offers anonymity. Helmets, gas masks and a host of other valuable equipment are available at any large Army-Navy surplus store. Kaufman's Surplus and Arms, Inc., 623

Broadway, New York, N.Y. 10012 is very well stocked. For 75 cents you can get their catalogue and order through the mail. It's in New York though and probably more expensive than a store in your locale. The surplus stores buy from wholesale distributors themselves, who in turn buy directly from the military. If you know a soldier or someone who is married to a soldier, they have access to the Post Dispensary or PX and can get all sorts of stuff at nothing prices. For 20 cents you can get an invaluable pamphlet from the Government Printing Office called *How to Buy Surplus Personal Property*. It has a complete list of regional surplus wholesalers. The closest one in the Northeast is the Naval Supply Center, Building 652, U.S. Naval Base, Philadelphia, Pa. and in Northern California, the Naval Supply Center, Building 502, Oakland, California. You can order by mail or in person and the prices are very low, even though it isn't as good as the stuff our brothers and sisters in the Viet Cong rip-off.

WALKIE-TALKIES

You should always go to a demonstration in a small group that stays in contact with each other until the demonstration is over. One way to keep in touch is to use walkie-talkies. No matter how heavy the vamping gets or how spread out are the crowds, you'll be able to communicate with these lightweight effective portable devices. The only disadvantage is cost. A half decent unit costs at least $18.00. It should have a minimum of 9 transistors and 100 milliwatts, although walkie-talkies can go as high as 5 watts and broadcast over 2 miles. Anything under 1 watt will not broadcast over ½ mile and considerably less in an area with tall buildings. The best unit you can buy runs about $300.00. If you ever deck a pig, steal his walkie-talkie even before you take his gun. A good rule is to avoid the bargain gyp-joints and go to a place that deals in electronic equipment.

The important thing to realize about all walkie-talkie networks is that if anyone can talk, anyone else can listen and vice versa. This applies to pigs as well as us. All walkie-talkies work on the Civilian Band which has 23 channels. The cheaper units are preset to channel 9 or 11. The pigs broadcast on higher channels, usually channel 22. More expensive sets can operate on alternative channels. By removing the front of the set, you can adjust the transmitter and receiver to pick up and receive police communications. Don't screw around with the inside though, unless you know what you are doing. Allied Radio, 100 N. Western Ave., Chicago, Illinois 60680, will send you a good free catalogue, as will most large electronic stores. Consider buying a number of sets and ask about group discounts. Practice a number of times before you actually use walkie-talkies in real action. Develop code names and words just like the pigs do. Once you get acquainted with this method of communications in the streets, you'll never get cut off from the action. Watch out in close combat though. The pigs always try to smash any electronic gear.

OTHER EQUIPMENT

A sign can be used to ward off blows. Staple it to a good strong pole that you can use as a weapon if need be. Chains make good belts, as do garrisons with the buckles sharpened. A tightly rolled-up magazine or newspaper also can be used as a defensive weapon.

Someone in your group should carry a first aid kit. A Medical Emergency Aeronautic Kit, which costs about $5.00 has a perfect carrying bag for street action.

Ideally you should visit the proposed site of the demonstration before it actually takes place. This way you'll have an idea of the terrain and the type of containment the police will be using. Someone in your group should mimeograph a map of the immediate vicinity which each person should carry. Alternative actions and a rendezvous point should be worked out. Everyone should have two numbers written on their arm, a coordination center number and the number of a local lawyer or legal defense committee. You should not take your personal phone books to demonstrations. If you get busted, pigs can get mighty Nosy when it comes to phone books. Any sharp objects can be construed as weapons. Women should not wear earrings or other jewelry and should tie their hair up to tuck it under a helmet. Wear a belt that you can use as a tourniquet. False teeth and contact lenses should be left at home if possible. You can choke on false teeth if you receive a sharp blow while running. Contact lenses can complicate eye damage if gas or Mace is used.

If it really looks heavy, you might want to pick up on a lightweight adjustable bullet-proof vest, available for $14.95 from Surplus Distributors, Inc., 6279 Van Nuys Blvd., Van Nuys, California 91401. Remember what the Boy Scouts say when they go camping: "Be Prepared". When you go to demonstrations you should be prepared for a lot more than speeches. The pigs will be.

Exam question: Who in this picture is comitting an act of violence: a) Anita b) the Bank c) the Seal

Trashing

Ever since the Chicago pigs brutalized the demonstrators in August of 1968, young people have been ready to vent their rage over Amerika's inhumanity by using more daring tactics than basic demonstrations. There is a growing willingness to do battle with the pigs in the streets and at the same time to inflict property damage. It's not exactly rioting and it's not exactly guerrilla warfare; it has come to be called "Trashing." Most trashing is of a primitive nature with the pigs having the weapon and strategy advantage. Most trashers rely on quick young legs and a nearby rock. By developing simple gang strategy and becoming acquainted with some rudimentary weapons and combat techniques, the odds can be shifted considerably.

Remember, pigs have small brains and move slowly, All formations, signals, codes and other procedures they use have to be uniform and simplistic. *The Army Plan for Containment and Control of Civil Disorders*, published by the Government Printing Office, contains the basic thinking for all city, county and state storm troopers. A trip to the library and a look at any basic text in criminology will help considerably in gaining an understanding of how pigs act in the street. If you study up, you'll find you can, with the aid of a bullhorn or properly adjusted walkie-talkie, fuck up many intricate pig formations. "Left flank-right turn!" said authoritatively into a bullhorn pointed in the right direction will yield all sorts of wild results.

You should trash with a group using a buddy system to keep track of each other. If someone is caught by a pig, others should immediately rush to the rescue if it's possible to do so without sustaining too many losses. If an arrest is made, someone from your gang should take responsibility for seeing to it that a lawyer and bail bread are taken care of. Never abandon a member of your gang.

Avoid fighting in close quarters. You run less risk by throwing an object than by personally delivering the blow with a weapon you hold in your hand. We suppose this is what pigs refer to as "dirty fighting." All revolutionaries fight dirty in the eyes of the oppressors. The British accused the Minutemen of Lexington and Concord of fighting dirty by hiding behind trees. The U.S. Army accuses the Viet Cong of fighting dirty when they rub a pointed bamboo shoot in infected shit and use it as a land mine. Mayor Daley says the Yippies squirted hair spray and used golf balls with spikes in them against his innocent blue boys. No one ever accused the U.S. of being sneaky for using an airforce in Southeast Asia or the Illinois State Attorney's office of fighting dirty when it murdered Fred Hampton and Mark Clark while they lay in bed. We say: all power to the dirty fighters!

WEAPONS FOR STREET FIGHTING

Spray Cans

These are a very effective and educating method of property destruction. If a liberated zone has been established or you find yourself on a quiet street away from the thick of things, pretty up the neighborhood. Slogans and symbols can be sprayed on rough surfaces such as brick or concrete walls that are a real bitch to remove unless expensive sandblasting is used.

The Slingshot

This is probably the ideal street weapon for the swarms of little Davids that are out to down the Goliaths of Pigdom. It is cheap, legal to carry, silent, fast-loading and any right size rock will do for a missle. You can find them at hobby shops and large sporting goods stores, especially those that deal in hunting supplies. Wrist-Rocket makes a powerful and accurate slingshot for $2.50. The Whamo Sportsman is not as good but half the price. By selecting the right "Y" shaped branch, you can fashion a home-made one by using a strip of rubber cut from the inner tube of a tire as the sling. A few hours of shooting stones at cans in the back yard or up on the roof will make you marksman enough for those fat bank windows and even fatter pigs.

Slings

A sling is a home-made weapon consisting of two lengths of heavy-duty cord each attached securely at one end to a leather patch that serves as a pocket to cradle the rock. Place the rock in the pouch and grab the two pieces of cord firmly in your hand. Whirl the rock round and round until gravity holds it firmly in the pouch. When you feel you have things under control, let one end of the cord go and the rock will fly out at an incredible speed. You should avoid using the sling in a thick crowd (rooftop shooting is best). Practice is definitely needed to gain any degree of accuracy.

Boomerangs

The boomerang is a neat weapon for street fighting and is as easy to master as the Frisbee. There is a great psychological effect in using exotic weapons such as this. You can buy one at large hobby stores. On the East Coast you can get one from Sportscraft, Bergenfield, New Jersey, for $1.69, and on the West Coast from Whamo, 835 El Monte St., San Gabriel, Calif., for $1.10.

Flash Guns

Electric battery-operated flash guns are available that will blind a power-crazy pig, thus distracting him long enough to rescue a captured comrade. Check out camping and boating supply stores.

Tear Gas and Mace

Personalized tear gas and mace dispensers are available for self-defense against muggers. Well, isn't a pig just an extra vicious mugger? Write J.P. Darby, 8813

New Hyde Park, New York, N.Y. 11040·for a variety of types and prices.

Tear gas shells are available for 12 gauge shotguns and .38 Special handguns, but it is highly inadvisable to bring guns to street actions. A far better weapon is a specially built projection device that shoots tear gas shells. Hercules Gas–Munitions Corp., 5501 No. Broadway, Chicago, Ill., sells compact units complete with cartridges for $6.95 that will fire up to 20 feet. Penguin Associates, Inc., Pennsylvania Avenue, Malvern, Penn., also has a variety of tear-gas propellant devices including a combination tear gas-billyclub item. All these companies will supply a catalogue and price list on request. Some states have laws against civilian use of tear gas devices. New York is one of them, and unfortunately these companies will not ship to states that forbid usage. If you want any of these items, and your state has restrictions, have a sister or brother in a neighboring state order for you. Just latching onto these catalogues can be a trip and a half in terms of getting your imagination hopping. For example, Raid, Black Flag and other insecticides shoot a 7 to 10 foot stream that burns the eyes. You can also dissolve Drano in water and squirt it from an ordinary plastic water pistol. This makes a highly effective defensive weapon. A phony letterhead of a Civil Defense unit will help in getting heavier anti-personnel weapons of a defensive nature.

Anti-Tire Weapons

Don't believe all those bullshit tire ads that make tires seem like the Supermen of the streets. Roofing nails spread out on the street are effective in stopping a patrol car. A nail sticking out from a strong piece of wood wedged under a rear tire will work as effectively as a bazooka. An ice pick will do the trick repeatedly but you've got to have a strong arm to strike home. Sugar in the gas tank of a pig vehicle will really fuck-up the engine.

Authentic Pig Gear

If you really get into it, you'll probably want to be as heavily prepared for trashing as are the pigs. Wouldn't you just know that the largest supplier of equipment to police in the world is in Chicago. Kale's, 550 W. Roosevelt Rd., Chicago, Ill. 60607, will send you, on request, the most complete catalogue you can get for trashing. Actual police uniforms, super-riot helmets, persuaders, chemical mace, a knuckle sap, which is a glove with powdered lead, billy clubs, secret holsters, a three-in-one mob stick that spits Mace, emits an electric shock and allows you to club to death a charging rhinoceros. You can also get the latest in handcuffs and other security devices. This catalogue is a must for the love-child of the 70's. If we want to get high we're going to have to fight our way up.

KNIFE FIGHTING

Probably one of the most favored street weapons of all time is the good old "shiv," "blade," "toe-jabber" or whatever you choose to call a good sticker. Remembering that today's pig is tomorrow's bacon, it's good to know a few handy slicing tips. The first thing to learn is the local laws regarding the possession of knives. The laws on possession are of the "Catch-22" vagueness. Cops can arrest you for having a small pocket knife and claim you have a concealed and deadly weapon in your possession. Here, as in most cases of law, it's not *what* you are doing, it's *who's* doing the what that counts. All areas, however, usually have a limit on length such as blades under 4" or 6" are legal and anything over that length concealed on a person can be considered illegal. Asking some hip lawyers can help here.

Unfortunately, the best fighting knives are illegal. Switchblades (and stilettos) because they can so quickly spring into operation, are great weapons that are outlawed in all states. If you want to risk the consequences, however, you can readily purchase these weapons once you learn how to contact the criminal

How to tie a knot with your toes

underworld or in most foreign countries. If both of these fail, go to any pawnshop, look in the window, and take your choice of lethal, illegal knives.

A flat gravity knife, available in most army surplus and pawn shops would be the best type available in regular over-the-counter buying. It's flat style makes for easy concealment and comfort when kept in a pocket or boot. It can be greased and the rear "heel" of the blade can be filed down to make it fly open with a flick of the wrist. A little practice here will be very useful.

Most inexperienced knife fighters use a blade incorrectly. Having seen too many Jim Bowies slash their way through walls of human flesh, they persist in carrying on this inane tradition. Overhead and uppercut slashes are a waste of energy and blade power. The correct method is to hold the knife in a natural, firm grip and jab straight ahead at waist level with the arm extending full length each time. This fencing style allows for the maximum reach of arm and blade. By concentrating the point of the knife directly at the target, you make defense against such an attack difficult. Work out with this jabbing method in front of a mirror and in a few days you'll get it down pretty well.

UNARMED DEFENSE

Let's face it, when it comes to trashing in the streets, our success is going to depend on our cunning and speed rather than our strength and power. Our side is all quarterbacks, and the pigs have nothing but linemen. They are clumsy, slobbish brutes that would be lost without their guns, clubs and toy whistles. When one grabs you for an arrest, you can with a little effort, make him let go. In the confusion of all the street action, you will then be able to manage your getaway.

There are a variety of defensive twists and pulls that are easy to master by reading a good, easily understandable book on the subject, such as George Hunter's *How To Defend Yourself* (see appendix). If a pig grabs you by the wrist, you can break the grip by twisting against his thumb. Try this on yourself by grabbing one wrist with your hand. See how difficult it is to hold someone who works against the thumb. If he grabs you around the waist or neck, you can grab his thumbs or another finger and sharply bend it backwards. By concentrating all your energy on one little finger, you can inflict pain and cause the grip to be broken.

There are a variety of points on the body where a firm amount of pressure skillfully directed will induce severe pain. A grip, for example, can be broken by jabbing your finger firmly between the pig's knuckles. (Nothing like chopped pigknuckles.) Feel directly under your chin in back of the jawbone until your finger rests in the V area, press firmly upward and backward towards the center of the head. There is also a very vulnerable spot right behind the ear lobe. Stick your fingers there and see. Get the point!

In addition to pressure points, there are places in the body where a sharp, well-directed whack with the side of a rigidly held palm can easily disable a person. Performed by an expert, such a blow can even be lethal. Try making such a rigid palm and practice these judo chops. The fist is a ridiculous weapon to use. It's fleshy, the blow is distributed over too wide an area to have any real effect and the knuckles break easily. You will have to train yourself to use judo chops instinctively, but it will prove quite worthwhile if you're ever in trouble. A good place to aim for is directly in the center of the chest cavity at its lowest point. Draw a straight line up about six inches starting from your belly button, and you can feel the point. The Adam's Apple in the center of the neck and the back of the neck at the top of the spinal column are also extremely vulnerable spots. With the side of your palm, press firmly the spot directly below your nose and above your upper lip. You can easily get an idea of what a short, forceful chop in this area would do. The side of the head in front of the ear is also a good place to aim your blow.

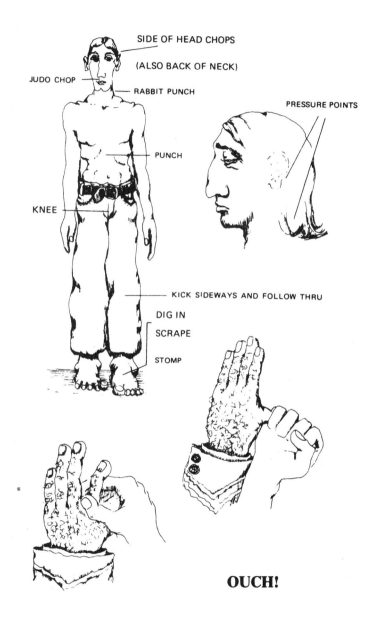

SIDE OF HEAD CHOPS

(ALSO BACK OF NECK)

JUDO CHOP

RABBIT PUNCH

PRESSURE POINTS

PUNCH

KNEE

KICK SIDEWAYS AND FOLLOW THRU

DIG IN

SCRAPE

STOMP

OUCH!

In addition to jabs, chops, twists, squeezes and bites, you ought to gain some mastery of kneeing and kicking. If you are being held in close and facing the porker, the old familiar knee-in-the-nuts will produce remarkable results. A feinting motion with the head before the knee is delivered will produce a reflexive reaction from your opponent that will leave his groin totally unprotected. Ouch!

Whether he has you from the front or the back, he is little prepared to defend against a skillfully aimed kick. The best way is to forcefully scrape the side of your shoe downward along the shinbone, beginning just below the knee and ending with a hard stomp on the instep of the foot. Just try this with the side of your hand and you will get an idea of the damage you can inflict with this scrape and stomp method. Another good place to kick and often the only spot accessible is the side of the knee. Even a half successful blow here will topple the biggest of honkers. Any of these easy to learn techniques of unarmed self defense will fulfill the old nursery rhyme that goes:

Catch a piggy by the toe
When he hollers
Let him go
Out pops Y-O-U

GENERAL STRATEGY RAP

The guideline in trashing is to try and do as much property destruction as possible without getting caught or hurt. The best buildings to trash in terms of not alienating too many of those not yet clued into revolutionary violence, are the most piggy symbols of violence you can find. Banks, large corporations, especially those that participate heavily in supporting the U.S. armed forces, federal buildings, courthouses, police stations, and Selective Service centers are all good targets. On campuses, buildings that are noted for warfare research and ROTC training are best. When it comes to automobiles, choose only police vehicles and very expensive cars such as Lamborghinis and Iso Grifos. Every rock or molotov cocktail thrown should make a very *obvious* political point. Random violence produces random propaganda results. Why waste even a rock?

When you know there is going to be a rough street scene developing, don't play into the pig's strategy. Spread the action out. Help waste the enemy's numbers. You and the other members of your group should already have a target or two in mind that will make for easy trashing. If you don't have one, setting fires in trash cans and ringing fire alarms will help provide a cover for other teams that do have objectives picked out. Putting out street lights with rocks also helps the general confusion.

After a few tries at trashing, you'll begin to overcome your fears, learn what to expect from both the pigs and your comrades, and develop your own street strategy. Nothing works like practice in actual street conditions. Get your head together and you'll become a pro. Don't make the basic mistake of just naively floating into the area. Don't think "rally" or "demonstration," think "WAR" and "Battle Zone." Keep your eyes and ears open. Watch for mistakes made by members of your gang and those made by other comrades. Watch for blunders by the police. In street fighting, every soldier should think like a general. Workshops should be organized right after an action to discuss the strength and weaknesses of techniques and strategies used. Avoid political bullshit at such raps. Regard them as military sessions. Persons not versed in the tactics of revolution usually have nothing worthwhile to say about the politics of revolution.

"... 5 pounds sulphur, 10 pounds potassium nitrate, 50 feet primer fuse, 2 rolls friction tape, 4 batteries, 1 clock ..."

People's Chemistry

STINK BOMB

You can purchase buteric acid at any chemical supply store for "laboratory experiments." It can be thrown or poured directly in an area you think already stinks. A small bottle can be left uncapped behind a door that opens into the target room. When a person enters they will knock over the bottle, spilling the liquid. Called a "Froines," by those in the know, an ounce of buteric acid can go a long way. Be careful not to get it on your clothing. A home-made stink bomb can be made by mixing a batch of egg whites, Drano, (sodium hydroxide) and water. Let the mixture sit for a few days in a capped bottle before using.

SMOKE BOMB

Sometimes it becomes strategically correct to confuse the opposition and provide a smoke screen to aid an escape. A real home-made smoke bomb can be made by combining four parts sugar to six parts saltpeter (available at all chemical supply stores). This mixture must then be heated over a very low flame. It will blend into a plastic substance. When this starts to gel, remove from the heat and allow the plastic to cool Embed a few wooden match heads into the mass while it's still pliable and attach a fuse.*

The smoke bomb itself is a non-explosive and non-flame-producing, so no extreme safety requirements are needed. About a pound of the plastic will produce thick enough smoke to fill a city block. Just make sure you know which way the wind is blowing. Weathermen—women! If you're not the domestic type, you can order smoke flares (yellow or black) for $2.00 a flare [12 inch] from Time Square Stage Lighting Co., 318 West 47th Street, New York, NY 10036.

CBW

LACE (Lycergic Acid Crypto-Ethelene) can be made by mixing LSD with DMSO, a high penetrating agent,

---

*You can make a good homemade fuse by dipping a string in glue and then rolling it lightly in gunpowder. When the glue hardens, wrap the string tightly and neatly with scotch tape. This fuse can be used in a variety of ways. Weight it on one end and drop a rock into the tank of a pig vehicle. Light the other end and run like hell.

and water. Sprayed from an atomizer or squirted from a water pistol, the purple liquid will send any pig twirling into the Never-Never Land of chromosome damage. It produces an involuntary pelvic action in cops that resembles fucking. Remember when Mace runs out, turn to Lace.

How about coating thin darts in LSD and shooting them from a Daisy Air Pellet Gun? Guns and darts are available at hobby and sports shops. Sharpening the otherwise dull darts will help in turning on your prey.

MOLOTOV COCKTAIL

Molotov cocktails are a classic street fighting weapon served up around the world. If you've never made one, you should try it the next time you are in some out-of-the-way barren place just to wipe the fear out of your mind and know that it works. Fill a thin-walled bottle half full with gasoline. Break up a section of styrofoam (cups made of this substance work fine) and let it sit in the gasoline for a few days. The mixture should be slushy and almost fill the bottle. The styrofoam spreads the flames around and regulates the burning. The mixture has nearly the. same properties as napalm. Soap flakes (not detergents) can be substituted for styrofoam. Rubber cement and sterno also work. In a pinch, plain gasoline will do nicely, but it burns very fast. A gasoline-kerosene mixture is preferred by some folks.

Throwing, although by far not the safest method, is sometimes necessary. The classic technique of stuffing a rag in the neck of a bottle, lighting and tossing is foolish. Often gas fumes escape from the bottle and the mixture ignites too soon, endangering the thrower. If you're into throwing, the following is a much safer method: Once the mixture is prepared and inside the bottle, cap it tightly using the original cap or a suitable cork. Then wash the bottle off with rubbing alcohol and wipe it clean. Just before you leave to strike a target, take a strip of rag or a tampax and dip it in gasoline. Wrap this

MOLOTOV (FOR PLACING)

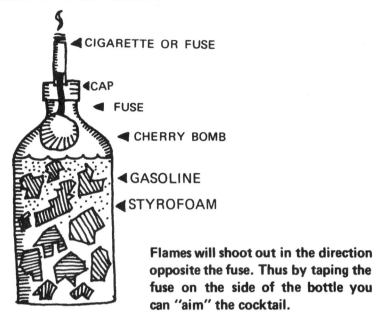

◀CIGARETTE OR FUSE

◀CAP

◀ FUSE

◀ CHERRY BOMB

◀GASOLINE

◀STYROFOAM

Flames will shoot out in the direction opposite the fuse. Thus by taping the fuse on the side of the bottle you can "aim" the cocktail.

MOLOTOV (FOR THROWING)

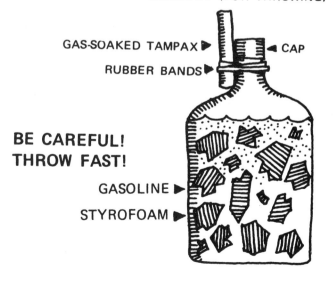

GAS-SOAKED TAMPAX ▶

◀ CAP

RUBBER BANDS ▶

BE CAREFUL! THROW FAST!

GASOLINE ▶

STYROFOAM ▶

fuse in a small plastic baggie and attach the whole thing to the neck of the capped bottle with the aid of several rubber bands. When you are ready to toss, use a lighter to ignite the baggie. Pull back your arm and fling it as soon as the tampax catches fire. This is a very safe method if followed to the letter. The bottle must break to ignite. Be sure to throw it with some force against a hard surface.

Naturally, an even safer method is to place the firebomb in a stationary position and rig up a timing fuse. Cap tightly and wipe with alcohol as before. The alcohol wipe not only is a safety factor, but it eliminates tell-tale fingerprints in case the Molotov doesn't ignite. Next, attach an ashcan fire cracker (M-80) or a cherry bomb to the side of the bottle using epoxy glue. A fancier way is to punch a hole in the cap and pull the fuse of the cherry bomb up through the hole before you seal the bottle. A dab of epoxy will hold the fuse in place and insure the seal. A firecracker fuse ignites quickly so something will have to be rigged that will delay the action enough to make a clean getaway.

When the firebomb is placed where you want it, light up a non-filter cancerette. Take a few puffs (being sure not to inhale the vile fumes) to get it going and work the unlighted end over the fuse of the firecracker. This will provide a delay of from 5 to 15 minutes. To use this type of fuse successfully, there must be enough air in the vicinity so the flame won't go out. A strong wind would not be good either. When the cancerette burns down, it sets off the firecracker which in turn explodes and ignites the mixture. The flames shoot out in the direction opposite to where you attach the firecracker, thus allowing you to aim the firebomb at the most flammable material. With the firecracker in the cap, the flames spread downward in a halo. The cancerette fuse can also be used with a book of matches to ignite a pool of gasoline or a trash can. Stick the unlighted end behind the row of match heads and close the cover. A firecracker attached to a gallon jug of red paint and set off can turn an office into total abstract art.

Commercial fuses are available in many hobby stores. Dynamite fuses are excellent and sold in most rural hardware stores. A good way to make a homemade fuse is described above under the Smoke Bomb section. By adding an extra few feet of fuse to the device and then attaching the lit cancerette fuse, you add an extra measure of caution. It is most important to test every type of fuse device you plan to use a number of times before the actual hit. Some experimentation will allow you to standardize the results. If you really want to get the job done right and have the time, place several molotov cocktails in a group and rig two with fuses (in case one goes out). When one goes, they all go . . .BAROOOOOOOOOOM!

STERNO BOMB

One of the simplest bombs to make is the converted sterno can. It will provide some bang and a widely dispersed spray of jellied fire. Remove the lid from a standard, commercially purchased can and punch a hold in the center big enough for the firecracker fuse. Take a large spoonful of jelly out of the center to make room for the firecracker. Insert the firecracker and pull the fuse up through the hole in the lid. When in place, cement around the hole with epoxy glue. Put some more glue around the rim of the can and reseal the lid. Wipe the can and wash off excess with rubbing alcohol. A cancerette fuse should be used. The can could also be taped around a bottle with Molotov mixture and ignited.

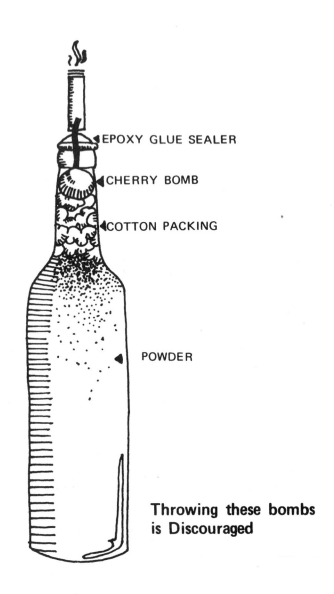

EPOXY GLUE SEALER

CHERRY BOMB

COTTON PACKING

POWDER

**Throwing these bombs
is Discouraged**

AEROSOL BOMB

You can purchase smokeless gunpowder at most
stores where guns and ammunition are sold. It is used for
reloading bullets. The back of shotgun shells can be
opened and the powder removed. Black powder is more

176

highly explosive but more difficult to come by. A graduate chemist can make or get all you'll need. If you know one that can be trusted, go over a lot of shit with him. Try turning him on to learning how to make "plastics" which are absolutely the grooviest explosive available. The ideal urban guerrilla weapons are these explosive plastic compounds.

A neat homemade bomb that really packs a wallop can be made from a regular aerosol can that is empty. Remove the nozzle and punch in the nipple area on the top of the can. Wash the can out with rubbing alcohol and let dry. Fill it gently and lovingly with an explosive powder. Add a layer of cotton to the top and insert a cherry bomb fuse. Use epoxy glue to hold the fuse in place and seal the can. The can should be wiped clean with rubbing alcohol. Another safety hint to remember is never store the powder and your fuses or other ignition material together. Powder should always be treated with a healthy amount of respect. No smoking should go on in the assembling area and no striking of hard metals that might produce a spark. Use your head and you'll get to keep it.

PIPE BOMBS

Perhaps the most widely used homemade concussion bombs are those made out of pipe. Perfected by George Metesky, the renown New York Mad Bomber, they are deadly, safe, easy to assemble, and small enough to transport in your pocket. You want a standard steel pipe (two inches in diameter is a good size) that is threaded on both ends so you can cap it. The length you use depends on how big an explosion is desired. Sizes between 3-10 inches in length have been successfully employed. Make sure both caps screw on tightly before you insert the powder. The basic idea to remember is that a bomb is simply a hot fire burning very rapidly in a tightly confined space. The rapidly expanding gases burst against the walls of the bomb. If they are trapped in a tightly sealed iron pipe, when they finally break out, they do so with incredible force. If the bomb itself is placed in a somewhat enclosed area like a ventilation shaft, doorway or alleyway, it will in turn convert this larger area into a "bomb" and increase the over-all explosion immensely.

When you have the right pipe and both caps selected, drill a hole in the side of the pipe (before powder is inserted) big enough to pull the fuse through. If you are using a firecracker fuse, insert the firecracker, pull the fuse through and epoxy it into place securely. If

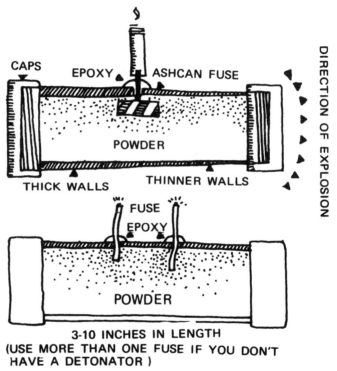

CAPS   EPOXY   ASHCAN FUSE

DIRECTION OF EXPLOSION

POWDER

THICK WALLS   THINNER WALLS

FUSE
EPOXY

POWDER

3-10 INCHES IN LENGTH
(USE MORE THAN ONE FUSE IF YOU DON'T HAVE A DETONATOR)

you are using long fusing either with a detonator (difficult to come by) timing device or a simple cancerette fuse, drill two holes and run two lines of fuse into the pipe. When you have the fuse rigged to the pipe, you are ready to add the powder. Cape one end snuggly, making sure you haven't trapped any grains of powder in the threads. Wipe the device with rubbing alcohol and you're ready to blast off.

A good innovation is to grind down one half of the

pipe before you insert the powder. This makes the walls of one end thinner than the walls of the other end. When you place the bomb, the explosion, following the line of least resistance, will head in that direction. You can do this with ordinary grinding tools available in any hardware or machine shop. Be sure not to have the powder around when you are grinding the pipe, since sparks are produced. *Woodstock Nation* contains instructions for more pipe bombs and a neat timing device (see pages 115-117).

GENERAL BOMB STRATEGY

This section is not meant to be a handbook on explosives. Anyone who wishes to become an expert in the field can procure a number of excellent books on the subject catalogued in the Appendix. In bombing, as in trashing, the same general strategy in regard to the selection of targets applies. Never use anti-personnel shrapnel bombs. Always be careful in placing the devices to keep them away from glass windows and as far away from the front of the building as possible. Direct them away from any area in which there might be people. Sophisticated electric timers should be used only by experts in demolitions. Operate in the wee hours of the night and be careful that you don't injure a night watchman or guard. Telephone in warnings before the bomb goes off. The police record all calls to emergency numbers and occasionally people have been traced down by the use of a voice-o-graph. The best way to avoid detection is by placing a huge wad of chewed up gum on the roof of your mouth before you talk. Using a cloth over the phone is not good enough to avoid detection. Be as brief as possible and always use a pay phone.

When you get books from companies or libraries dealing with explosives or guerrilla warfare, use a phony name and address. Always do this if you obtain chemicals from a chemical supply house. These places are being increasingly watched by the F.B.I. Store your material and literature in a safe cool place and above all, keep your big mouth shut!

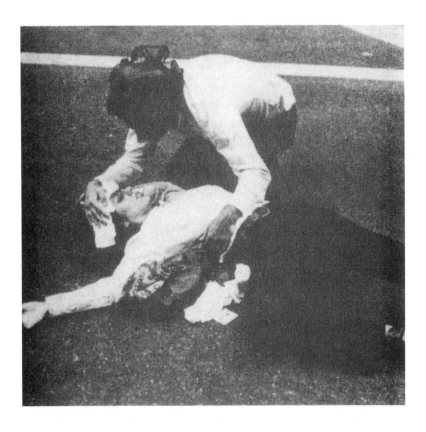

Now if the head is bleeding, do you tighten a tourni-quet around the neck?

First Aid For Street Fighters

Without intending to spook you, we think it is becoming increasingly important for as many people as possible to develop basic first aid skills. As revolutionary struggle intensifies, so will the number and severity of injuries increase. Reliance on establishment medical facilities will become risky. Hospitals that border on "riot" areas are used by police to apprehend suspects. All violence-induced injuries treated by establishment doctors might be reported. Knife and gunshot wounds in all states by law must be immediately phoned in for investigation. At times a victim has no choice but to run such risks. If you can, use a phony name, but everyone should know the location of sympathetic doctors.

Chaos resulting from the gassing, clubbing and shooting associated with a police riot also makes personal first aid important. Most demonstrations have medical teams that run with the people and staff mobile units, but often these become the target of assault by the more vicious pigs. Also, in the confusion, there is usually too much work for the medical teams. Everyone must take responsibility for everyone else if we are to survive in the streets. If you spot someone lying unconscious or badly injured, take it upon yourself to help the victim. Immediately raise your arm or wave your Nation flag and shout for a medic. If the person is badly hurt, it is best not to move him, or her, but if there is the risk of more harm or the area is badly gassed, the victim should be moved to safety. Try to be as gentle as possible. Get some people to help you.

WHAT TO DO

Your attitude in dealing with an injured person is extremely important. Don't panic at the sight of blood. Most bloody injuries look far worse than they are. Don't get nervous if the victim is unconscious. If you're not able to control your own fear about treating someone, call for another person. It helps to attend a few first aid classes to overcome these fears in practice sessions.

When you approach the victim, identify yourself. Calmly, but quickly figure out what's the matter. Check to see if the person is alive by feeling for the pulse. There are a number of spots to check if the blood is circulating, under the chin near the neck, the wrists, and ankles are the most common. Get in the habit of feeling a normal pulse. A high pulse (over 100 per minute) usually indicates shock. A low pulse indicates some kind of injury to the heart or nervous system. Massaging the heart can often restore the heartbeat, especially if its loss is due to a severe blow to the chest. Mouth-to-mouth resuscitation should be used if the victim is not breathing. Both these skills can be mastered in a first aid course in less than an hour and should become second nature to every street fighter.

When it comes to dealing with bleeding or possible fractures, enlisting the victim's help as well as adopting a firm but calm manner will be very reassuring. This is important to avoid shock. Shock occurs when there is a serious loss of blood and not enough is being supplied to the brain. The symptoms are high pulse rate; cold, clammy, pale skin; trembling or unconsciousness. Try to keep the patient warm with blankets or coats. If a tremendous amount of blood has been lost, the victim may need a transfusion. Routine bleeding can be stopped by firm direct pressure over the source of bleeding for 5 to 10 minutes. If an artery has been cut and bleeding is severe, a tourniquet will be needed. Use a belt, scarf or torn shirtsleeve. Tie the tourniquet around the arm or leg directly above the bleeding area and tighten it until the bleeding stops. Do not loosen the tourniquet. Wrap the injured limb in a cold wet towel or ice if available and move the person to a doctor or hospital before irreparable damage can occur. Don't panic, though, you have about six hours.

A painful blow to a limb is best treated with an ice pack and elevation of the extremity by resting it on a pillow or rolled-up jacket. A severe blow to the chest or side can result in a rib fracture which produces sharp pains when breathing and/or coughing up blood. Chest X-rays will eventually be needed. Other internal injuries can occur from sharp body blows such as kidney injuries. They are usually accompanied by nausea, vomiting, shock and persistent abdominal pain. If you feel a bad internal injury has occurred, get prompt professional help.

Head injuries have to be attended to with more attention than other parts of the body. Treat them by stopping the bleeding with direct pressure. They should be treated before other injuries as they more quickly can cause shock. Every head injury should be X-rayed and the injured person should be watched for the next 24 hours as complications can develop hours after the injury was sustained. After a severe blow to the head, be on the look-out for excessive sleepiness or difficulty in waking. Sharp and persistent headaches, vomiting and nausea, dizziness or difficulty maintaining balance are all warning signs. If they occur after a head injury, call a doctor.

If a limb appears to be broken or fractured, improvise a splint before moving the victim. Place a stiff backing behind the limb such as a board or rolled-up magazine and wrap both with a bandage. Try to avoid moving the injured limb as this can lead to complicating the fracture. Every fracture must be X-rayed to evaluate the extent of the injury and subsequent treatment.

Bullet wounds to the abdomen, chest or head, if loss of consciousness occurs are extremely dangerous and must be seen by a doctor immediately. If the wound occurs in the limb, treat as you would any bleeding with direct pressure bandage and tourniquet only if nothing else will stop the bleeding.

If you expect trouble, every person going to a street scene should have a few minimum supplies in addition to those mentioned in the section on Demonstrations for protection. A handful of bandaids, gauze pads (4x4), an ace bandage (3 inch width), and a roll of 1/2 inch adhesive tape can all easily fit in your pocket. A plastic bag with cotton balls pre-soaked in water will come in handy in a variety of situations where gas is being used, as will a small bottle of mineral oil. You should write the name, phone. number and address of the nearest movement doctor on your arm with a ballpoint pen. Your arm's getting pretty crowded, isn't it? If someone is severely injured, it may be better to save their life by taking them to a hospital, even though that means probable capture for them, rather than try to treat it yourself. However, do not confuse the police with the hospital. Many injured people have been finished off by the porkers, and that's no joke. It is usually better to treat a person yourself rather than let the pigs get them, unless they have ambulance equipment right there and don't seem vicious. Even then, they will often wait until they get two or three victims before making a trip to the hospital.

If you have a special medical problem, such as being a diabetic or having a penicillin allergy, you should wear a medi-alert tag around your neck indicating your condition. Every person who sees a lot of street action should have a tetanus shot at least once in every five years.

Know just this much, and it will help to keep down serious injuries at demonstrations. A few lessons in a first aid class at one of the Free Universities or People's Clinics will go a long way in providing you with the confidence and skill needed in the street.

MEDICAL COMMITTEES

Here is a partial list of some Medical Committees for Human Rights. They will be glad to give you first aid instructions and often organize medical teams to work demonstrations. A complete list is available from the Chicago office.
BALTIMORE, MARYLAND, 21215 - 6012 Wallis Ave.

BERKELEY, CALIFORNIA, 94609 - 663 Alcatrz
BIRMINGHAM, ALABAMA, 35205 - 2122 9th Ave. South
CHICAGO, ILLINOIS - 1512 E. 55th St.
CLEVELAND, OHIO, 44112 - Outpost, 13017 Euclid Ave.
DETROIT, MICHIGAN, 48207 - 1300 E. Lafayette
HARTFORD, CONN., 06112 - 161 Ridgefield St.
LOS ANGELES, CALIF. - PO Box 2463, Sepulveda, Calif. 91343 (mail)
NASHVILLE, TENN., 37204 - 3301 Lealand Land
NEW HAVEN, CONN., - 30 Bryden Terrace, Hamden, Conn. 06514 (mail)
NEW ORLEANS, LA., 70130 - 623 Bourbon St.
NEW YORK, NY, 10014 - 15 Charles St.
PHILADELPHIA, PA., 19119 - 6705 Lincoln Drive
PITTSBURGH, PA., 15222 - 617 Empire Building
SAN FRANCISCO, CALIF., 94115 - 2519 Pacific Ave.
SYRACUSE, NY, 13210 - 931 Comstock Ave.
WASHINGTON, D.C. - 3410 Taylor St., Chevy Chase, Md. 20015 (mail)

Now it says here that under certain conditions a molotov cocktail can definitely be considered a defensive weapon.

Hip-Pocket Law

LEGAL ADVICE

Any discussion about what to do while waiting for the lawyer has to be qualified by pointing out that from the moment of arrest through the court appearances, cops tend to disregard a defendant's rights. Nonetheless, you should play it according to the book whenever possible as you might get your case bounced out on a technicality. When you get busted, rule number one is that you have the right to remain silent. We advise that you give only your name and address. There is a legal dispute about whether or not you are obligated under the law to do even that, but most lawyers feel you should. The address can be that of an office if you're uptight about the pigs knowing where you live.

When the pigs grab you, chances are they are going to insult you, rough you up a little and maybe even try to plant some evidence on you. Try to keep your cool. Any struggle on your part, even lying on the street limp, can be considered resisting arrest. Even if you beat the original charge, you can be found guilty of resisting and receive a prison sentence. Often if the pigs beat you, they will say that you attacked them and generally charge you with assault.

If you are stopped in the street on suspicion (which means you are black or have long hair), the police have the right to pat you down to see if you are carrying a weapon. They cannot search you unless they place you under arrest. Technically, this can only be done in the police station where they have the right to examine your possessions. Thus, if you are in a potential arrest situation, you should refrain from carrying dope, sharp objects that can be classified as a weapon, and the names and phone numbers of people close to you, like your dealer, your local bomb factory, and your friends underground.

Forget about talking your way out of it or escaping once you're in the car or paddy wagon. In the police station, insist on being allowed to call your lawyer. Getting change might be a problem, so you should always have a few dimes hidden. Since many cases are dismissed because of this, you'll generally be allowed to make some calls, but it might take a few hours. Call a close friend and tell him to get all the cash that can be quickly raised and head down to the court house. Usually the police will let you know where you'll be taken. If they don't, just tell your friend what precinct you're being held at, and he can call the central police headquarters and find out what court you'll be appearing in. Ask your friend to also call a lawyer which you also should do if you get another phone call. Hang up and dial a lawyer or defense committee that has been set up for demonstrations. The lawyer will either come to the station or meet you in court depending on the severity of the charge and the likelihood you'll be beaten in the station. When massive demonstrations are occuring where a number of busts are anticipated, it's best to have lawyers placed in police stations in the immediate vicinity.

The lawyer will want to know as many details as possible of the case so try and concentrate on remembering a number of things since the pigs aren't going to let you take notes. If you can, remember the name and badge number of the fink that busted you. Sometimes they'll switch arresting officers on you. Remember the time, location of the bust and any potential witnesses that the lawyer might be able to contact.

If you are unable to locate a lawyer, don't panic, the court will assign you one at the time of the arraignment. Legal Aid lawyers are free and can usually do as good a job as a private lawyer at an arraignment. Often they can do better, as the judge might set a lower bail if he sees you can't afford a private lawyer. The arraignment is probably the first place you'll find out what the charges are against you. There will also be a court date set and bail established. The amount of bail depends on a variety of factors ranging from previous convictions to the judge's hangover. It can be put up in collateral, i.e., a bank book, or often there is a cash alternative offered which amounts to about 10% of the total bail.

Your friend should be in the court with some cash (at least a hundred dollars is recommended). For very high bail, there are the bail bondsmen in the area of the courthouse who will cover the bail for a fee, generally not to exceed 5%. You will need some signatures of solid citizens to sign the bail papers and perhaps put up some collateral. For bail over $50,000 check out the possibility of putting up state bonds.

Once you get bailed out, you should contact a private lawyer, preferably one that has experience with your type of case. If you are low on bread, check out one of the community or movement legal groups in your area. It is not advisable to keep the legal aid lawyer beyond the arraignment if at all possible.

If you're in a car or in your home, the police do not have a right to search the premises without a search warrant or probable cause. Do not consent to any search without a warrant, especially if there are witnesses around who can hear you. Without your consent, the pigs must prove probable cause in the court. Make the cops kick in the door or break open the trunk themselves. You are under no obligation to assist them in collecting evidence, and helping them weakens your case.

LAWYERS GROUPS

National Lawyers Guild

The "Guild" provides various free legal services, especially for political prisoners. If you have any legal hassles, call and see if they'll help you. You can call the one nearest you and get the name of a good lawyer in your area.

BOSTON – 70 Charles St.
DETROIT – 5705 N. Woodward St.
LOS ANGELES – c/o Haymarket, 507 N. Hoover St.
NEW YORK - 1 Hudson St.
SAN FRANCISCO – 197 Steiner St.

Outside of these areas, there are no offices, but people to contact in the following cities are:

FLINT, MICH., Carl Bekofske, 1003 Church St.
PHILADELPHIA, PA. – A. Harry Levitan, 1412 Fox Building
WASHINGTON, D.C. – S. David Levy, 2812 Pennsylvania Ave., N.W.

American Civil Liberties Union

The ACLU is not as radical as the Guild, but will in most instances provide good lawyers for a variety of civil liberty cases such as censorship, denial of permits to demonstrations, and the like. But beware of their tendency to win the legal point while losing the case. Here is a list of some of their larger offices.

ALABAMA – Box 1972, University, Alabama 35486
CALIFORNIA – ACLU of Northern California, 503 Market St., San Francisco, Calif. 94105 (EX 2-4692)
COLORADO – 1452 Pennsylvania St., Denver, Colorado 80203 (303-TA5-2930)
GEORGIA – 5 Forsyth St. N.W., Atlanta, Georgia 30303 (404-523-5398)
ILLINOIS – 6 S. Clark, Chicago, Illinois 60603 (312-236-5564)
MICHIGAN – 234 State St., Detroit, Mich. 48226 (313-961-4662)
MONTANA – 2707 Glenwood Land, Billings, Montana 59102 (406-657-2328)
NEW MEXICO – 131 La Vega S.W., Albuquerque, New Mexico 87105 (505-877-5286)

NEW YORK — 156 Fifth Ave., New York, NY 10010 (212-WA9-6076)
NORTH DAKOTA — Ward County (Minot), Box 1000, Minot, North Dakota 58701 (702-838-0381)
OHIO — Suite 200, 203 E. Broad St., Columbus, Ohio 43215
WASHINGTON, D.C. — (NCACLU) 1424 16th St. NW, Suite 501, Washington, D.C. 20036 (202-483-3830) (202-483-3830)
WEST VIRGINIA — 1228 Seventh St., Huntington, West Virginia 25701
WISCONSIN — 1840 N. Farwell Ave., Rm. 303, Milwaukee, Wisc. 53202 (414-272-4032)

To obtain a complete list of all the ACLU chapters, write: American Civil Liberties Union, 156 5th Avenue, New York, NY 10010, or call them at (212) WA 9-6076.

JOIN THE ARMY OF YOUR CHOICE

The first rule of our new Nation prohibits any of us from serving in the army of a foreign power with which we do not have an alliance. Since we exist in a state of war with the Pig Empire, we all have a responsibility to beat the draft by any means necessary.

First check out your medical history. Review every chronic or long-term illness you ever had. Be sure to put down all the serious infections like mono or hep. Next, make note of your physical complications. When you have assembled a complete list, get a copy of *Physical Deferments* or one of the other draft counseling manuals and see if you qualify. If you have a legitimate deferment, document it with a letter from a doctor.

The next best deal is a Consciencious Objection status (C.O.) or a psychiatric deferment (psycho). The laws have been getting progressively broader in defining C.O. status during the past few years. The most recent being, "sincere moral objections to war," without necessarily a belief in a supreme being. There are general

YES SIR!

guidelines sent out by the National Office of Selective Service that say it is a matter of conscience. The decision, however, is still pretty much in the hands of the local board. Visit a Draft Counseling Center if you feel you have a chance for this type of story. They'll know how your local board tends to rule. There are still some more cases to be heard by the Supreme Court before objection to a particular war is allowed or disallowed. It is not grounds for deferment as of now.

Psychos are our specialty. Chromosome damage has totally wiped out our minds when it comes to concentrating on killing innocent people in Asia. When you get your invite to join the army, there are lots of ways you can prepare yourself mentally. Begin by staggering up to a cop and telling him you don't know who you are or where you live. He'll arrange for you to be chauffered to the nearest mental hospital. There you repeat your performance, dropping the clue that you have used LSD in the past, but you aren't sure if you're on it now or not. In due time, they'll put you up for the night. When morning comes, you bounce out of bed, remember who you are, swear you'll never drop acid again and thank everyone who took care of you. Within a few hours, you'll be discharged. Don't be uptight about thinking how they'll lock you up forever cause you really are nuts. The hospitals measure victories by how quickly they can throw you out the door. They are all overcrowded anyway.

In most areas, a one-night stand in a mental hospital is enough to convince the shrink at the induction center that you're capable of eating the flesh of a colonel. Just before you go, see a sympathetic psychiatrist and explain your sad mental shape. He'll get verification that you did time in a hospital and include it in his letter, that you'll take along to the induction center.

When you get to the physical examination, a high point in any young man's life, there are lots of things working in your favor. Here, long hair helps; the army doesn't want to bother with trouble-makers. Remember this even though a tough looking sergeant runs down bullshit about "how they're gonna fix your ass" and "anybody with a trigger finger gets passed." He's just auditioning for the Audie Murphy movies, so don't believe anything he lays down.

Talk to the other guys about how rotten the war in Vietnam is and how if you get forced to go, you'll end up shooting some officers. Tell them you'd like the training so you can come back and take up with the Weathermen.

Check off as many items as can't be verified when given the forms. Suicide, dizzy spells, bed-wetting, dope addiction, homosexuality, hepatitus. Be able to drop a few symptoms on the psychiatrist to back up your story of rejection by a cold and brutal society that was indifferent, from a domineering father that beat you, and mother that didn't understand anything. Be able to trace your history of bad family relationships, your taking to the streets at 15 and eventually your getting "hooked." Let him "pry" things out of you, if possible. Show him your letter if you had the foresight to get one.

Practice a good story before you go for the physical with someone who has already beat the system. If your local board is fucked up, you can transfer to an area that disqualifies almost everyone who wants out, such as the New York City boards. If you can't think of anything you can always get FUCK ARMY tatooed on the outside of the baby finger of your right hand and give the tough sergeant a snappy salute and a hearty "yes sir!"*

CANADA, SWEDEN & POLITICAL ASYLUM

If you've totally fucked up your chances of getting a deferment or already are in the service and considering

*If unfortunately you get hauled in. The Army gives you a life insurance policy. By making Dan Berrigan or Angela Davis the beneficiary you might avoid front-line duty.

ditching, there are some things that you should know about asylum.

There are three categories of countries that you should be interested in if you are planning to ship out to avoid the draft or a serious prison term. The safest countries are those with which Amerika has mutual offense treaties such as Cuba, North Korea and those behind the so-called Iron Curtain. The next safest are countries unfriendly to the U.S. but suffer the possibility of a military coup which might radically affect your status. Cambodia is a recent example of a border-line country. Some cats hijacked a ship bound for Vietnam and went to Cambodia where they were granted asylum. Shortly thereafter the military with a good deal of help from the CIA, took over and now the cats are in jail. Algeria is currently a popular sanctuary in this category.

Sweden will provide political asylum for draft dodgers and deserters. It helps to have a passport, but even that isn't necessary since they are required by their own laws to let you in. There are now about 35,000 exiles from the Pig Empire living in Sweden. The American Deserters Committee, Upplandsgaten 18, Stockholm, phone 08-344663, will provide you with immediate help, contacts and procedural information once you get there. If you enter as a tourist with a passport, you can just go to the local police station, state you are seeking asylum and fill out a form. It's that simple. They stamp your passport and this allows you to hustle rent and food from the Swedish Social Bureau. It takes six months for you to get working papers that will permit you to get employment, but you can live on welfare until then with no hassle. The following places can be contacted. for additional help. They are all in Stockholm:

Reverend Tom Hayes 82-42-11 or 21-45-86
Kristina Nystrom of the Social Bureau 08-230570
Bengt Suderstrom 31-84-32 (legal)
Hans-Goran Franck 10-25-02 (legal)

Canada does not offer political asylum but they do not support the U.S. foreign policy in Southeast Asia so they allow draft dodgers and deserters to the current tune of 50,000 to live there unmolested. Do not tell the officials at the border that you are a deserter or draft dodger, as they will turn you in. Pose as a visitor. To work in Canada you have to qualify for landed immigration status under a point system.

There will be a number of background questions asked and you have to score 50 points or better to pass and qualify. You get one point for each year of formal education, 10 points if you have a professional skill, 10 points for being between 18-35 years of age, more points for having a Canadian home and job waiting for you, for knowing English or French and a wopping 15 points for having a stereotyped middle class appearance and life-style. Letters from a priest or rabbi will help here. Some entry points are easier than others. Kingsgate, for example, just north of Montana is very good on weekdays after 10:00 P.M.

The best approach if you are considering going to Canada is to write or, better still, visit the Montreal Council to Aid War Resisters, Case Postale 5, Westmount, Montreal, 215 Quebec or American Deserters Committee, 3837 Blvd., Saint Laurent, St. Louis, Montreal 3, Quebec. They will provide you with the latest info on procedures and the problems of living in Canada as a war resister. If you can't make it up there, see a local anti-war organization for counseling. If you are already in the army, you should find out all you need to know before you ditch. It's best to cross the border while you're on leave as it might mean the difference between going AWOL and desertion if you decide to come back. In any event, no one should renounce their citizenship until they have qualified for landed immigration status as that would classify the person as a non-resident and make it possible for the Canadian police to send you back, which on a few rare occasions has happened.

Because there have been few cases of fugitives from the U.S. seeking political asylum, there is not a clear and simple formula that can be stated. Germany, France, Belgium and Sweden will often offer asylum for obvious political cases, but each case must be considered individually. Go there incognito. Contact a movement organization or lawyer and have them make application to the government. Usually they will let you stay if you promise not to engage in political organizing in their country. In any event if they deport you these countries are good enough to let you pick the country to which you desire to be sent.

We feel it's our obligation to let people know that life in exile is not all a neat deal, not by a long shot. You are removed from the struggle here at home, the problems of finding work are immense and the customs of the people are strange to you. Most people are unhappy in exile. Many return, some turn themselves in and others come back to join the growing radical underground making war in the belly of the great white whale.

Canada welcomes hard-working middle class immigrants.

If 8 oz. is 49 cents and 12 oz. is 69 cents ....

Steal Now, Pay Never

SHOPLIFTING

This section presents some general guidelines on thievery to put you ahead of the impulse swiping. With some planning ahead, practice and a little nerve, you can pick up on some terrific bargains.

Being a successful shoplifter requires the development of an outlaw mentality. When you enter a store you should already have cased the joint so don't browse around examining all sorts of items, staring over your shoulder and generally appearing like you're about to snatch something and are afraid of getting caught. Enter, having a good idea of what you want and where it's located.

Camouflage is important. Be sure you dress the part by looking like an average customer. If you are going to rip-off expensive stores (why settle for less), act like you have a chauffeur driven car double parked around the corner. A good rule is dress in the style and price range of the clothes, etc., you are about to shoplift. The reason we recommend the more expensive stores is that they tend to have less security guards, relying instead on mechanical methods or more usually on just the sales people. Many salespeople are uptight about carrying out a bust if they catch you. A large number are thieves themselves, in fact one good way to steal is simply explain to the salesclerk that you're broke and ask if you can take something without paying. It's a great way to radicalize shop personnel by rapping to them about why they shouldn't give a shit if the boss gets ripped off.

The best time to work out is on a rainy, cold day during a busy shopping season. Christmas holiday is shoplifter's paradise. In these periods you can wear heavy overcoats or loose raincoats without attracting suspicion. The crowds of shoppers will keep the nosy "can-I-help-you's" from fucking up your style.

Since you have already checked out the store before hitting it, you'll know the store's "blind-spots" where you can be busy without being observed too easily. Dressing rooms, blind alley aisles, and washrooms are some good spots. Know where the cashier's counter is located, where the exits to the street and storage rooms are to be found, and most important, the type of security system in use.

If you are going to snatch in the dressing room, be sure to carry more than one item in with you. Don't leave tell-tale empty hangers behind. Take them out and ditch them in the aisles.

An increasingly popular method of security is a small shoplifting plastic detector attached to the price tag. It says "Do Not Remove" and if you do, it electronically triggers an alarm in the store. If you try to make it out the door, it also trips the alarm system. When a customer buys the item, the cashier removes the detector with a special deactivation machine. When you enter the store, notice if the door is rigged with electronic eyes. They are often at the waist level, which means if the item is strapped to your calf or tucked under your hat, you can walk out without a peep from the alarm. If you trigger the alarm either inside the store or at the threshold, just dash off lickitty-split. The electronic eyes are often disguised as part of the decor. By checking to see what the cashier does with merchandise bought, you can be sure if the store is rigged. Other methods are undercover pigs that look like causal shoppers, one-way mirrors and remote control television cameras. Undercover pigs are expensive so stores are usually understaffed. Just watch out (without appearing to watch out) that no one observes you in action. As to mirrors and cameras, there are always blind spots in a store created when displays are moved around, counters shifted, and boxes piled in the aisles. Mirrors and cameras are rarely adjusted to fit these changes. Don't get turned off by this security jazz. The percentage of stores that have sophisticated security systems such as those described is very small. If you work out at lunch time, the security guards and many of the sales personnel will be out of the store. Just before closing is also good, because the clerks are concentrating on going home.

By taking only one or two items, you can prevent a bust if caught by just acting like a dizzy klepto socialite getting kicks or use the "Oh-gee-I-forgot-to-pay" routine. Stores don't want to hassle going into court to press charges, so they usually let you go after you return the stuff. If you thought ahead, you'll have some cash ready to pay for the items you've pocketed, if caught. Leave your I.D. and phone book at home before going shopping. People rarely go to jail for shoplifting, most if caught never even see a real cop. Just lie like a fucker and the most you'll get is a lecture on law and order and a warning not to come back to that store or else.

TECHNIQUES

The lining of a bulky overcoat or loose raincoat can be elaborately outfitted with a variety of custom-made large pockets. The openings to these pockets are not visible since they are inside the coat. The outside pockets can be torn out leaving only the opening or slit. Thus you can reach your hand (at counter level) through the slit in your coat and drop objects into the secret pockets sewn into the lining. Pants can also be rigged with secret pockets. The idea is to let your fingers do the walking through the slit in your coat, while the rest of the body remains the casual browser. You'll be amazed at how much you can tuck away without any noticeable bulge.

Another method is to use a hidden belt attached to the inside of your coat or pants. The belt is specially designed with hooks or clothespins to which items can be discretely attached. Ditching items into hidden pockets requires a little cunning. You should practice before a mirror until you get good at it.

A good idea is to work with a partner. Dig this neat duet. A man and woman walk into a store together looking like a respectable husband and wife. The man purchases a good belt or shirt and engages the salesman in some distracting conversation as he rings up the sale. Meanwhile, back in the aisle, "wife" is busy rolling up two or three suits. Start from the bottom while they are still on the rack and roll them up, pants and jackets together, the way you would roll a sleeping bag. The sleeves are tied around the roll making a neat little bundle. The bundle is then tucked between your thighs. The whole operation takes about a minute and with some practice you can walk for hours with a good size bundle between your legs and not appear like you just shit in your pants. Try this with a coat on in front of a mirror and see how good you get at it.

Another team method is for one or more partners to distract the sales clerks while the other stuffs. There are all sorts of theater skits possible. One person can act drunk or better still appear to be having an epileptic fit. Two people can start a fight with each other. There are loads of ways, just remember how they do it in the next spy movie you see.

One of the best gimmicks around is the packaging technique. Once you have the target item in hand, head for the fitting room or other secluded spot. Take out a large piece of gift wrapping and ribbon. Quickly wrap up the item so it will look like you brought it in with you. Many stores have their own bags and staple the cash register receipt to the top of the bag when you make a purchase. Get a number of these bags by saving them if you make a purchase or dropping around to the receiving department with a request for some bags for your Christmas play or something. Next collect some sales receipts, usually from the sidewalk or trash cans in front of the store. Buy or rip-off a small pocket stapler for less than a dollar. When you get the item you want, drop it in the bag and staple it closed, remembering to attach the receipt. This is an absolutely perfect method

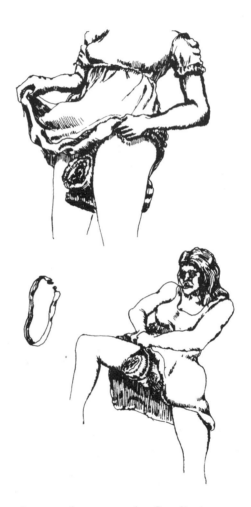

and takes just a few seconds. It eliminates a lot of unsightly bulges in your coat and is good for warm-weather heisting.

A dummy shopping bag can be rigged with a bit of ingenuity. The idea is to make it look like the bag is full when there's still lots of room left. Use strips of cardboard taped to the inside of the bag to give it some body. Remember to carry it like it's filled with items, not air. Professional heisters often use a "booster box," usually a neatly wrapped empty package with one end that opens upon touch. This is ideal for electrical

appliances, jewelry, and even heavy items such as portable television sets. The trick side can be fitted with a spring door so once the toaster is inside the door slams shut. Don't wear a black hat and cape and go around waving a wand yelling "Abracadabra," just be your usual shlep shopper self. If you can manage it, the trick side just can be an opening without a trick door. Just carry the booster box with the open side pressed against your body. Briefcases, suitcases and other types of carrying devices can all be made to hold items. Once you have something neatly tucked away in a bag or box, it's pretty hard to prove you didn't come in with it.

ON THE JOB

By far the easiest and most productive method of stealing is on the job. Wages paid to delivery boys, sales clerks, shippers, cashiers and the like are so insulting that stealing really is a way of maintaining self-respect. If you are set on stealing the store dry when you apply for the job, begin with your best foot forward. Make what employment agencies call a "good appearance." Exude cleanliness, Godliness, sobriety and all the other WASPy virtues third grade teachers insist upon. Building up a good front will eliminate suspicion when things are "missing."

Mail clerks and delivery boys can work all sorts of neat tricks. When things get a little slow, type up some labels addressed to yourself or to close friends and play Santa Claus. Wrap yourself a few packages or take one that is supposed to go to a customer and put your label over theirs. Blame it on the post office or on the fact that "things get messed up 'cause of all the bureaucracy." It's great to be the one to verbalize the boss's own general feelings before he does when something goes awry. The best on-the-job crooks always end up getting promoted.

Cashiers and sales persons who have access to money can pick up a little pocket change without too much effort, no matter how closely they are watched by supervisors. Women can make use of torn hems to stash coins and bills. Men can utilize cuffs. Both can use shoes and don't forget those secret little pockets you learned about in the last section. If you ring up items on a cash register, you can easily mistake $1.39 for 39¢ or $1.98 for 98¢ during the course of a hectic day. Leave pennies on the top shelf of the cash register and move one to the far right side every time you skip a dollar. That way at the end of the day, you'll know how much to pocket and won't have to constantly be stuffing, stuffing, stuffing.

If you pick up trash or clean up, you can stick all sorts of items into wastebaskets and later sneak them out of the store.

There are many ways of working heists with partners who pose as customers. See the sections on free food and clothing for these. There are also ways of working partnerships on the job. A cashier at a movie theater and a doorman can work out a system where the doorman collects the tickets and returns them to the cashier to sell again.

A neat way to make a large haul is to get a job through an agency as a domestic for some rich slob. You should use a phony identification when you sign up at the agency. Once you are busy dusting the town house, check around for anything valuable to be taken home.

Pick up the phone, order all sorts of merchandise, and have it delivered. A friend with a U-haul can help you really clean up.

CREDIT CARDS

Any discussion of shoplifting and forgeries inevitably leads to a rap on credit cards; those little shiny plastic wonder passes to fantasy land that are rendering cash obsolete. There are many ways to land a free credit card. You can get one yourself if your credit is good, or from a friend: report it stolen and go on a binge around town. Sign you name a little funny. Super underworld types might know where you can purchase a card that's not too hot on the black market. You might heist one at a fashionable party or restaurant. If you're a hat check girl at a night club, don't forget to check out pockets and handbags for plastic goodies.*

Finally, you can redo a legitimate card with a new number and signature and be sure that it's on no one's "hot list." Begin by removing the ink on the raised letters with any polyester resin cleaner. Next, the plastic card should be held against a flat iron until the raised identification number is melted. You can use a razor blade to shave off rough spots. This combination of razor blade and hot iron, when worked skillfully, will produce a perfect blank card. When the card is smooth as new, reheat it using the flat iron and press an addressograph plate into the soft plastic. The ink can be replaced by matching the original at any stationary store. If this is too hard, you can buy machines to make your own credit cards, which are made for small

---

*The absolute best method is to have an accomplice working in the post office rip off the new cards that are mailed out. They get to know quickly which envelopes contain new credit cards. Since the person never receives the card it never dawns on them to report it stolen. This gives you at least a solid month of carefree spending and your signature will be perfect.

department stores. Granted, this method is going to require some expertise, but once you've learned to successfully forge a credit card, you can buy every item imaginable, eat fancy meals, and even get real money from a bank.

Whether your credit card is stolen, borrowed or forged, you still have to follow some guidelines to get away without any hassle. Know the store's checking method before you pass the hot card. Most stores have a fifty-dollar limit where they only call upstairs on items costing fifty dollars or more. In some stores it's less. Some places have a Regiscope system that takes your picture with each purchase. You should always carry at least one piece of back-up identification to use with the phony card as the clerk might get suspicious if you don't have any other ID. They can check out a "hot list" that the credit card companies send out monthly, so if you're uptight about anything watch the clerk's movements at all times. If things get tight, just split real quick. Often, even if a clerk or boss thinks it's a phony, they'll OK the sale anyway since the credit card companies make good to the stores on all purchases; legit or otherwise. Similarly, the insurance companies make good to the credit companies and so on until you get to a little group of hard working elves in the basement of the U.S. Mint who do nothing but print free money and lie to everybody about there being tons of gold at Fort Knox to back up their own little forging operation.

Monkey Warfare

If you like Halloween, you'll love monkey warfare. It's ideal for people uptight about guns, bombs and other children's toys, and allows for imaginative forms of protesting, many of which will become myth, hence duplicated and enlarged upon. A syringe (minus the needle) or a cooking baster can be filled with a dilute solution of epoxy glue. Get the two tubes in a hardware store and squeeze into a small bottle of rubbing alcohol. Shake real good and pour into the baster or syringe. You have about thirty minutes before the mixture gets too hard to use. Go after locks, parking meters, and telephones. You can fuck up the companies that use IBM cards by buying a cheap punch or using an Exacto knife and cutting an extra hole in the card before you return it with your payment. By the way, when you return payments always pay a few cents under or over. The company has to send you a credit or another bill and it screws up their bookkeeping system. Remember, *always* bend, fold, staple or otherwise mutiliate the card. By the way, if you ever find yourself in a computer room during a strike, you might want to fuck up the school records. You can do this by passing a large magnet or portable electro-magnet rapidly back and forth across the reels of tape, thus erasing them. And don't miss the tour of the IBM plant, either.

Another good bit is to rent a safe deposit box (only about $7.00 a year) in a bank using a phony name. They usually only need a signature and don't ask for identification. When you get a box, deposit a good size dead fish inside the deposit box, close it up and return it to its proper niche. From then on, forget about it. Now think about it, in a few months there is going to be a hell-of-a-smell from your small investment. It's going to be almost impossible to trace and besides, they can never open the box without your permission. Since you don't exist, they'll have no alternative but to move away. Invest in the Stank of Amerika savings program. Just check out Lake Erie and you'll see saving fish isn't such a dumb idea. If you get caught, tell them you inherited the fish from your grandmother and it has sentimental value.

There are lots of things you can send banks, draft boards and corporations that contribute to pollution via the mails. It is possible to also have things delivered. Have a hearse and flowers sent to the chief of police. We know someone who had a truckload of cement dumped in the driveway of her boss under the fib that the driveway was going to be repaired.

By getting masses of people to use electricity, phones or water at a given time, you can fuck up some not-so-public utility. The whole problem is getting the word out. For example, 10,000 people turning on all their electrical appliances and lights in their homes at a given time can cause a black-out in any major city. A hot summer day at about 3:00 PM is best. Five thousand people calling up Washington, D.C. at 3:00 PM on a Friday (one of the busiest hours) ties up the major trunk lines and really puts a cramp in the government's style of carrying on. Call (202) 555-1212, which is information and you won't even have to pay for the call. If you call a government official, ask some questions like "How many kids did you kill today?" or "What kind of liquor do Congressmen drink?" or offer to take Teddy Kennedy for a ride. A woman can cause some real excitement by calling a Congressman's office and screaming "Tell that bastard he forgot to meet Irene at the motel this afternoon."

A Washington call-in would work even better by phoning direct to homes of the big boys. For starters you can call collect the following: *

*Any group who elopes with any of the persons listed is entitled to a free copy of this book. Anyone who parlays all 10 in a lift-off can have all the royalties. Send ears for verification.

212

Richard M. Nixon - El Presidente - (202) 456-1444
Spiro T. Agnew - El Toro - (202) 265-2000 ext. 6400
John N. Mitchell - El Butcher - (202) 965-2900
Melvin R. Laird - El Defendo - (301) 652-4449
Henry A. Kissinger - El Exigente - (202) 337-0042
William P. Rogers - El Crapper - (301) 654-7125
Earl G. Wheeler - El Joint Bosso - (703) 527-6119
William C. Westmoreland - El Pollutoni - (703) 527-6999
Richard M. Helms - El Assassin - (301) 652-4122
John N. Chafee - El Sinko Swimmi - (703) 536-5411

A great national campaign can be promoted that asks people to protest the presidential election farces on Inauguration Day. When a president says "So help me God," rush in and flush the toilet. A successful Flush for God campaign can really screw up the water system.

If you want to give Ma Bell an electric permanent, consider this nasty. Cut the female device off an ordinary extension cord and expose the two wires. Unscrew the mouthpiece on the phone and remove the voice amplifier. You will see a red and a black wire attached to two terminals. Attach each of the wires from the extension cord to each one from the phone. Next plug in the extension cord to a wall socket. What you are doing is sending 120 volts of electricity back through equipment which is built for only 6 volts. You can knock off thousands of phones, switchboards and bugging devices if all goes right. It's best to do this on the phone in a large office building or university. You certainly will knock out their fuses. Unfortunately, at home your own phone will probably be knocked out of commission. If that happens, simply call up the business office and complain. They'll give you a new phone just the way they give the other seven million people that requested them that day.

Remember, January is Alien Registration Month, so don't forget to fill out an application at the Post Office, listing yourself as a citizen of Free Nation. Then when they ask you to "Love it or leave it," tell them you already left!

Okay General Mitchell, let's see you dance

Piece Now

It's ridiculous to talk about a revolution without a few words on guns. If you haven't been in the army or done some hunting, you probably have a built-in fear against guns that can only be overcome by familiarizing yourself with them.

HANDGUNS

There are two basic types of handguns or pistols: the revolver and the automatic. The revolver carries a load of 5 or 6 bullets in a "revolving" chamber. The automatic usually holds the same number, but some can hold up to 14 bullets. Also, in the automatic the bullets can be already packed in a magazine which quickly snaps into position in the handle. The revolver must be reloaded one bullet at a time. An automatic can jam on rare occasions, or misfire, but with a revolver you just pull the trigger and there's a new bullet ready to fire. Despite pictures of Roy Rogers blasting a silver dollar out of the sky, handguns are difficult to master a high degree of accuracy with and are only good at short ranges. If you can hit a pig-size object at 25 yards, you've been practicing.

Among automatics, the Colt 45 is a popular model with a long record of reliability. A good popular favorite is a Parabellum 9 mm, which has the advantage of a double action on the first shot, meaning that the hammer does not have to be cocked, making possible a quick first shot without carrying a cocked gun around. By the way, do not bother with any handgun smaller than a .38 caliber, because cartridges smaller than this are too weak to be effective.

Revolvers come in all sizes and makes, as do automatics. The most highly recommended are the .38 Special and the .357 Magnum. Almost all police forces use the .38 Special. They are light, accurate and the small-frame models are easy to conceal. If you get one, use high velocity hollow pointed bullets, such as the Speer DWM (146 grain h.p.) or the Super Vel (110 grain h.p.). The hollow point shatters on contact, insuring a kill to the not-so-straight shooters. Smith and Wesson makes the most popular .38 Special. The Charter Arms is a favorite model. The .357 Magnum is an extremely powerful handgun. You can shoot right through the wall of a thick door with one at a distance of 20 yards. It has its own ammo, but can also use the bullets designed for the .38. Both guns are about the same in price, running from $75-$100 new. An automatic generally runs about $25 higher.

RIFLES

There are two commonly available types of rifles; the bolt action and the semi-automatic. War surplus bolt action rifles are cheap, and usually pretty accurate, but have a slower rate of fire than a semi-automatic. A semi-automatic is preferable in nearly all cases. The M-1 carbine is probably the best semi-automatic for the money (about $80). It's light, short, easy to handle, and has only the drawback of a cartridge that's a little underpowered. Among bolt actions, the Springfield, Mauser,. Royal Enfield, Russian 7.62, and the Lee Harvey Oswald Special, the Mannlicher-Carcano, are all good buys for the money (about $20).

One of the best semi-automatics is the AR-18, which is the civilian version of the military M-16. In general, this is a fantastic gun with a high rate of fire, minimal recoil, high accuracy, light weight, and easy maintenance. If kept clean, it will rarely jam, and the bullet has astounding stopping power. It sells for around $225.

SHOTGUNS

The shotgun is the ideal defensive weapon. It's perfect for the vamping band of pigs or hard-heads that tries to lynch you. Being a good shot isn't that necessary because a shotgun shoots a bunch of lead pellets that spread over a wide range as they leave the barrel. There are two common types: the pump action and the semi-automatic. Single shot types and double-barrel types do not have a high enough rate of fire for self-defense.

The pump action is easy to use and reliable. It usually holds about five shells in a tube underneath the barrel. For self-defense you should use 00 buckshot shells. Shotguns come in various gauges, but you will want the largest commonly available, the 12 gauge. The Mossberg Model 500 A is a super weapon in this category which sells for about $90. When buying one, try to get a shotgun with a barrel as short as possible up to the legal limit of 18 inches. It is easy to cut down a longer barrel, too. This increases the area sprayed.

The semi-automatic gun is not used too much for self-defense, as they usually hold only three shells. With some practice, you can shoot a pump nearly as fast as a semi-automatic, and they are much cheaper. See the gun books catalogued in the Appendix for more information.

There are many other good guns available, and a great deal to know about choosing the right gun for the right situation. Reading a little right wing gun literature will help.

OTHER WEAPONS

If you are around a military base, you will find it relatively easy to get your hands on an M-79 grenade launcher, which is like a giant shotgun and is probably the best self-defense weapon of all time. Just inquire discreetly among some long-haired soldiers.

TRAINING

Owning a gun ain't shit unless you know how to use it. They make a hell of a racket when fired so you just can't work out in your den or cellar, except with a BB gun, which is good in between real practice sessions. find some friends who served in the military or are into hunting or target-shooting and ask them to teach you the fundamentals of gun handling and safety. If you're over 18, you can practice on one of your local firing ranges. Look them up in the Yellow Pages, call and see if they offer instructions. They are usually pretty cheap to use. In an hour, you can learn the basics you need to know about guns and the rest is mostly practice, practice, just like in the westerns. Contact the National Rifle Association, Washington, D.C. and ask for information on forming a gun club. If you can, you are entitled to great discounts, have no trouble using ranges and get excellent info on all matters relating to weapons.

A secluded place in the country outside city limits, makes an ideal range for practicing. Shoot at positioned targets. A good idea is to blow up balloons and attach them to pieces of wood or boxes. Position yourself downstream alongside a running brook. A partner can go upstream and release the balloons into the water. As they rush downstream, they simulate an attacker charging you and make excellent moving targets. Watch out for ricochetting bullets. Have any bystander stand by behind you. A clothesline with a pulley attachment can be rigged up to also allow practice with a moving target.

GUN LAWS

Once you decide to get a gun, check out the local laws. There are federal ones, but they're not stricter than any state ordinance. If you're unsure about the laws, send 75¢ to the U.S. Government Printing Office for the manual called *Published Ordinances: Firearms*. It runs down the latest on all state laws. In most states you can buy a rifle or shotgun just for the bread from a store or individual if you are over 18 years old. You can get a handgun when you can prove you're over 21, although you generally need a special permit to carry it concealed on your person or in your car. A concealed weapon permit is pretty hard to get unless you're part of the establishment. You can keep a handgun in your home, though. It's also generally illegal to walk around with a loaded gun of any type. Once you get the hang of using a gun, you'll never want to go back to the old peashooter.

Let's see now, you run the fuse thru the clock face and fasten it to your left toe ....

The Underground

Amerika is just another Latin dictatorship. Those who have doubts, should try the minimal experience of organizing a large rock festival in their state*, sleeping on some beach in the summer or wearing a flag shirt. Ask the blacks what it's been like living under racism and you'll get a taste of the future we face. As the repression increases so will the underground—deadly groups of stoned revolutionaries sneaking around at night and balling all day. As deadly as their southern comrades the Tupamaros. Political trials will only occur when the heavy folks are caught. Too many sisters and brothers have been locked up for long stretches having maintained a false faith in the good will of the court system. Instead, increased numbers have chosen to become fugitives from injustice: Bernadine Dohrn, Rap Brown, Mark Rudd, hundreds of others. Some including Angela Davis, Father Berrigan and Pun Plamondon have been apprehended and locked in cages, but most roam freely and actively inside the intestines of the system. Their growth leads to persistent indigestion for those who sit at the tables of power. As they form into active isolated cells they make apprehension difficult. Soon the FBI will have a Thousand Most Wanted List. Our heroes will be hunted like beasts in the jungle. Anyone who provides information leading to the arrest of a fugitive is a traitor.

Well fellow reader, what will you do when Rap or Bernadine call up and ask to crash for the night? What if

*Unless you want to use our music to attack our politics as the governor of Oregon did to drain support away from demonstrations against the AmeriKKKan Legion. In such a situation the concert should be sabotaged along with political education as to why such an action nas been taken. Don't let the pigs separate our culture from our politics.

221

the Armstrong Brothers want to drop some acid at your pad or Kathy Boudin needs some bread to keep on truckin'? The entire youth culture, everyone who smiles secretly when President Agnew and General Mitchell refer to the growing number of "hot-headed revolutionaries", all the folks who hope the Cong wins, who cheer the Tupamaros on, who want to exchange secret handshakes with the Greek resistance movement, who say " It's about time" when the pigs get gunned down in the black community, all of us have an obligation to support the underground. They are the vanguard of our revolution and in a sense this book is dedicated to their courage.

If you see a fugitive's picture on the post office wall take it home for a souvenir. But watch out, because this is illegal. Soon the FBI will be printing all our posters for free. Right on, FBI! Print up wanted posters of the war criminals in Washington and undercover agents (be absolutely sure) and put them up instead. Since the folks underground move freely among us, we must be totally cool if by chance we recognize a fugitive through their disguise. If they deem it necessary to contact you, they will make the first move. If you are very active in the aboveground movement, chances are you are being watched or tapped and it would be foolhardy to make contact. The underground would be meaningless without the building of a massive community with corresponding political goals. People above ground demonstrate their love for fugitives by continuing and intensifying their own commitment.

If the FBI or local subversive squad of the police department is asking a lot of questions about certain fugitives, get the word out. Call your underground paper or make the announcement at large movement gatherings or music festivals; the grapevine will pass the information on to those that need to know.

If you're forced to go undergound, don't think you need to link up with the more well-known groups such as the Weathermen. If you go under with some close friends, stick together if it's possible. Build contacts with aboveground people that are not that well known to the authorities and can be totally trusted.

You should change the location in which you operate and move to a place where the heat on you won't be as heavy. A good disguise should be worked out. The more information the authorities have on you and the heavier the charges determine how complete your disguise should be. There are some good tips in the books on make-up listed in the Appendix. Only in rare cases is it necessary to abandon the outward appearance of belonging to the youth culture. In fact, even J. Edgar Freako admits that our culture is our chief defense. To infiltrate the youth culture means becoming one of us. For an FBI agent to learn an ideological cover in a highly disciplined organization is relatively easy. To penetrate the culture means changing the way they live. The typical agent would stand out like Jimmy Stewart in a tribe of Apaches.

In the usual case the authorities do not look for a fugitive in the sense of carrying on a massive manhunt. Generally, people are caught for breaking some minor offense and during the routine arrest procedure, their fingerprints give them away. Thus for a fugitive having good identification papers, being careful about violations such as speeding or loitering, and not carrying weapons or bombing manuals become an important part of the security. It is also a good idea to have at least a hundred dollars cash on you at all times. Often even if you are arrested you can bail yourself out and split long before the fingerprints or other identification checks are completed.

If by some chance you are placed on the "10 Most Wanted List" that is a signal that the FBI are indeed conducting a manhunt. It is also the hint that they have uncovered some clues and feel confident they can nab you soon. The List is a public relations gimmick that Hooper, or whatever his name is, dreamed up to show the FBI as super sleuths, and compliment the bullshit image of them that Hollywood lays down. Most FBI agents are southerners who majored in accounting or some other creative field. When you are placed on the List, go deeper underground. It may become necessary to curtail your activities for a while. The manhunt lasts only as long as you are newsworthy since the FBI is very media conscious. Change your disguise, identification and narrow your circle of contacts. In a few months, when the heat is off, you'll be able to be more active, but for the time, sit tight.

IDENTIFICATION PAPERS

An amateur photographer or commercial artist with good processing equipment can make passable phony identification papers. Using a real I.D. card, mask out the name, address, and signature with thin strips of paper the same color as the card itself. Do a neat gluing job. Next, photograph the card using bright overhead lighting to avoid shadows, or xerox it. Use a paper of a color and weight as close to the real thing as you can get. If you use phony state and city papers such as birth certificate or driver's license, choose a state that is far away from the area in which you are located. Have a complete understanding of all the information you are forging. Dates, cities, birthdays and other data are often part of a coding system. Most are easy to figure out simply by studying a few similar authentic cards.

Almost all I.D. cards use one or another IBM Selectric type to fill in the individual's papers. You can buy the exact model used by federal and state agencies for less than $20.00 and install the ball in 5 seconds on any Selectric machine. When you finish the typing operation, sign your new name and trim the card to the size you want. Rub some dirt on the card and bend it a little to eliminate its newness.

Another method is to obtain a set of papers from a close friend of similar characteristics. Your friend can replace the originals without too much trouble. In both cases it might be advisable to get authentic papers using the phonies you have in your possession. In some states getting a license or voting registration card is very easy. Library cards and other supplementary I.D.'s are simple to get. A passport should not be attempted until you definitely have made up your mind to split the country. That way agencies have less time to check the information and you can decide on the disguise to be used for the picture. Unless you expect to get hotter than you are right now, in which case, get it now.

It is wise to have two sets of identification to be on the safe side but *never* have both in your possession at the same time. If you sense the authorities are close to nailing you and choose to go underground, prepare all the identification papers well in advance and store them in a secure place. Inform no one of your possible new identity.

Before you start passing phony I.D.'s to cops, banks and passport offices, you should have experience with lesser targets so you feel comfortable using them. There are stiff penalties for this if you get caught. A few better methods than the ones listed above exist, but we feel they should not be made this public. With a little imagination you'll have no trouble. Dig!

COMMUNICATION

Living underground, like exile, can be extremely lonely, especially during the initial adjustment period when you have to reshuffle your living habits. Psychologically it becomes necessary to maintain a few close contacts with other fugitives or folks aboveground. This is also necessary if you plan to continue waging revolutionary struggle. This means communication. If you contact persons or arrange for them to contact you, be super cool. Don't rush into meetings. Stay OFF the phone! If you must, use pay phones. Have the contact person go to a prescribed booth at prescribed time. Knowing the phone number beforehand, you can call from another pay phone. The pay phone system is superior to debugging devices and voice scramblers. Even so, some pay phones, that local police suspect bookies use, are monitored.

Keep your calls short and disguise your voice a bit. If you are a contact and the call does not come as scheduled, don't panic. Perhaps the booth at the other end is occupied or the phone you are on is out of order. In New York, the latter is usually true. Wait a reasonable length of time and then go about your business. Another contact will be made. Personal rendezvous should take place at places that are not movement hangouts or heavy pig scenes. Intermediaries should be used to see if anyone was followed. Just groove on a few good spy flicks and you'll figure it all out.

Communicating to masses of people above ground is very important. It drives the MAN berserk and gives hope to comrades in the struggle. The most important message is that you are alive, in good spirits and carrying on the struggle. The communications of the Weathermen are brilliantly conceived. Develop a mailing list that you keep well hidden in case of a bust. You can devise a system of mailing stuff in envelopes (careful of fingerprints) inside larger envelopes to a trusted contact who will mail the items from another location to further camouflage your area of operation. A host of communication devices are available besides handwritten notes and typed communications. Tape recorders are excellent but better still are video-tape cassette machines. You can wear masks, do all kinds of weird theatrical stuff and send the tapes to televison stations. At times you might want to risk being interviewed by a newsman, but this can be very dangerous unless you conceive a super plan and have some degree of trust in the word of the journalist. Don't forget a grand jury could be waiting for him with a six months contempt or perjury charge when he admits contact and does not answer their questions.

The only other advice is to dress warm in the winter and cool in the summer, stay high and

I WAS BORN down SOUTH on a CHICKEN FARM near Nashville, TennessEE;

'Twern't nobody there But a sky full of Air, Seventeen billion CHICKENS and ME.

And then one day I said, "Hey, hey, HEY, Think I'll DROP a little LSD."

It BLEW my MIND.

I got real KIND,

And set my CHICKENS FREEEEE!

And there was Chickens in the PASTURE,

Chickens in the BARN,

Chickens in the CAULIFLOWER,

& Chickens in the CORN;

CHICKENS drivin' CADILLACS to WASHINGTON, D.C.,

WASHINGTON D.C. →
← WASHINGTON A.C.

WHEN I SET MY CHIIICKENNNS FREE!

liberate!

fuck new york

HOUSING

You can always sleep up in Central Park during the daytime, although the muggers come out to play at night. Free night crashing can be found in the waiting room of the Pennsylvania Railroad station, 34th St. and 7th Ave. The cops will leave you alone until about 7:00 AM when they kick you out. You can put your rucksack in a locker for twenty-five cents to avoid it being ripped-off.

The Boys Emergency Shelter, 69 St. Marks Place, (777-1234) provides free room and board for males 16-20 years of age. The Living Room can be found on the same block. It's a heavy religious scene, but they will help with room and board. Their hours are 6:30 PM to 2:00 AM, phone 982-5988. Also on the Lower East Side is the Macauley Mission at 90 Lafayette St.

On the West Side, there's a poet named Delworth at 125 Sullivan St. that houses kids if he's got room. The Judson Memorial Church, Washington Square South always has one or more housing programs going. If you're really hard up, try the Stranded Youth Program, 111 W. 31st St. (554-8897). Teenagers 16-20 are sent home; if you don't want to go back but need room and board, give them phony identification.

The Graymoor Monastery (CA 6-2388) offers free room and board for young people in the country. They provide transportation.

FOOD

Hunt's Point Market, Hunt's Point Ave. and 138th St. in the Bronx will lay enough fruit and vegetables on your family to last a week or more. Lettuce, squash, carrots, canteloupe, grapefruit, even artichokes and mushrooms all crated. You'll need a car or truck and they only give stuff away in the early morning. Just tell them you're doing a free food thing and it's yours. Outasight!

The large slaughterhouse area is in the far West Village, west of Hudson and south of 14th St. Get a letter from a clergyman saying you need meat for a church-sponsored meal.

The fish market is located on Fulton and South Streets under the East River Drive overpass in lower Manhattan. You can always manage to find some sympathetic fisherman early in the morning who will lay as much fish on you as you can cart away.

If you pick up on a car, take a trip to Long Island City. There you will find the Gordon Baking Company at 42-25 21st, Pepsi Cola at 4602 Fifth Ave., Borden Company at 35-10 Steinway St. and Dannon Yogurt at 22-11 38th Ave. All four places give out samples for free if you call or write ahead and explain how it's for a block party.

Along 2nd and 3rd Avenues on the upper east side are a host of swank bars with free hors-d'oeuvres beginning at five. All Longchamps are good, as is Max's Kansas City.

For real class, check the back pages of the New York Times for ocean cruises and those swinging bon voyage parties. If you look kind of straight or want to disguise yourself and see the other half at it, sneak into conventions for drinks, snacks and all kinds of free samples. Call the New York Convention Bureau, 90 E. 42nd St. MU 7-1300 for info. You can also get free tickets to theater events here at 9:00 AM on weekdays.

Other free meals can be gotten at the various missions.

Bowery Mission — 227 Bowery (674-3456). Pray and eat from 4:00 to 6:00 PM only. Heavy religious orientation.
Catholic Worker — 36 E. First St. Soup line from 10:00 to 11:00 AM. Clothes for women on Thursday from 12:00 to 2:00 PM. Clothes for men after 2:00 PM weekdays. Sometimes lodging.
Holy Name Center for Homeless Men — 18 Bleeker St. (CA 6-5848 or CA 6-2338) Clothes and morning showers from 7:00 to 11:00 AM.
Macauley Mission — 90 Lafayette St. (CA 6-6214) Free room and board. Free food Saturdays at 5:00 PM. Sometimes free clothes.
Moravian Church — 154 Lexington Ave. (MU 3-4219 or 533-3737) Free spaghetti dinner on Tuesday at 1:00 PM.
Quakers — 328 E. 15th St. Meals at 6:00 PM Tuesdays.
Wayward — 287 Mercer St. Free meals nightly.

The International Society For Krishna Consciousness is located at 41 Second Ave. Every morning at 7:00 AM a delicious cereal breakfast is served free along with chanting and dancing. Also at noon, more food and chanting and on Monday, Wednesday and Friday at 7:00 PM, again food and chanting. Then it's all day Sunday in Central Park Sheepmeadow (generally) for still more chanting (sans food). Hari Krishna is the freest high going if you can get into it and dig cereal and of course, more chanting.

The Paradox Restaurant, at 64 E. 7th St. is a neat cheap health joint that will give you a free meal if you help peel shrimp or do the dishes.

MEDICAL CARE

The latest dope on family planning and the new abortion law can be obtained from Planned Parenthood, 300 Park Ave. (777-2015). They provide a free directory on city-wide services in this area. The Black Panther Free Health Clinic on 180 Sutter Ave. in Brooklyn is radical medicine in action. If you ripped off this book, why not send them or another group mentioned in this book a check so they can continue serving the people. Two fantastic clinics on the Lower East Side are the St. Marks People's Clinic at 44 St. Marks Place (533-9500), open weekdays 6-10 PM and NENA at 290 E. Third St. (677-5040) which also functions as a switchboard for the area.

The Beth Israel Teenage Clinic at 17th St. and 1st Ave. (673-3000 ext. 2424) services young people. Millie at the Village Project, 88 2nd Ave. can arrange for free glasses. The New York University Dental Clinic, 421 First Ave. will give you the cheapest dental care in Gotham. Stuyvesant-Poly Clinic, 137 Second Ave. (674-0232) has an emergency day clinic with the quickest service. Dial-a-freakout is 324-0707. Ambulance service is at 440-1234. You ought to know the cops accompany ambulance calls. The following is a list of the New York City Health Department Centers. They provide a number of free services including X-rays, venereal examinations and treatment, shots for children's diseases, vaccinations, tetanus shots and a host of other services.

Manhattan
Central Harlem—2238 Fifth Ave. AU 3-1900
East Harlem—158 E. 115th St. TR 6-0300
Lower East Side—341 E. 25th St. MU 9-6353
Manhattanville—21 Old Broadway MO 5-5900
Morningside—264 W. 118th St. UN6-2500
Washington Heights—600 W. 168th St. WA 7-6300

Bronx
Morrisania—1309 Fulton St. WY 2-4200
Mott Haven—349 E. 140th St. MO 9-6010
Tremont-Fordham—1826 Arthur Ave. LU 3-5500
Westchester-Pelham—2527 Glebe Ave. SY 2-0100

Brooklyn
Bedford—485 Throop Ave. GL 2-7880
Brownsville—259 Briston St. HY 8-6742
Bushwick—335 Central Ave. HI 3-5000
Crown Heights—1218 Prospect Place SL 6-8902
Flatbush-Gravesend—1601 Ave. S NI 5-8280
Ft. Greene—295 Flatbush Ave. Ext. 643-8934
Red Hook-Gowanus—250 Baltic St. 643-5687
Sunset Park—514 49th St. GE 6-2800
Williamsburg-Greenpoint—151 Mayier St. EV 8-3714

Queens
Astoria-Maspeth—12-16 31st Ave. L.I.C. AS 8-5520
Corona-Flushing—34-33 Junction Blvd., Jackson Heights HI 6-3570
Jamaica—90-37 Parsons Blvd. OL 8-6600
Rockaway—67-10 Rockaway Beach Blvd., Arvenne NE 4-7700

Richmond
51 Stuyvesant Place SA 7-6000

The key to getting overall medical care for free is to pick up on a Medicaid card. You can apply at any metropolitan hospital. After filling out a long form and waiting three weeks you'll get your card in the mail. Have a good story when interviewed about why you're not working or only making under $2900 a year. There is an age limit in that only folks over 21 can qualify, but the rule is liberally enforced and younger people can get the card with the right hardship story.

LEGAL AID

The Lawyer's Commune is a group of revolutionary young lawyers pledged to make a limited income and handle the toughest political cases. They handle all our cases. Find them at 640 Broadway on the fifth floor (677-1552).

New York radicals are fortunate in having a number of good legal assistance agencies. One of the following is bound to be able to help you out of a jam.

Emergency Civil Liberties Committee—25 E. 26th St. 683-8120 (civil liberties)
Legal Aid Society—100 Centre St. BE 3-0250 (criminal matters)
Mobilization for Youth Legal Services—320 E. Third St. 777-5250 (all types of services)
National Lawyers Guild—5 Beekman St. 277-0385 or 227-1078 (political)
New York Civil Liberties Union—156 Fifth Ave. 929-6076 (civil liberties)
New York University Law Center Office—249 Sullivan St. GR 3-1896 (civil matters)

DRAFT COUNSELING

Bronx

Claremont Neighborhood Center — 169th St. and Washington Ave. 588-1000. Hours are from 2:00 to 10:00 weekdays.

Brooklyn

Black Anti-Draft Union — 448 Nostrand Ave.

Church of St. John the Evangelist — 195 Mayier St. 387-8721

Society for Ethical Culture — 53 Prospect Park West SO 8-2972

Manhattan

American Friends Service Committee — 15 Rutherford Place 777-4600

Chelsea Draft Information — 346 W. 20th St. WA 9-2391

Community Free Draft Counseling Center — 470 Amsterdam Ave. 787-8500

Greenwich Village Peace Center — 137 W. Fourth St. 533-5120

Harlem Unemployment Center — 2035 Fifth Ave. 831-6591

LEMPA 105 Avenue B 477-9749

New York Civil Liberties Union — 156 Fifth Ave. 675-5990

New York Workshop in Nonviolence — 339 Lafayette St. 227-0973

Resistance — 339 Lafayette St. 674-9060

Union Theological Seminary — 606 W. 122nd St. MO 3-9090

War Resisters League — 339 Lafayette St. 228-0450

Westside Draft Information — 602 Columbus Ave. (89th St.) 874-7330

Woman's Strike for Peace — 799 Broadway 254-1925

PLAY

Botanical Gardens

Conservatory Gardens — Central Park, 105th St. and Fifth Ave. Seasonal display. LE 4-4938
Brooklyn Botanic Gardens — Flatbush and Washington Aves. Oriental Garden, Rose Garden, Native Wild Flower Garden, Rock Garden, Conservatory. Seasonal display. MA 2-4433.

New York Botanical Gardens, Bronx Park, 200th St., east of Webster Ave. Gardens and Conservatories. Seasonal displays. Parking fee: $1.00 on Saturday, Sunday and holidays. Open: Grounds — 10:00 AM to dark, Greenhouses — 10:00 AM to 4:00 PM. 933-9400.

Queens Botanical Gardens, 43-50 Main St., between Dahilia and Elder Aves, Flushing. TU 6-3800.

These gardens are really beautiful places to fuck around for a day. The best ones are the Bronx and Brooklyn. Bring a picnic, a few friends, some grass, and plant the seeds. It's all free.

Zoos

Central Park — 64th St. and Fifth Ave. Free. Open 11 AM to 5 PM.

Children's Zoo — 64th St. and Fifth Ave. Open 10 AM to 5 PM. Admission is 10 cents. No tickets are sold after 4:30 PM. Free story-telling sessions with motion pictures or color slides at 3:30 PM, Mondays through Fridays.

Bronx Park — Fordham Road and Southern Blvd. WE 3-1500. Open daily from 10 AM to 5 PM. November,

December, January closes at 4:30 PM. Admission on Tuesdays, Wednesdays and Thursdays is 25 cents for adults and children over 5 years. Free on other days and all legal holidays. Children's Zoo closes November 1st.

Barrett Park Zoo – in Richmond, Broadway, Glenwood Place and Clove Road. Open daily 10 AM to 5 PM. GI 2-3100.

Unlike the barbaric cages in Central Park, the 18-acre Flushing Meadow Zoo in Queens has been designed so that visitors can view the animals and birds in their natural surroundings, without bars. Take the Main Street Flushing Line Subway (train number 7) from Times Square to 111th St. in Queens. Bronx Zoo which is the largest in the United States and Flushing Meadow Zoo are fantastic.

Beaches

Brooklyn – Coney Island Beach and Boardwalk ES 2-1670

Manhattan Beach – Oriental Blvd., from Ocean Ave. to Makenzie St. DE 26794

Bronx – Pelham Bay Park – Orchard Beach and Boardwalk TI 5-1828

Queens – Jacob Riis Park – Jamaica Bay, Beach 149 to Beach 169 GR 4-4600

Rockaway Beach – First St. to 149th St. GR 4-3470

Richmond – Great Kills Park – Hylan Blvd., Great Kills EL 1-1977

South Beach and Boardwalk – Ft. Wadsworth to Miller Field, New Dorp YU 7-0709

Wolf's Pond Park – Holten and Cornelia Avenues, Princes Bay YU 4-0360

Go to the beach on weekdays as it usually is very crowded on the weekends. The best beach by far is Rockaway. It has pretty good waves.

Swimming Pools

MANHATTAN – OUTDOOR POOLS

Carmine Street Pool – Clarkson St. and Seventh Ave. WA 4-4246

Colonial Pool – Bradhurst Ave. and W. 145th St. WA 6-8109

East 23rd Street Pool – Asser Levy Place MU 5-1026

Hamilton Fish Pool – E. Houston and Sheriff Streets GR 7-3911

Highbridge Pool – Amsterdam Ave. and W. 173rd St. WA 3-2360

John Jay Pool – 77th St., east of York Ave. at Cherokee Place. RE 7-2458

Lasker Memorial Pool – Central Park, 110th St. and Lenox Ave. 348-6297

Thomas Jefferson Pool – 111th St. and First Ave. LE 4-0198

West 59th Street Pool – between West End and Amsterdam Avenues. CI 5-8519

MANHATTAN – INDOOR POOLS

Baruch Pool – Rivington St. and Baruch Place GR 3-6950

East 54th Street Pool – 342 E. 54th St. and Second Ave. PL 8-3147

Rutgers Place Pool – 5 Rutgers Place GR 3-6567

West 28th Street Pool – 407 W. 28th St. CH 4-1896

West 134th Street Pool – 35 W. 134th St. AU 3-4612

BROOKLYN – OUTDOOR POOLS

Betsy Head Pool – Hopkinson and Dumont Avenues DI 2-2977

McCarren Pool – Driggs Ave. and Lorimer St. EV 8-2367

Red Hook Pool – Bay and Henry Streets TR 5-3855

Sunset Pool – Seventh Ave. and 43rd St. GE 5-2627

BROOKLYN – INDOOR POOLS
Brownsville Recreation Center – Linden Blvd. and Christopher Ave. HY 8-1121
Metropolitan Avenue Pool – Bedford Ave., no phone; call SO 8-2300
St. John's Recreation Center – Prospect Place and Schenectady Avenues HY 3-3948

BRONX – OUTDOOR POOLS
Crotona Pool – E. 173rd St. and Fulton Ave. LU 3-3910

BRONX – INDOOR POOLS
St. Mary's Recreation Center Pool – St. Ann's Ave. and E. 145th St. CY 2-7254

QUEENS – OUTDOOR POOLS
Astoria Pool – 19th St. and 23rd Drive, Astoria AS 8-5261
Flushing Meadow Amphitheatre – Long Island Expressway and Grand Central Parkway, Swimming pool and diving pool. 699-4228.

RICHMOND – OUTDOOR POOLS
Faber Pool – Faber St. and Richmond Terrace GI 2-1524
Lyons Pool – Victory Blvd. and Murray Hulbert Ave. GI 7-6650

The pools are generally crowed but on a warm summer day you don't care. The pools are open on weekdays from 10 AM to 12:30 PM. There is a free period for children 14 years of age and under. No adults are admitted to the pool areas during this free period. After 1 PM on weekdays and all day on Saturdays, Sundays and holidays there is a 15 cents charge for children under 14 years and a 35 cents charge for children over 14 years.

Free Cricket Matches

At both Van Cortland Park in the Bronx and Walker Park on Staten Island every Sunday afternoon there are free cricket matches. Get schedule from British Travel Association, 43 W. 61st St. At Walker Park, free tea and crumpets are served during intermission. I say!

Free Park Events

All kinds of activities in the Parks are free. Call 755-4100 for a recorded announcement of the week's events. The freak center is the rowing pond around 70th St. and Bethesda Fountain around 72nd St. in Central Park, although it floats. Busts are non-existent. A complete list of all recreational facilities can be obtained by calling the New York City Department of Parks.

Museums

American Academy of Arts and Letters, American Numismatic Society, and the American Geographical Society are all located at Broadway and 155th St.

Asia House Gallery — 112 E. 64th St. Art objects from the Far East.

Brooklyn Museum — Eastern Parkway and Washington Ave. Egyptian stuff best in the world outside Egypt. Take IRT (Broadway line) express train to Brooklyn Museum station. (Don't miss the Gardens in back.)

The Cloisters — Weekdays 10 AM to 5 PM, Sundays 1 PM to 6 PM. Take IND Eighth Avenue express (A train) to 190th Str. station and walk a few blocks. The number 4 Fifth Avenue bus also goes all the way up and it's a pleasant ride. One of the best trip places in medieval setting.

Frick Museum — 1 E. 70th St. Great when you're stoned. Closed Mondays.

The Hispanic Society of America — Broadway between 15th and 16th Streets. The best Spanish art collection in the city.

Marine Museum of the Seaman's Church — 25 South St.. All kinds of model ships and sea stuff. Also the Seaport Museum on 16 Fulton St.

Metropolitan Museum — 5th Ave. and 82nd St.

Museum of the American Indian — Broadway at 155th St. Largest Indian museum in the world. Open Tuesday to Sunday 1 to 5 PM. Take IRT (Broadway line) local to 157th St. station.

Museum of the City of New York — 103rd St. and 5th Ave. LE 4-1672

Museum of Modern Art — 11 W. 53rd St. CI 5-3200. Monday is free.

Museum of Natural History — Central Park West and 79th St. Great dinosaurs and other stuff. Weekdays 10-5 PM, Sunday 1-5 PM.

Museum of the Performing Arts — Lincoln Center, Amsterdam Ave. and 65th St. 799-2200

New York Historical Society — 77th St. and Central Park West. TR 3-3400

Chase Manhattan Museum of Money — 1256 6th Ave. All banks, especially Chase Manhattan ones are museums when you get right down to it. Liberate them!

Music

About the closest you can come to good free rock music is the Summer Musical Festival in Central Park. There are concerts every Monday, Wednesday, Friday and Saturday in the months of July and August. It only costs $1.00 or $2.00, and everybody in the music world plays at least once. The concerts are held at the Wollman Ice Skating Ring. Occasionally there are free rock concerts in Central Park.

The Greenwich House of Music located at 46 Barrow St. in the West Village puts on free concerts and recitals every Friday at 8:30 PM. For a complete schedule send a stamped, self-addressed envelope.

The Frick Museum, 1 E. 70th St., BU 8-0700, has concerts every Sunday afternoon. The best of the classical offerings. You must hassle a little. Send a self-addressed stamped envelope that will arrive on Monday before the date you wish to go. One letter, one ticket. The Donnell Library, 20 W. 53rd St. also presents free classical music. The schedule is found in "Calendar of Events" at any library.

The Juilliard School presents a variety of free stuff: orchestral, opera, dance, chamber music, string quartets and soloists. Performances take place most Friday evenings at 8:30 PM, from November through May.

The Museum of the City of New York, 5th Ave. between 103rd St. and 104th St. every Sunday at 2:30 PM, October through April. Phone first: LE 4-1672. Classical.

From December through April, glee clubs string groups, and classical singers also perform on Sundays at 2:30 PM at the New York Historical Society, 170 Central Park West (near 77th St.), Phone TR 3-3400 for schedule.

Classical concerts by assorted soloists and groups are presented free every Sunday from October through June at 2 PM, at the Brooklyn Museum, Eastern Parkway and Washington Ave. NE 8-5000.

Television Shows

You can sometimes pick up tickets to television shows at the New York Convention and Visitors Bureau, 90 E. 42nd St. For the bigger and better shows you have to write direct to the studios. If you do write, do it as far in advance as possible. CBS, 51 W. 52nd St., asks you to write two months in advance. Sometimes you can get last-minute tickets for the Ed Sullivan Theater, 1697 Broadway. For NBC shows, write NBC Ticket Division, 30 Rockefeller Plaza. There is also a ticket desk on the NBC Mezzanine of 30 Rockefeller Plaza where tickets are given out for the day shows on a first-come-first-served basis. It's open Monday through Friday from 9-5. ABC, 1330 Sixth Ave. ask you to write two to three weeks in advance for tickets. You can get tickets up to the day of the show by calling in or visiting the ticket office of ABC, 79 W. 66th St. or 1330 6th Ave. (LT 1-7777). Metromedia also gives out free tickets to their shows and you can get them by writing to WNEW-TV, 205 E. 67th St. (LE 5-1000).

Theater

The Dramatic Workshop, Studio number 808, Carnegie Hall Building, 881 7th Ave. at 56th St. Free on Friday, Saturday and Sunday at 8:15 PM. JU 6-4800 for information.

New York Shakespeare Festival, Delacourte Theater, Central Park. Every night except Monday. Performance begins at 8:00 PM, but get there before 6:00 PM to be assured of tickets.

Pageant Players, the Sixth Street Theater Group and other street theater groups perform on street corners and in parks. Free theater is also provided at the United Nations Building and the Stock Exchange on Wall Street. If you enjoy seventeenth century comedy.

The Equity Library Theatre gives performances of

old Broadway hits at the Masters Institute, 103rd St. and Riverside Drive. They perform Tuesday through Sunday at 8:30 PM and Sunday at 2:30 PM. Free tickets are not always available so phone ahead (MO 3-2038) for reservations. No shows during the summer.

The Museum of Performing Arts, 111 Amsterdam Ave. offers plays, dance programs and music. Shows start at 6:30 PM. Tickets are handed out at 4:00 PM. Saturday shows start at 2:30 PM. You can write for a calendar of events to 1865 Broadway or call 799-2200.

Movies

The New York Historical Society, Central Park West and 77th St. presents Hollywood movies every Saturday afternoon. TR 3-3400 for a schedule.

At the Metropolitan Museum, Fifth Ave. and 82nd St., you can see art films every Monday at 3:00 PM. TR 9-5500 for a schedule.

New York University has a very good free movie program as well as poetry, lectures, and theatre presentations. Call the Program Director's Office 598-2026 for a schedule.

The Film Library in the Donnell Library, 20 W. 53rd St., 790-6463, has a wide variety of films which may be borrowed free of charge. The Library system also presents film programs throughout the year. Pick up a Calendar of Events which lists the free showings at all the branches.

The Museum of Modern Art is free every Monday and they have a free film showing at 2 and 5 PM. Get a schedule at the Museum. They have the largest movie collection in the world.

The Museum of Natural History, Central Park West between 77th and 81st St. (TR 3-1300), presents travel and anthropological films on Wednesday and Saturday afternoons at 2:00 sharp, from October through May.

Every movie that plays in New York has a series of screenings for critics, film buyers and friends of the folks that made it. Look in the Yellow Pages under Motion

Picture Studios and Motion Picture Screening Rooms. Once you get the feel of it, you'll quickly learn who shows what, where and when. They always let you in free and if not give some gull story. (See Free Entertainment section). If you see previews in a theater or notice a publicity build-up in the newspapers, the movie is being screened at one or more of the rooms.

INFORMATION

Daily News—220 E. 42nd St., will answer any questions you put to them. Well almost! General information: 883-1122; Sports: 883-1133; Travel: 883-1144; Weather: 883-1155.

For the latest news call the wire services. AP is PL 7-1312, UPI is MU 2-0400.

The New York Times Research Bureau, 229 W. 43rd St., 556-1651, will research news questions that pertain to the past three months.

Liberation News Service at 160 Claremont Ave., will give you up-to-the-minute coverage of radical news. Call 749-2200.

UNDERGROUND PAPERS

East Village Other—20 E. 12th St., 225-2130
Liberation—339 Lafayette St., 674-0050
Other Scenes—Box 8, Village Station, 242-3888
Rat—241 E. 14th St., 228-4460
Win—339 Lafayette St., 674-0050
Others, call Underground Press Syndicate, Box 26, Village Station, 691-6073

MISCELLANEOUS

Dial-a-Beating—911, Dial-a-Demonstration—924-6315, Dial-a-Satellite—TR 3-0404, Time—NERVOUS, Weather—WE 6-1212.

The Switchboard—989-0720, at the Alternate U, is open 6 PM to 3 AM.

THE SUBWAY SYSTEM

The first thing to do is get familiar with the geography of stops you use most frequently. Locate the token cage. Check to see whether the exits are within easy view of the teller, off to the side, or blocked from view by concrete pole-supporters. Next learn the type of turnstile in use. Follow the hints laid down in the Free Transportation section.

The rush hours are always the easiest times. Just go through the exits as people push open the door. Also at crowded hours, people go single file past the turnstiles, one after another in a steady stream. Get in line and go under. The people will block you from view and won't do anything. Even a cop won't give you much hassle. Some subway stations have concrete supports that block the teller's view. Where these exist, slip through the exit nearest the pole or slide by the turnstile.

Turnstile jumping is such a skill, it's going to be added to the Olympics. There are three basic styles common to New York and most cities and each needs a slightly different approach.

The Old Wooden Cranker—(Traditional) You have to go under or sail over this type. Going under is a smoother trip. Going over is trickier since you need both hands free to hurdle and it's a quicker, more noticeable motion.

New-Aluminum-Bar-Turnstiles-Which-Turn-Both-Ways-For-Exit-and-Entrance—Approach it with confidence. Pretend you're putting in a token with your right hand and pull the bar toward you one third of the way with your left hand. Go through the space left between the bars and the barrier. Not for heavyweights!

New-Aluminum-Bar-Turnstiles-Which-Can-Be-Used-Only-For-Entrance—They won't pull towards you, and so, you must go either under or over them.

NOTE: There is no way to tell a New-Aluminum-Bar-Turnstile-Which-Turns-Both-Ways-For-Exit-and-Entrance from a New-Aluminum-Bar-Turnstile-Which-Can-Be-Used-

Only-For-Entrance unless there is a sign. You have to try it first. Therefore, it is important to remember which kind is in use at your local station so your technique will be smooth. Once you're through, remember in your mind you've paid. Ignore everybody who tries to stop you or tell you different. If someone shouts just keep on truckin' on toward your track. Don't stop or run. Insist you are right if you ever get caught. We have been doing it for years, got caught twice and let go both times when other passengers insisted we paid. Everybody hates the subways, even the tellers.

FREEBIES

Clothing Repairs

All Wallach stores feature a service that includes sewing on buttons, free shoe horns, and shoe laces, mending pants pockets and linings, punching extra holes in belts, and a number of other free services.

Furniture

By far the best place to get free furniture in New York is on the street. Once a week in every district, the Sanitation Department makes bulk pick-ups. The night before, residents put out all kinds of stuff on the street. For the best selection try the West Village on Monday nights, and the East Seventies on Tuesday nights. On Wednesday night there are fantastic pick-ups on 35th St. in back of Macy's. Move quickly though, the guards get pissed off easily; the truckers couldn't care less. This street method can furnish your whole pad. Beds, desks, bureaus, lamps, bookcases, chairs, and tables. It's all a matter of transportation. If you don't have access to a car or truck, it's worth it to rent a station wagon and make pick-ups.

Ghosts

If you would like to meet a real ghost, write Hans Holtzer, c/o New York Committee for Investigation for Paranormal Research, 140 Riverside Drive, New York, NY. He'll put you in touch for free.

Free Lessons

Lessons in a variety of skills such as plumbing, electricity, jewelry-making, construction and woodworking are provided by the Mechanics Institute, 20 W. 44th St. Call or write them well in advance for a schedule. You must sign up early for lessons as they try to maintain small courses. MU 7-4279.

Poems

are free. Are you a poem or are you a prose?

Liberated Churches

Saint Mark's in the Bowery, Second Ave. and 10th ST. (674-6377); Washington Square Methodist Church, 133 W. Fourth St., Greenwich Village (777-2528); Judson Memorial Church, Washington Square South (725-9211).

Flowers

At about 9:30 AM, free flowers in the Flower District on Sixth Ave. between 22nd St. and 23rd St. Once in a while, you can find a potted tree that's been thrown out because it's slightly damaged.

The Staten Island Ferry—Not free, but a nickel each way for a five mile ocean voyage around the southern tip of Manhattan is worth it. Take IRT (Broadway line) to South Ferry, local only. Ferry leaves every half-hour day and night.

Drugs

In the area along Central Park West in the Seventies and Eighties are located many doctor's offices. Daily they throw out piles of drug samples. If you know what you're looking for, search this area.

Books

You can always use the library. The main branch is on Fifth Ave. and 42nd St. The Public Library prints a leaflet entitled "It's Your Library" which lists all the 168 branches and special services the library provides. You can pick it up at your nearest branch. They also publish a calendar of events every two weeks which is available free. If you have any questions call 791-6161.

You can get free posters, literature and books from the various missions to the United Nations located on the East Side near the UN Building. The Cuban Mission,

6 E. 67th St., will give you free copies of *Granma,* the Cuban newspaper, *Man and Socialism in Cuba*, by Che Guevara and other literature.

Map

A free subway map is available at any token booth. Good if you're new in the city and don't know your way around.

Pets

ASPCA, 441 E. 92nd St. and York Ave., TR 6-7700. Dogs, cats, some birds and other pets. Tell them you're from out of town if you want a dog and you will not have to pay the $5.00 license fee. Have them inspect and innoculate the pet, which they do free of charge. A good place to look for free pets is in the Village Voice under their column Free Pets.

Radio Free New York

WBAI FM, 99.5 on your dial. 30 E. 39th St. (OX 7-8506).

Free Schools

Alternative University, 69 W. 14th St. (989-0666). A good radical school offering courses in karate, Mao, medical skills and other courses. They will send you a catalogue listing current courses.

Bottega Artists Workshop, 1115 Quentin Road, Brooklyn, 336-3212 has art taught by professionals for a free.

GENERAL SERVICES

Contact—220 E. Seventh St. Open 3 to 10 PM. Raps, contacts, mailing addresses, counseling, sometimes food.
Traveler's Aid—204 E. 39th St. MU 4-5029
Village Project—88 Second Ave. Open 2 to 6 PM. Same as Contact.

Con Edison's number is 679-6700.

fuck chicago

HOUSING

Contrary to rumors, none of us have ever been to Chicago. None-the-less, we have some friends who have visited the area. In Chicago, everyone 17 or under must be off the streets by 10:30 PM and by 11:30 PM on Fridays and Saturdays. Don't sleep in Lincoln Park during political conventions, but other nights it's O.K. Wasn't it Hillel who asked, "Why is this night different from all other nights?" And wasn't it Mayor Richard J. Daley who responded, "Cause I say get your ass out of the park!"

The Chicago Seed (929-0133) will give you the best advice on crashing and the local heat scene. Grace Lutheran Church, 555 W. Beldon St., and the Looking Glass at 1725 W. Wilson also have crashing places or know where you can find free room and board.

You won't get hassled if you sack out in the Union Station on Adams Street just over the bridge. There are loads of folks crashing in abandoned buildings along La Salle and other streets. Also the rooftops are cool. Stay off the streets though, unless you've got good identification.

FOOD

SCLC (Operation Breadbasket) has a free breakfast program every morning Monday through Friday from 7–10 AM at St. Anna Church, 55th St. and La Salle St., and also at Christ the King Lutheran Church located at 3700 Lake Park.

You can get free samples of cheese, meat, and coffee everyday at the Stop and Shop food store located on Washington between Dearborn and State Streets. At the Treasure Island grocery store located on Broadway, two blocks north of Belmont, free coffee and cookies are offered for the people. Halloway House at 27 W. Randolph gives coupons good for coffee. Also at the Guild Bookstore at 25 W. Jackson Blvd., and from the machines at the 4th through 14th floors of the Playboy Building.

There are real cheap restaurants. One is a truck-stop in Skokie called Karl's Cafe. It's just north of Oakton on Skokie Highway. It's open until 6:00. You get a whole lot of food for $1.00. Also, under the viaduct at Milwaukee and Damen is a small restaurant with Polish food. You can get a great meal for $1.35. It's worth a visit. It closes early in the evening. Another cheap restaurant is Paul and Ernie's on North Lincoln, just south of Wrightwood. You can have a beef dinner for about 70 cents.

A good place to pick up free vegetables and fruits is at the wholesale market on Randolph St. or S. Water St. on Friday afternoons. Many of the food factories such as Kraft Dairy Products give away free samples and cases for "charity." Check them out.

It is possible to steal food from the 2nd floor Federal Building Cafeteria at Adams and Dearborn and the National Cafeteria at Clark and Van Buren. These cafeterias usually have long lines and you can eat while standing and just pay for the coffee.

If you have a place to cook and store food, there are a few places that have pretty cheap food. The east gate of International Harvester, located at 1015 W. 120th St. is unbelievable. Dig these bargains! 10 pounds of T-bone steaks (boxed) for $5.25 at midnight. at 4 PM, the produce man brings a different combination of goods. A typical bill of fare might include tomatoes, cucumbers, strawberries, etc. at $1.00 for 10 pounds of any item. The produce might vary from day to day, but the prices stay the same. On Thursdays at noon and 4 PM, the Lennell cookie man comes around. It's $1.25 per box. At 7 PM, the sausage man arrives and the standard price is

$2.00. The standard size is 3 to 4 pounds. He has salami, liver sausage, polish sausage, and usually odd lunchmeat such as bologna or summer sausage. All the food is sold out of trucks, and the prices might not be exact, but they're pretty close.

Eggs are about 3 dozen for $2.00 on Randolph west of Halsted. Orange juice is pretty cheap at the Del Farm on Broadway. Wonder Bread thrift store on Diversey; Butternut, 87th St. and Ridgeland and 1471 W. Wilson, and Silvercup, 55th and Federal, offer bread and rolls at big discounts. The Cicero Bottling Company at 31st St. and 48 Court sell a case of 12 quart bottles for $2.00. Mamas Cookies, 7400 S. Kostner give 5 pounds for $1.50. At Burhops, State and Grand, you can get cheap 5-pound boxes of steak. The Railroad Salvage around Madison and Halsted has dented cans (with stuff inside) for big discounts. It is also a good place for paper products. Campbell Soup, 2250 W. 55th St., open Tuesday and Thursday, will give you cases free or at discounts if you tell them it's for charity or look straight. Two good spots for all around shopping are the Hi-Lo on Lincoln, north of Irving. There's lots of stuff for 10 cents. Marathon Products at Randolph and Halsted is another good place.

If you can survive on just one meal a day, you're set. The city has just opened 14 free lunch centers throughout the town. They are located at:

Antgeld Urban Progress Center—967 E. 132nd St.
Area II Multi-Service Center of DHR—1500 N. North Park
Division Street Urban Progress Center—1940 W. Division
DHR Woodlawn District Office—6317 S. Maryland
Englewood District Office of DHR—6003 S. Halsted
Garfield Neighborhood Service Program— 9 S. Kedzie
Halsted Urban Progress Center—1935 S. Halsted
Lawndale Urban Progress Center—3818 W. Roosevelt
Madden Park Fieldhouse—500 E. 37th St.
Martin Luther King Urban Progress Center—4741 S. King Drive

Montrose Urban Progress Center—901 W. Montrose
North Kenwood CCUO Office—4155 S. Lake Park
South Chicago Urban Progress Center—9231 S. Houston
Southern District DHR Office—2108 E. 71st St.

The free hot meals consist of meat, potatoes, a vegetable, desert, fruit, and coffee or milk. You have to give them a name and an address.

MEDICAL CARE

All three major universities have excellent clinics that do most kinds of medical work for free. The University of Chicago maintains a clinic at 950 E. 59th St. The University of Illinois has one located at 840 S. Wood. In addition to good medical care, Northwestern University Clinic offers very cheap dental treatment. The clinic is at 303 E. Chicago. Call the main switchboard of the schools and ask for the clinics to check out services and hours.

A V.D. clinic is open every weekday and late on Wednesdays at 27 E. 26th St. and N. North Park. Chronic diseases are treated at 2974 N. Clybourn. Free chest X-rays are available at City Hall downtown, everyday. For mental health problems, try the clinic at 1900 N. Sedgwick (642-3531).

Drug education is offered by Earth Mother on Wednesdays at the Grace Church, 555 W. Belden. Information and help with bad trips can be obtained through Just Us, 61 N. Parkside (378-7618) or LSD Rescue Service, 7717 N. Sheridan (338-6750). Chicago has a number of good clinics maintained by movement and community groups spread throughout the city for the people that live in the area. The Black Panther Party runs the Spurgeon "Jake" Winters Free People's Clinic at 3850 W. 16th St. (522-3220).

The Young Patriots Uptown Health Service located at 4408 N. Sheridan (334-8957) serves the people in that community. The Young Lords maintain the Dr. E. Betances Free People's Health Center at Peoples Church,

258

834 W. Armitage (549-8505). The Latin American Defense Organization has a clinic on 2353 W. North Avenue, (276-0900). The growing Student Health Organization administers a number of small clinics in various communities. Call them at 493-2741 or drop into their office at 1613 E. 53rd St. At the Holy Covenant Church, on Wilton and Diversey, you can get medical assistance at the Free People's Clinic as well as help with legal, housing, family planning and nutrition problems. Call 348-6842. All these clinics provide a variety of services and operate on different schedules. Call them first to be sure they are open.

LEGAL AID

Chicago has a number of good law schools and you can often get some assistance or referral by calling them and speaking to the editor of the law school paper. You can go to the bathroom for free in the Julius J. Hoffman Room at Northwestern University Law School.

The Law Student Commune, 357 E. Chicago, 649-8462, is a group of young radical lawyers and law students trying to bring legal assistance into the streets. The People's Law Office, 2156 N. Halsted, 929-1880, operates the same way. For community problems, call the Lincoln Park Rights Center, 525-9775, or the Community Legal Counsel, 726-0157. The ACLU maintains a large chapter in Chicago at 6 S. Clark, 236-5564, and handles cases where civil liberties are affected.

DRAFT COUNSELING

American Friends Service Committee   407 S. Dearborn St. 427-2533
Austin Draft Counseling Center   5903 Fulton 626-9385
Chicago Area Draft Resisters (Cadre)   519 W. North Ave. 664-6895

Chicago Circle Draft Information Organization —
University of Illinois, 317 Chicago Circle Center
663-2557
Hyde Park Draft Information Center — Quaker House,
5615 S. Woodlawn Ave. 363-1248
Kennedy-King Draft Counseling Center 7047 S.
Stewart — 488-0900, ext. 36
Lawndale Draft Counseling — 4049 W. 28th St.
277-3140
Loyola Draft Counseling Center 6525 N. Sheridan
274-3000, ext. 378
Mandel Legal Aid Clinic 6020 S. University Ave.
324-5181
Ravenswood Draft Counseling — Barry Memorial
Methodist Church, 4754 N. Leavitt 784-3273
Roosevelt Selective Service Counseling Organization —
Roosevelt University Student Senate Office, Rm. 204,
430 S. Michigan Ave. 922-3580, ext. 334
South Side Draft Information (Mt. Carmel Book Dist.)
2355 W. 63rd St. 925-3686
Uptown Hull House Draft Information Service — 4520
N. Beacon St. 561-8033
Wellington Avenue Congregational Church Draft
Counseling Center 615 W. Wellington Ave. 935-0642.

PLAY

Parks

Lincoln Park stretches along Lake Michigan in the
Northern section of the city. It has a Conservatory and
Zoo, opened 9 AM to 5 PM. Just south of the zoo is the
gathering place for free rock concerts, be-ins, and the
like. There is also a zoo in the Brookfield section at
8400 W. 31st St. The Morton Arboretium located on
Route 53 in Lisle is open every day till sunset. The
Shedd Aquarium is located at 1200 South Lake Shore
Drive at Roosevelt.

Music

   The Auditorium and Opera House sometimes offers free concerts on Sunday and weeknights. Hang around the lobby and claim there are tickets in your name at the box office. Even if it's a pay concert you can generally bluff your way inside. The Center for New Music, 2263 N. Lincoln, usually has free concerts on Sunday and Monday at 8 PM. WGLD is the local underground station. The Universal Life Church Coffee House, 1049 W. Polk, has free rock and folk music on the weekends. Free City Music sponsors free rock concerts during the spring and summer in Lincoln Park.

MUSEUMS

The Art Institute — Adams and Michigan. Opens daily at 10 AM. Great art museum.

Chicago Academy of Science—Lincoln Park at 2001 N. Clark. (LI 9-0606) Open daily from 10 AM to 5 PM.

Field Museum of Natural History—Roosevelt Road at Lake Shore Drive. Time of opening varies from day to day; call 922-9410. Thursday, Saturday and Sunday admission is free.

Museum of Contemporary Art—237 E. Ontario (943-7755) OPen daily.

Museum of Science and Industry—57th St. in the Hyde Park area. (MU 4-1414) Open daily from 9 AM to 5 PM. Our all-time favorite museum.

The Oriental Institute—University of Chicago campus, 1155 E. 58th St. (643-0800) Open daily, except Monday, from 10 AM to 5 PM.

Poetry

The Other Door Coffee House, 3124 N. Broadway, features nightly poetry readings and music. Call 348-8552. Cafe Pergolesi, 3404 N. Halsted, features poetry readings, baroque music and an art gallery. There is no cover or minimum. Open 6 to 12 PM, and till 1:00 AM on Saturday.

Theater

The Playhouse North, 315 W. North Ave. features free theater. For $1.00, you can see various groups perform at the Harper Theater Coffee House at 5238 S. Harper. Second City, 1616 N. Wells, has free improvisations after their evening performances every evening except Fridays. Free children's theater can be seen at La Dolores, 1980 North Orchard, Mondays and Wednesdays at 1 PM. Call 664-2352.

Movies

The Biograph Theater, 2433 N. Lincoln Ave. shows double bills for $1.25 and has a penny candy counter. John Dillinger got ambushed when he left the place. Free Newsreel films can be seen Wednesdays at 8 PM at the Neighborhood Commons, Wisconsin and Freemart. Newsreel, 2744 N. Lincoln (248-2018) provides movement films for free or low cost to groups.

Alice's Revisited, 950 N. Wrightwood, is a restaurant that shows free movies. On Fridays and Saturdays at 8 PM they have free folk-rock-blues music. Saturdays they also have free children's theater. Tuesdays they have psychodrama, also for free. Call 528-4250 for more info.

INFORMATION

The Switchboard number is 281-7197.

Underground Papers

Rising Up Angry – 2261 N. Lincoln 472-1791
Second City – 2120 N. Halsted 549-8760
The Chicago Seed – 950 W. Wrightwood 929-0133

The Seed features a column called "Making It," which deals with survival in the Windy City. It is probably the best of its type in the country.

The Black Panther Party office is located at 2350 W. Madison (243-8276).

COMMUNITY PRINTING

Agitprop – no office; phone 929-0133
Chicago Print Co-op. – 6710 N. Clark
J. S. Jordan Memorial Printing Co-op. – 6710 N. Clark
Omega Posters – 711 S. Dearborn
Red Star Press – 180 N. Wacher

SCHOOLS

The People's School, 4409 N. Sheridan (561-6737), offers free courses in many areas of survival and radical politics. The White Panther Party, 787-1962, offers courses in street fighting, history of American radicalism, and dialectic sexism.

FREEBIES

Clothes

The Concerned Citizens Survival Front, 2512 N. Lincoln Ave. has clothes. Try the dry cleaners on Armitage east of Halsted along the south side of the street. They give away unclaimed stuff. Also Brazil Cleaners at 3943 Indiana. The Eugene Blue Jean Store at 7017 Paulina has jeans, old army shirts and other items for less than a dollar.

Furniture

The Lake Shore Drive area on collection days has furniture. Call the bureau of Streets and Sanitation for a collection schedule.

Free Store

At 727 S. Laflin, you'll find a genuine free store that gives away everything you can imagine. It has a tendency to be a floating free store though.

Money

Pick up some underground papers at any of the offices listed and hawk them on the streets. You can pull in $6-$10 an hour if you work at it.

fuck los angeles

HOUSING

There are several crash pads and communes that will put you up for a few nights. Call the Free Clinic at 938-9141. Floor space is available at the Sans Souce Temple on S. Ardmore. Women's Emergency Lodge at 912 W. 9th St. (627-5571) will put up women without a place to stay or make referrals. Resistance (386-9645) and Green Power (HO 9-5184) wiill be helpful if you have to crash. Sleeping on the beaches is out, but the roofs are cool. The Midnite Mission at 396 S. Los Angeles (624-9258) has room and board for some boarders. The parks and streets are certain bust material. The L.A. pigs are matched in brutality only by their fellow hoggers in Chicago and South Africa. Every L.A. cop is nine feet of solid chrome. Bite his toes and down he goes.

FOOD

Green Power Feeds Millions is a unique organization serving the needs of the people. They provide food for festivals, concerts, demonstrations, be-ins, sit-ins and similar events for free. In addition they supply a number of communes and serve food every Sunday in Griffith Park, the central get-together spot in Los Angeles. Call them at HO 9-5184 or 938-9141 for information and also to offer your help.

Free vegetarian lunch can be found at the W. Hollywood Presbyterian Church at Sunset and Mariel (874-1816). For supper, try the Midnite Mission, 396 S. Los Angeles Street; God Squas, 1412 N. Crescent Heights Blvd (near Sunset), and His Place, Sunset and La Cienega.

The Half-Price Bakery at Third and Hill St. gives away free bakery goods late at night and you can always bum a meal in any Clifton's Cafeteria with a good story.

The Watts Trojan House is a free store that provides not only food, but clothing and a variety of other items and service. They are located at 1822 E. 103rd St. The County Welfare Department at 2707 S. Grand (near Adams Street) has a liberal food stamp program (746-0522).

MEDICAL CARE

The Free Clinic at 115 N. Fairfax Ave. (938-9141) is very popular and provides a number of services at various hours such as:

Job Co-ops—Monday thru Friday, 10:00-4:00 PM.
Medical—Monday thru Friday, 5:30-10:00 PM. Saturday 12:30-5:00 PM.
Dental—Monday thru Thursday, 7-10 PM.
Counseling-Psychiatric, Monday thru Friday, 6-10 PM.
Legal—Monday thru Friday, 7-10 PM
Draft—Monday thru Thursday, 7:30-10:00 PM.
Pregnancy and Abortion—Monday, Tuesday, Thursday, 7:30. Saturday 1:30 PM
Birth Control—Monday thru Friday, 6-7 PM. Saturday 2-3 PM.

The Foothill Clinic, 547 E. Union in Pasadena (795-8088) offers similar services free of charge. Call them for a schedule of hours. Venereal Diseases are treated in the evenings at a clinic maintained by the Committee to Eradicate Syphillis. They are found at 5205 Melrose Ave., Hollywood (870-2524).

In Venice use the free Youth Clinic at 905 Venice Blvd. (near Lincoln). The services are varied and they are only open evenings. Call 399-7743 and they'll help you.

For specialized problems try:

Drugs—Narcotics Anonymous (463-3123)
Abortion—The Woman's Center, 1027 S. Crenshaw (near Olympic Blvd.) Wednesdays at 7:30 PM.
Mental—Central City Community Mental Health Center, 4272 S. Broadway (232-2441) Suicide Prevention Center, 2521 W. Pico (381-5111).

District Health Centers provide many free services. For exact information, call the center or write to: County of Los Angeles Health Department, Public Health Education Division, 220 N. Broadway, Los Angeles, California 90012. Ask for a list and information about their health services.

EAST LOS ANGELES– 670 S. Ferris Ave. 261-3191.
Subcenter -Maravilla -915 N. Bonnie Beach Pl. 264-6910.
HOLLYWOOD-WILSHIRE–5202 Melrose Ave. 464-0121. Subcenter—West Hollywood—621 N. San Vicente Blvd. 652-3090.
NORTH HOLLYWOOD 5300 Tujunga Ave. 766-3981. Subcenters--Pacoima--13300 Van Nuys Blvd. 899-0231. Tujunga 7747 Foothill Blvd. 352-1417.
SOUTH—1522 E. 102 St. 564-6801
Subcenter Florence-Firestone- 8019 Compton Ave. 583-6241.
SOUTHEAST -4920 Avalon Blvd. 231-2161.
SOUTHWEST 3834 S. Western Ave. 731-8541.

LEGAL AID

The Legal Aid Foundation of Los Angeles at 106 3rd St. (628-9126) provides help in civil matters.

The ACLU of Southern California is located at 323 W. Fifth St. (MA 6-5156).

DRAFT COUNSELING

AFSC 980 N. Fair Oaks, Pasadena 91103 (791-1978)
Black Community Draft Assistance -7228 S. Broadway, LA 90003 (778-0710)
Catholic Peace Assn.--911 Malcolm Ave., Westwood 90024 (474-2683)
Counterdraft--PO Box 74881, LA 90004
East LA Peace Center—409 N. Soto, LA 90033 (261-2047)
Episcopal Draft Counseling Center- 514 W. Adams Blvd., LA 90004 (748-4662)

Fellowship for Reconciliation 4356½ Melrose, LA 90029 (666-0145)

First Unitarian Church–2936 W. Eighth St., LA 90005 (389-1356)

Free Clinic–115 N. Fairfax, LA 90036 (938-9141)

L.A. Comm. for Defense of Bill of Rights–(MA 5-2169)

L.A. Draft Help–1018 S. Hill St., LA (RI 7-5461)

Myra House–191 N. Sunkist, West Covina (338-9636)

Northeast Peace Center–5682 York Blvd., LA 90042 (257-2004)

Peace House–724 Morengo, Pasadena 91103 (449-8228)

Resistance–507 N. Hoover, LA 90004

The Resistance–11317 Santa Monica Blvd., Westwood 90024 (478-2374)

SFVSC–Student Service Center, Admissions and Records Office, San Fernando Valley State College, Northridge (349-1200, ext. 1181)

UCLA Draft Counseling Center–UCLA Law School, 405 Hilgard Ave., LA 90024 (746-6092)

USC Counseling Center–Gould Law School, University Park, Student Union Bldg., Rm. 217 (746-6092)

Valley Peace Center–7105 Hayvenhurst, Van Nuys 91406 (787-6925). Tuesday and Wednesday evenings.

Venice Draft Info Center–73 Market St., Venice 90291 (399-5812)

War Resisters League–1046 N. Sweetzer, LA 90069 (654-4491)

Westside Jewish Community Center–5870 W. Olympic Blvd., LA 90046 (938-2531)

Women Strike for Peace–5899 W. Pico Blvd., LA 90019 (937-0236)

PLAY

Beaches

Los Angeles has 14 miles of beaches extending from north of Pacific Palisades to Cabrillo Beach in San Pedro.

Will Rogers Beach State Park, 15100 Pacific Coast

Highway, Pacific Palisades, extends north three miles from the Santa Monica city limits to a point near Topanga Canyon. This beach has a large, popular surfing area.

Venice Beach, 2100 Ocean Front Walk, Venice, extends from the Santa Monica city limits south to Marina Del Rey. Six acres have been developed into a park with picnic areas, shuffleboard courts and the Venice Beach Pavilion. The huge Venice Fishing Pier is located here, and there is an area for surfing.

Isidore B. Dockweiler Beach State Park, 11401 Vista del Mar Ave. extends from Marina del Ray, south of the city of El Segundo. This beach has 700 fire pits and a surfing area.

Cabrillo Beach, 3720 Stephen White Drive, San Pedro, located at the northern end of Los Angeles Harbor, has picnic areas, fire pits and a section for surfing.

Royal Palms Beach, 1799 Paseo del Mar is equipped with picnic areas and fire pits.

Parks

Griffith Park is the largest park and the favorite gathering spot of the local hip community. It's next to the Ventura and State Freeways.

Arroyo Seco Park is located along the Arroyo Seco and has picnic, recreational and bowling-on-the-green facilities. You'll also find the Los Angeles Zoo at 5333 Zoo Drive in the park.

Brand Park and Memory Garden opposite the old Mission San Fernando is a real strange place to go.

Echo Park has the largest artificial lake in Los Angeles. Fishing programs for kids are conducted each summer and electric boats are available for rent.

Hancock Park, located on Wilshire Blvd. between Odgen and Curson, has the LaBrea Tar Pits with prehistoric animal and plant fossils all over the place.

The Exposition Park Rose Garden on Exposition Blvd. is a seven-acre sunken rose garden that smells great.

Founded by Hubert Eaton as "the first step up to heaven," Forest Lawn Memorial Park, overlooking beautiful downtown Glendale has to be the wildest spot around. It is pure L.A. with the largest collection of reproduced statuary in the world. Jean Harlow, Sabu, Clark Gable and other loved ones are tucked away here. You can turn on in front of the Jean Hersholt Memorial, fuck in the Aisle of Benevolence located in the Great Mausoleum, and trip out on a stereo sermon emanating from the giant Mystery of Life sculpture. Far-fucking-out!

Museums

There are over fifty free museums in the greater Los Angeles area. We are listing those of special interest.

California Museum of Science and Industry—Exposition Park, 749-0101.

Hollywood Wax Museum—6767 Hollywood Blvd. (near Grauman's Chinese Theater).

Los Angeles County Museum of Art—5905 Wilshire Blvd. in Hancock Park, 937-2590.

Music

Every Sunday there are free music concerts in Griffith Park.

Movies

U.C.L.A. has a free experimental film series every year. Call them at 825-4321 for a schedule.

INFORMATION

The Switchboard in Los Angeles has a 24-hour-a-day service called the Hot Line. It's located at 4650 Sunset Blvd. (663-1015). Call them for the latest in what's going down in the area. The L.A. Free Press at 7813 Beverly Blvd. 937-1970, is always a good source of information. The Black Panther Party Headquarters can be found at 4115 S. Central Ave., 235-4127, or at 9818 Anzac, in Watts, 567-8027. The Traveler's Aid Society has offices in the Greyhound Bus Terminal and International Airport. They provide all kinds of services and information to lost souls or visitors. Generally

FREEBIES

Clothes

The following spots offer clothes, furniture and other household items at low prices:

Goodwill Industries- 235 So. Broadway 228-1748; 5208 Whittier 264-1638

St. Vincent de Paul Society--727 N. Broadway 627-8147; 210 San Fernando Rd. 221-6151

The Volunteers of Amerika maintain a number of thrift stores throughout the area. Try 8609 S. Broadway or call 750-9251 for the store near you.

The Salvation Army also has a chain of stores. The main store is at 801 E. 7th St. 620-1270. They can help you there or let you know where you can shop in your area.

Money

You can sell a pint of blood for $10.00 at the Red Cross Blood Bank, 1200 S. Vermont (384-5261).

Pets

All sorts of free pets are available at the ASPCA, 5026 W. Jefferson (731-2491).

Identification

Los Angeles has a curfew law but you can get a suitable I.D. with photo for $3.50 at Twelfth and Hill Streets.

fuck san francisco

HOUSING

The nights are chilly in San Francisco but there are places that offer a free night's lodging. To avoid overcrowding they tend to employ a ticket system. By showing up in the late afternoon, you are generally assured a place to stay that night. The following places work it this way:

Brother Juniper's Inn--1736 Haight, tickets on a first-come, first-serve basis.

Holy Order of Man--937 Fillmore, no tickets.

Hospitality House--148 Leavenworth, for people under 18, generally filled.

Pinehurst Emergency Lodge--2685 30th Ave., for unwed mothers and women with children.

St. Mary's Church--660 California, tickets at 6:00 PM.

St. Patrick's Church--756 Mission, tickets at 6:00 PM

St. Vincent De Paul - 235 Minna, tickets at 4:00 PM for single men only.

Salvation Army Harbor Light – 290 Fourth St., no tickets.

Traveler's Aid, 38 Mason, 771-0880, will assist in finding temporary shelter. Young runaways will find it cool to try All Saint's Church, 1350 Walker (863-9718) for both room and board. Also Huckleberry's for Runaways, 1347 7th Ave. (731-3921) will provide these and other services such as counseling.

If you're going to settle for a while in San Francisco, you might have difficulty finding an apartment to rent. Try the Federal Housing Information Center, 100 California (556-5900). They maintain a free listing.

The Community Design Center, 215 Haight (863-3718) provides free advice on architectural and design of pads inside and out once you locate a place.

speaking, you can find a Traveler's Aid Station in every place that large numbers of travelers can be found.

FOOD

During the day you can cop a free meal at St. Anthony's, 55 Jones, that is of standard mission quality. Similarly, the Worldwide Brotherhood, Inc. at 1219 Fillmore, serves three free meals at 11:15 AM, 3:00 PM and 7:00 PM. Sacred Heart Convent, Fillmore and Hayes has sandwiches and milk every morning at 10:00 AM. The Hare Krishna Temple at 518 Frederick St. (731-9671) serves whole wheat chapatis, vegetables, fruits, dhal and rice every day at 11:30 AM. Bring them an offering of flowers, money, or incense as they don't have that much bread to sustain indefinite freeloading.

The Peinel Mission is found in Natoma Alley at 3rd St. and Market, near the Mission Street side. Doors open at 7:30 PM and they serve excellent sandwiches and coffee. They'll even let you wrap some up and take them back to your pad. Holy Order of Man, 937 Fillmore has a a hot meal free every night beginning at 8:00 PM, as does the Lifeline Mission at 917 Folsom. The Andor Rescue Mission starts serving at 7:00 PM on weekdays. They are located at 1253 McAllister and also feature shower facilities for both men and women between 3:00 and 5:00 PM.

The Good Karma Cafe at Eighteenth Street and Dolores has free macrobiotic meals on Sundays from 2-5 PM. At 1 PM every Sunday an excellent dinner with mostly freaks dining, can be found at the Glide Church, 2330 Ellis. In the evenings they dish out free familia to anybody who wants some. Free salad and cheap sandwiches can be found at the Everloving Trading Post, 1428 Haight.

There are a number of really cheap restaurants in San Francisco such as Dishop's as 315 Divisadero that offers a meal for a quarter. The All Saint's Church at 1350 Walker has a complete hot full-course dinner every Wednesday night for only a dollar. The Ruby Palace, 631 Kearny, has all the Chinese food you can eat for $1.60. Ginn's Cafe, 115 6th St. has a variety of meals for under a dollar. The People's Restaurant, 260 Valencia, features great, cheap, Mexican food.

The Produce Market between 3rd St. and Bayshore just under the freeway going south is the wholesale fruit and vegetable area. Early in the morning you can pick up all sorts of free stuff from the different sheds. Farmers Market. 100 Alemeny Blvd. should also be a hit. The **Salvation** Army Welfare Bureau at 178 Valencia (863-6520) gives away stacks of free groceries to families. You'll have to fill out an application but once you qualify, you can keep coming back.

Day-old bread can be picked up for next to nothing at the shipping door of the Larabum Bakery, 365 3rd Ave. The Canned Food Distribution Center, 1350 Folsom, offers dented cans and inexpensive meats at low discount prices. Big Bonus supermarkets at 2627 Army, 1158 Howard, and 555 S. Van Ness, have the cheapest prices to be found in commercial stores.

If you're already settled and interested in joining one of the various food buying conspiracies, call 621-3788 or ask around the Everlovin' Trading Post or Sonoma Natural Foods at 3214 Folsom. Basta Ya serves a children's breakfast at 7:00 AM at St. Peter's Church, 24th St. and Alabama, and at St. John's Church, 14th St. and Julian. The Black Panther Party provides the same service at Hunter's Point Community Center, 1492 Jerrold and Sacred Heart Church, Fell and Fillmore.

MEDICAL CARE

The Canon Kip Community House located on 8th St. at Natoma (861-6801) has a free clinic and dispensary open weekdays in the morning. The Haight-Ashbury Free Clinic, which is the oldest hip community center in the world is located on 558 Clayton St. (431-1714). The hours are 6-10 PM during the week; however they offer a variety of special services during the day. Call them for a schedule. Los Siete People's Clinic at 2990 22nd St. (258-3655) provides medical care and conducts classes. The clinic is open every weekday evening. Another free clinic serving the people is the Every Man's Free Clinic, 120 Church (626-9548) which operates on Monday, Wednesday and Friday in the evenings.

There are numerous neighborhood clinics that treat residents. A few worth trying are:

Hunter's Point Community Health Center—5815 Third St. 822-3130.
Mission Community Free Clinic—240 Chadwell 552-3870.
Mission Neighborhood Clinic—17th St. and Shotwell 552-3870
Potero Hill Clinic—953 Dettaro 826-8080.

The city maintains free preventative health centers that have a number of services including vaccinations and birth control devices. Check out the following:
Bayview—Hunter's Point, Outer Mission, 1525 Silver Ave. 587-3664
Mission—3850 17th St. 558-3905
Northeast—Chinatown, N. Beach—799 Pacific Ave. 558-3158
Sunset—Richmond, Parkside—1990 41st Ave. 558-3246·
Westside—Haight Ashbury, W. Add.—Marina, 1901 Pierce St. 558-3256.

These can provide you with birth control pills on a monthly basis. More help with birth control problems can be obtained at the Planned Parenthood Center, 2340 Clay (922-1720). They will also help you determine if you qualify for a theraputic abortion which is the only way the operation can be performed legally in the state. The Society for Humane Abortion will, for a five dollar donation, provide you with counseling on how to obtain an out-of-state or out-of-the-country abortion. Theraputic abortions are granted, however, with not as much difficulty as one might expect. You have to prove that your mental health is being impaired by your pregnancy. They are performed free if you are on welfare or qualify for it. If you decide you need an abortion, go to San Francisco General Hospital at 22nd and Potrero. Ask for the Social Service Department where a social worker will listen to your depressing tale. Lay it on heavy enough and you'll qualify. If you have complications from any type of abortion whether it be internal bleeding or feelings of depression, visiting the Post-Abortion Care Center at 555 Arguello can help. Their services are free and they also do pregnancy tests.

The Department of Public Health, 101 Grove (558-6161) offers various free services at centers throughout the city. Call them. There is a free Children's Clinic at 330 Ellis (771-6300). You can get free chiropractic work at 931 Sutter. Call 391-1848 for an appointment. Psychiatric aid is available at the Center for Special Problems, 2107 Van Ness (558-4801).

Dental care is provided free or very cheap at the clinic maintained by the University of California Dental School. Located in the Medical Science Building, Room 606 at 3rd Ave. and Parnassus (666-1173). Call them also for referrals to low-priced dentists.

For emergency bad trips, call Crisis Clinic at 566-1050. Contemplating suicide? Call 751-4866. An ambulance will rush to your place by calling 431-2830, and Dial-a-Beating is 553-0123.

LEGAL AID

The Neighborhood Legal Assistance at 532 Natoma (626-5285) provides help in all civil cases such as evictions and other landlord hassles. Free for low income folks who live south of Market in the Tenderloin District. Legal Aid Society is located at 690 Market (421-7337). Juvenile Defense, 1830 Fell St. (387-3575) provides help for young people under 18 years of age with criminal cases pending. The ACLU has its offices at 503 Market (EX 2-4962).

The Citizen's Alert, 330 Ellis (776-9669) maintains

a 24-hour-a-day phone service that will record police harassment and make lawyer referrals if you get busted. Youth Emergency Service (293-4073) performs the same service for young people.

The On Bail Project can be found inside the Hall of Justice, 850 Bryant, Room 304 (552-2202). They can generally arrange for your release on your own recognizance without putting up any bail. There are some cases they won't handle and you must be over 18 for this service but it's worth trying as soon as you're arraigned.

DRAFT COUNSELING

Black Draft Counsel -1373 Page 863-8786
CCOC—437 Market St. 397-6917
Chinatown Draft Help—854 Kearny 781-9622
Draft Help 3684 18th, near Dolores Park 863-0775
Ecumenical House (Dean Anderson)- 190 Denslowe Drive 333-4920
409 House (Episcopal Peace Fellowship) 409 Clayton (621-9553)
Lawyer's Panel—Draft resistance work. 626-7877
Marin Draft Help- 406 San Amselmo St. 454-8026
Quaker Draft Counseling- Near Walnut and Vine 843-9725
San Francisco Resistance -483 Guerrero St. 626-1910
War Resister's League—833 Haight 626-6976
Women for Peace- 50 Oak St. 861-4118

If you have to split for Canada from the West Coast, head for Vancouver, British Columbia. The Georgia Straight, Vancouver's great underground newspaper, is at 217 Carroll (off Hastings) and will provide information about the Draft Dodger Hostels in the area. If you arrive at night, try the Cool-Aid Crash House (3 day limit) at the corner of Burrand and 7th Ave. Look fairly straight for the border crossing and be careful about hitching through Washington as local ordinances and state laws are said to be enforced by the blue meanies.

Parks

All kinds of free recreational events take place in

the parks. You can call 558-4268 and the Public Information Datebook will inform you of the week's free activities. Golden Gate Park is the largest around and the traditional gathering place ever since the first Be-in was held there on January 14, 1967. The features are duck ponds, a Zoo, an Aquarium, Japanese Tea Gardens and loads of ball fields and picnic areas. Free music can generally be heard every Sunday afternoon.

The San Francisco Zoological Gardens on Sloat Blvd. and Great Highway is worth a visit, as is the Strybing Botanical Gardens on South Drive at 9th Ave. The Conservatory, JFK Drive and Arguello Blvd. features a luscious tropical plant paradise.

Pools—Indoor

BALBOA- San Jose Ave. and Havelock St. 585-1677
COFFMAN--Visitacion Ave. and Hahn St. 586-8570
GARFIELD- 26th and Harrison Sts. 824-4949
HAMILTON—Geary Blvd. and Steiner St. 931-2450
LARSEN- 19th Ave and Wawona St. 661-1475
NORTH BEACH -Mason and Lombard St. 421-7466
ROSSI--Arguello Blvd. and Anza St. 751-9411

Rates: 10 cents for under 18 years in the daytime and 25 cents at night; 50 cents for over 18 years. You can rent a suit and towel for 15 cents. Telephone 558-3643 for additional information.

PLAY
Museums

California Palace of the Legion of Honor- Main entrance to Lincoln Park, 34th Ave. and Clement St. 221-5610.
California Historical Society 2090 Jackson. 567-1848.
M.H. De Young Memorial Museum Golden Gate Park 558-3598.
San Francisco Art Institute--800 Chestnut St. 771-7020.
San Francisco Museum of Art McAllister St. at Van ' Ness Ave. Civic Center. 863-8800.

Movies

One of the best movie scenes in town is the free series at City University. It runs every Thursday night at 8:00 PM. You don't have to be a student.

Music

Free Jam Session and Jazz Dance Happenings every Sunday at 2:00 PM at the Black Light Explosion Company, 331 Grove. For information call 621-4685. Now, get together with some friends and make your own music.

INFORMATION

For the latest dope on the hip community scene, try one of the underground newspapers. Good Times at 2377 Bush Street (922-9881) usually has some folks around who can help you. The Haight-Ashbury Tribune, 1778 Haight (387-2733) will also assist. Another paper serving San Francisco is the Oracle which is found at 460 Magnolia Ave. in Larkspur. Papers can be sold on the streets in all the Bay Area.

The Switchboard at 1830 Fell is one of the oldest and best run. Call 387-3575. They have real 24-hour, 7-days-a-week service. There are several other switchboards throughout the area. Check the Switchboard section of this book.

The weather info number is 936-1212 and time can be had by calling POPCORN.

Newsreel, 450 Alabama (863-6197) offers free showing of radical films as well as engaging in production and distribution. The Radical Education Project has seminars, conferences for church and movement people and free literature. Located at 330 Ellis St. 4th Fl. (333-4920). The San Francisco Black Panther Party Chapter is at 1336 Fillmore St. (922-0095).

The Rip-Off Press is at 698 Golden Gate. (775-7975). They charge real low and do some stuff free.

FREEBIES
Clothes

Try Everlovin Tradin Post, Anchor Rescue Mission, the 409 House, Holy Order of Man and St. Vincent De Paul for all kinds of free clothing. Their addresses can be found above in various sections.

Low priced clothing can be gotten at the Salvation

Army, 1500 Valencia and at Goodwill Industries, 986 Howard and 2279 Mission.

The Free Store is currently located at 457 Haight (861-6840) but has a tendency to float a little. Cost Plus at Fisherman's Wharf is the easiest rip-off in town.

Furniture
Behind the Goodwill Industries store on Howard St. you can find a construction site where all kinds of items can be found that will convert quickly into furniture. Next to the King Paper Co., Potrero and Alameda (near Whitefront) you can pick up the greatest assortment of wooden cable drums for tables and lamps. Go there when it's dark.

Butchertown, Burke and Jennings is a fantastic junk yard with all kinds of automobile and truck parts. You can purchase stuff for low prices or trade them for other junk.

Pets
ASPCA is located at 2500 16th St.

Books
The San Francisco Public Library is in the Civic Center.

Welfare
Every Wednesday at 8:00 PM a Welfare Rights Group meets at 409 Clayton (621-9553). People there can help prepare you before you head for the line at the Welfare Office. The line is at 585 Bush.

Blood Bank
The best blood bank is the San Francisco General Hospital at 22nd Street and Potrero (648-8200). You must be over 21 but they pay $20 a pint.

Food Stamps
Go to 1360 Mission or call 558-5662 for info on the liberal food stamp program.

Bridge Trip
North on the Golden Gate Bridge is a free trip and you have to pay double coming back. So if you're into jumping, approach the bridge from the South. Right Onnnnnnn!

appendix

organizations that serve the people

American Serviceman's Union, Room 538, 156 Fifth Ave., New York, NY—A group that's working to organize American servicemen into a union.

Berkeley Free Church, 2389 Oregon St., Berkeley, California—Publishes a complete list of liberated churches. Write to Berkeley Free Church, Free Church Publications, Box 9177, Berkeley, California 94709. The name of the directory is *Win With Love.*

Black Panther Party, 1048 Peralta, West Oakland, California—A Black revolutionary self-defense organization. They are a national party that has started free breakfast programs, free clinics, liberation schools and related projects.

Boston Area Ecology Action, 925 Mass. Ave., Cambridge, Mass.—They work to raise ecological consciousness through guerrilla theater, public school education, use of power and land resources, and supermarket resistance.

Bread and Roses, 1145 Mass. Ave., Cambridge, Mass.—A socialist women's liberation organization composed of work and discussion collectives.

Cooperative Services, Inc., 7404 Woodward, Detroit, Michigan—Helps start co-ops and provides services once they are on their feet.

Gay Liberation Front, 2398 Bancroft, Berkeley, California—Working to educate about homosexuality and organizing the gay community in a fight against oppression. Literature available.

The G.I. Office, PO Box 9746, Washington, D.C. 20015, (202) 244-2831—handles complaints against the military from G.I.s getting a raw deal.

Holding Together, 1230 Queens Road, Berkeley, California 94708—Organizing to aid political fugitives and prisoners.

Movement for a Democratic Military (MDM), 429 J St., San Diego, California—An organization for G.I.s that provides a press service for underground information on military counseling and legal aid; and a packet of information outlining how to organize an area, an underground paper, how to leaflet a base, and how to set up a counseling office.

Movement Speaker's Bureau, 365 W. 42nd St., New York, NY—Handles engagements for radical speakers. They publish a colorful catalogue that describes the speakers and their topics. Send 50¢ to cover the cost of mailing the catalogue.

National Welfare Rights Organization, 1419 H St. NW, Washington, D.C.—The national coalition of local welfare recipient groups. Acts as a center for information, leadership training and other services for affiliated welfare recipient organizations. Also coordinated national actions.

New Mobilization Committee to End the War in Vietnam, 1029 Vermont Ave. NW, Washington, D.C.—The major national coalition of anti-war groups. They organize national demonstrations and have a considerable amount of literature available for organizing.

Radical Student Union, 7105 Hayvenhurst Ave., Van Nuys, California—A group of high school students in the Los Angeles area working to form a student union which would unify people in the area. Has some national contacts.

United American Indian, PO Box 26149, San Francisco, California—Publishes the *Warpath Indian* and organizes around Indian rights.

War Resister's League, 339 Lafayette St., New York, NY—WRL supports draft and tax resistance, publishes radical pacifist literature.

Venceramos Brigade, PO Box 1137, Manhattanville Station, New York, NY—Organizes groups of young people into work brigades for helping with the sugar cane harvest and other agricultural projects in Cuba.

The Weathermen, Times Square, New York, NY—Organizes bombings, political assassinations, jail breaks, bank robberies and other activities. There is one inside the vault of every Bank of Amerika waiting to turn you on. Go there soon.

White Panther Party, 1520 Hill St., Ann Arbor, Michigan—A national Marxist—Leninist **cadre-building** organization organizing the youth culture into a new nation (Woodstock Nation). They publish the exciting new *Sun/Dance* paper.

Women's Center, 36 West 22nd St., New York, NY—A meeting place for women's liberation groups throughout the country. Literature is available as well as help in starting a local women's liberation group.

Young Lords Party, 1768 Madison Ave., New York, NY—A national Puerto Rican organization. They want freedom for their people as well as an independent socialist Puerto Rico. They publish the paper *Palante,* organize rent strikes, medical clinics and street demonstrations.

Young Patriots, 4400 N. Sheridan, Chicago, Ill.—A group of revolutionary greasers engaged in community organizing in Chicago. They publish the paper *Rising Up Angry.*

Youth International Party, PO Box C, Old Chelsea Station, New York, NY 10011—The national communications center for Yippie chapter, collectives and gangs, organizing the destruction of the Empire. Provides posters, flags, buttons to Yippie chapters for a small amount. Also send out a Dope Sheet.

A complete list of organizations such as these can be obtained by writing to U.S. Directory Service, Research Guides and Directories, PO Box 1832, Kansas City, Mo. 64141. Request the *Guide to the American Left.* ($4.00)

other books worth stealing

SURVIVE!

CHAPTER 1: FREE FOOD

Bradford Angier, GOURMET COOKING FOR FREE, Stackpole Books, Cameron & Kelker Streets, Harrisburg, Pennsylvania 17105, 1970; 190 pp.; $4.95. There's free food around you waiting to be eaten. Learn how to cook what's already there.

COOKING GOOD FOOD, The Order of the Universe Pub, Box 203, Prudential Center Station, Boston, Mass. 02199, 34 pp.; $1.50. Eastern recipes and ways of preparing different foods.

COOKING WITH GRAINS AND VEGETABLES PLUS, The Order of the Universe Pub, Box 203, Prudential Center Station, Boston, Mass. 02199, 29 pp.; $1.00. Mystical, health food freaks will dig this book.

Euell Gibbons, *STALKING THE WILD ASPARAGUS,* David McKay Co., New York, 1962; 303 pp.; $2.95. There's free food everywhere. Shows how to identify edible plants and where to locate them.

Marie Roberson Hamm, *THE MONEY IN THE BANK COOKBOOK,* The MacMillan Company 866 Third Ave., New York, NY 10022, 1969; 250 pp.; $1.25. Has hundreds of cheap recipes.

Franklin Jay F. Rosenberg, *THE IMPOVERISHED STUDENTS BOOK OF COOKERY, DRINKERY, AND HOUSEKEEPERY*, Doubleday & Company, 501 Franklin Ave., Garden City, Long Island, New York, 11531, 1965; 48 pp.; $1.50. A short understandable introduction to cheap food preparation.

Marion A. Wood, Katherine W. Harris, *QUANTITY RECIPES*, Cornell Home Economics Extension, New York State College of Human Ecology, Mailing Room, Building 7, Research Park, Cornell University, Ithaca, New York 14850, 1945; 233 pp.; $1.00. Great for large communes.

CHAPTER 2: FREE CLOTHING AND FURNITURE

BOTTLE CUTTER, Fleming Bottle and Jug Cutter, 2110 S.W. 173rd Place, Seattle, Washington 98166, $3.00. A great gimmick. Cuts bottles into useable glasses.

Robert Campbell, *HOW TO WORK WITH TOOLS AND WOOD*, Pocket Books, A Division of Simon & Schuster, Inc., 630 Fifth Ave., New York, NY 10020, 1965; 448 pp.; 75¢. A comprehensive introduction to working with hand tools.

Charles H. Hayward, *CARPENTRY FOR BEGINNERS*, Emerson Book, Inc., 251 W. 19th St., New York, NY 10011. 1969; $4.50. Good book to learn how to make simple tables, chairs, bookcases, etc.

Leo P. McDonnell, *HAND WOODWORKING TOOLS*, Delmar Publishers, Inc., Box 5087, Albany, NY 12205, 1962; 294 pp.; $5.00. A great book on handworking tools. Goes into individual tools in great detail.

John D. Wilson, *PRACTICAL HOUSE CARPENTRY*, McGraw Hill, New York, 1957; $2.95. Methods of construction, building are clearly shown with some good quality illustrations.

CHAPTER 3: FREE TRANSPORTATION

Ed Buryn, *HITCH-HIKING IN EUROPE*, Hannah Associates, San Francisco, California, 1969; 72 pp.; $1.75.

Tom Grimm, *HITCHHIKER'S HANDBOOK*, Vagabond Press, Ltd., PO Box 83, Laguna Beach, California 92652, 1970; 72 pp.; $2.00. Goes into greater depth on the art of hitchhiking.

Peter Kocalanos, *TRAVELER'S DIRECTORY*, Peter Kocalanos, 51-02 39th Ave., Woodside, New York, 11377, 1970; 56 pp.; $3.00. Directory of people you can stay with throughout the world. Write for details. Highly recommended.

CHAPTER 4: FREE LAND

Michael Frome, *NATIONAL PARK GUIDE*, Rand McNally and Company, New York, 1970; 176 pp.; $2.95. A good complete guide to all national parks.

GUIDEBOOK TO CAMPGROUNDS, Rand McNally and Company, New York, 1970; 303 pp.; $3.95. Lists more than 150,000 U.S. and Canadian campgrounds with over 55,000 campsites.

CHAPTER 5: FREE HOUSING

Bradford Angier, *HOW TO BUILD YOUR HOME IN THE WOOD*, Hart Publishing Company, Inc., New York, 1952; 310 pp.; $2.45. Great for freaks who want to build their dream home in the country.

Bradford Angier, *HOW TO STAY ALIVE IN THE WOODS*, The MacMillan Company, 866 Third Ave., New York, NY 10022, 1956; 285 pp.; 95¢. Good book for survival in the forests.

Steve Baer, *DOME COOKBOOK*, Lama Cookbook Fund, Corrales, New Mexico, 1968; 40 pp.; $1.00. If you're into building a dome, this book is for you. Well conceived.

Jeanie Darlington, *GROW YOUR OWN*, The Bookworks, 1611 San Pablo Ave., Berkeley, California 94702, 1970; 87 pp.; $1.75. A great beginner's book on organic farming.

Anthony Greenbank, *THE BOOK OF SURVIVAL*, The New American Library, Inc., 1301 Avenue of the Americas, New York, NY 10019, 1967; 233 pp.; 95¢. This is a practical book. The threats it deals with are close and real; burning buildings, freaked humans, dogs, floods, poisons—genuine homely hazards.

HANDBOOK FOR BUILDING HOMES OF EARTH, U.S. Department of Commerce, Clearinghouse for Federal Scientific and Technical Information, Springfield, Virginia 22151; $3.00. A non-technical account of field experiences with formulas and procedures for different types of earth buildings.

Reginald and Gladys Laubin, *THE INDIAN TIPI*, University of Oklahoma Press, Sales Office, Faculty Exchange, Norman, Oklahoma 73069, 1957; 208 pp.; $4.95. The one and only book on tipis.

LOW-COST WOOD HOMES FOR RURAL AMERICA – CONSTRUCTION MANUAL, Superintendent of Documents, U.S. Government Printing Office, Washington, D.C. 20402, 1969; 112 pp.; $1.00. A good manual with hundreds of groovy drawings on wood house construction.

L.W. Neubauer, *ADOBE CONSTRUCTION METHODS*, Agricultural Publications, 207 University Hall, University of California, Berkeley, California 94720, 1964; 35 pp.;

25¢. (They also have hundreds of other good publications; send for their catalogue.) Gives details on laying bricks, fireplaces, foundations, floors, and walls.

J.I. Rodale and Staff, *THE ENCYCLOPEDIA OF ORGANIC GARDENING*, Rodale Books, Inc., 33 E. Minor St., Emmaus, Pennsylvania 18049, 1968; 1145 pp.; $10.00. A good book for the more advanced organic gardening freaks.

J.I. Rodale and Staff, *HOW TO GROW VEGETABLES AND FRUITS BY THE ORGANIC METHOD*, Rodale Books, Inc., 33 E. Minor St., Emmaus, Pennsylvania 18049, 1961; 926 pp.; $10.00. The Bible of growing your own food.

Calvin Rutstrum, *WILDERNESS CABIN*, The MacMillan Company, Front and Brown Streets, Riverside, New Jersey 08075, 1961; 169 pp.; $5.95. Explains how to go into the woods, and with very few tools, erect a shelter.

SOIL-CEMENT–ITS USE IN BUILDING, United Nations, Sales Section, New York, NY 10017, 1964; 85 pp.; $1.50. Booklet on the stabilization of earth and cement.

WHOLE EARTH CATALOG 558 Santa Cruz Ave., Menlo Park, California 94025, $8.00 a year; 2 big catalogs, 4 $1.00 catalogs (Jan., March, July, Sept.). The Sears Roebuck of the new Nation. Ten years ahead of its time.

CHAPTER 6: FREE EDUCATION

THE BIG ROCK CANDY MOUNTAIN, Portola Institute, Inc., 1115 Merrill St., Menlo Park, California 94025. A new publication similar to the popular Whole Earth Catalog, but devoted to "resources for ecstatic education." The catalogue reviews schools, teaching methods, games, tapes and records. It highlights new approaches that "make the student himself the content of his learning." $4.00 per copy, $18.00 per year subscription—two issues plus four supplements.

EDUCATOR'S GUIDE TO FREE FILMS, Educator's Progress Service, Randolph, Wisconsin 53956, 1968; 784 pp.; $10.75. This is an invaluable reference if you are interested in film education. The book has indices of contents, film listings, cross-index; titles, subject, source and availability.

W. Matthews, R. Bartholmew, *FREE MATERIAL FOR EARTH SCIENCE TEACHERS,* Prentice-Hall, Inc., 70 5th Ave., New York, NY 10011, 1964; $1.50. If you're into science the free materials offered here are great.

NEW SCHOOLS EXCHANGE, 2840 Hidden Valley, Santa Barbara, California 93103—The best single source of information on free schools: where they are, how to start one, problems to anticipate, and almost anything else you need to know.

NEW SCHOOLS MANUAL, New Directions Community School, 445 Tenth St., Richmond, Ca. 94801; $1.00. Explains how one group of free school people have worked out the various problems of setting up a school in California. It deals with such things as credentials, diplomas, incorporation, bookkeeping, admission to college, and taxes.

Gordon Salisbury, *CATALOG OF FREE TEACHING MATERIALS,* Catalog of Free Teaching Materials, PO Box 1075, Ventura, Calif. 93001, 1970; 392 pp.; $2.50. Thousands of posters and pamphlets for free.

Robert L. Schain, Murray Polner, *WHERE TO GET AND TO USE FREE AND INEXPENSIVE TEACHING AIDS,* Atherton Press, 70 5th Ave., New York, NY 10011, $1.95. Offers some interesting shit. Its use is intended for schools and teachers.

J. Pepe Thomas, *FREE AND INEXPENSIVE EDUCATIONAL AIDS*, Dover Publications, Inc., 180 Varick Street, New York, NY 10014, 1962; $1.75. Thousands of posters and pamphlets for free.

CHAPTER 7: FREE MEDICAL CARE

Lawrence Lader, *ABORTION*, Beacon Paperback, 1960; 264 pp.; $1.95. The best general source of information on the subject.

McGill Students' Society, *BIRTH CONTROL HANDBOOK*, Students' Society of McGill University, 3480 McTavish St., Montreal, Quebec, Canada, 1969; 46 pp.; individual copies for postage—10¢. Fantastic. Best book on birth control available.

Eugene Schoenfeld, *DEAR DOCTOR HIPPOCRATES* Grove Press, New York, 1968; 112 pp.; 95¢. Questions and answers on stuff you might want to know but don't know who to ask about medical problems.

CHAPTER 8: FREE COMMUNICATION

Free, *REVOLUTION FOR THE HELL OF IT*, Pocket Books, 1968; 271 pp.; $1.25. Good ideas on communication especially television, guerrilla theater and nose-picking. Written by a close friend.

GUERRILLA STREET THEATRE, A collection of 28 guerrilla and street theatre pieces are available by sending a large self-addressed, stamped envelope (24¢) to Henry Lesnick, 915 West End Ave., Apt. 8F, New York, NY 10025.

Joe McGinniss, *THE SELLING OF THE PRESIDENT 1968*, Trident Press, 1969, Pocket Books, 1970, 278 pp.; $1.25. Gives a good understanding of the use of T.V.

Marshall McLuhan, *MECHANICAL BRIDE*, Beacon Press, 239 pp.; 1961; $2.95. Essential reading.

Marshall McLuhan, *UNDERSTANDING MEDIA: THE EXTENSIONS OF MAN,* McGraw Hill Publications, 1965; 346 pp.; $1.95. The classic in this field.

CHAPTER 10: FREE MONEY

ENCYCLOPEDIA OF U.S. GOVERNMENT BENEFITS, William H. Wise & Co. Inc., 336 Mountain Road, Union City, New Jersey 07087, $10.00. The Feds do not advertise these programs very much. To find out if you're eligible for benefits or have access to some service, you have to do a lot of research. This book helps.

Marianna O. Lewis, Ed. *THE FOUNDATION DIRECTORY,* Russell Sage Foundation, 230 Park Ave., New York, New York 10017, 1967; 1198 pp.; $12.00. The reference book of foundations. Gives addresses, finances, offices, purposes, and activities.

J. Richard Taft, *UNDERSTANDING FOUNDATIONS,* McGraw-Hill Book Company, Princeton Road, Highstown, New Jersey 08520, 1967; 205 pp.; $2.95. It tells you some about how to raise money and where to look.

CHAPTER 11: FREE DOPE

John Dominick, *THE DRUG BUST,* The Light Company, 259 W. 15th St., New York, NY 10011, 1970, 96 pp.; $1.00. The most complete coverage of what to do if, and how not to be.

Bill Drake, *THE CULTIVATOR'S HANDBOOK OF MARIJUANA,* The Augur Publishing Company, Room 202, 115 E. 11th, Eugene, Oregon 97401, 1970; 88 pp.; $2.50. Explains how and why grass grows.

David Ebin, *THE DRUG EXPERIENCE,* Grove Press, Inc., New York, 1961; 385 pp.; $1.75. Describes what happens when you take drugs.

Dave Fleming, *THE COMPLETE GUIDE TO GROWING MARIJUANA*, Sundance Press, PO Box 99393, San Francisco, California 94109, 1970; 43 pp.; $1.00. A great complete guide that makes clear all the aspects of growing your own.

Richard R. Lingeman, *DRUGS FROM A TO Z: A DICTIONARY*, McGraw Hill Books Company, New York, 1969; 277 pp. Lists drugs that get you high.

Panama Rose, THE HASHISH COOKBOOK, Gnaoua 1966; 20 pp.; $1.65. For the yippies who like to eat and get high at the same time.

John Rosevear, *POT*, Citadel Press, 222 Park Avenue South, New York, NY 10003, 1970; 160 pp.; $1.95. Gives good description of the hows, wheres, and whys of pot.

TRIP OUT BOOK, Trips Unlimited, Box 36347–CN, Hollywood, California, 90036. $2.00. Gives the formulas for LSD, mescalene, DMT, peyote, and cannabis extract.

CHAPTER 12: FREEBIES (ASSORTED)

THE CANYON COLLECTIVE, PO Box 78, Canyon, California 94516, 1970; 24 pp.; 5¢ . This great tabloid covers a wide range of topics related to building alternative structures and struggle.

CONSUMER'S REPORTS, Consumer Union, Mount Vernon, NY 10550. $6.00/year (monthly). Whenever you buy something, check out consumer's reports. They tell you the best buys for your money.

Mike and Marilyn Ferguson, *CHAMPAGNE LIVING ON A BEER BUDGET*, G.P. Putnam's Sons, 200 Madison Ave., New York, NY 10016. 1968; 247 pp.; 75¢. Similar to *HOW TO LIVE ON NOTHING*.

Frederick O'Hara, *OVER 2,000 FREE PUBLICATIONS*,

The New American Library, 1301 Avenue of the Americas, New York, NY 10019, 1968; 352 pp.; 95¢. Worth picking up for a reference book.

Joan Ranson Shortney, *HOW TO LIVE ON NOTHING*, Simon & Schuster, New York, NY, 1961; 336 pp.; 75¢. A good how-to-do-it book.

VOCATIONS FOR SOCIAL CHANGE, Vocations for Social Change, Inc., Canyon, California 94516. Send a donation for this newsletter printed bi-monthly by great people. It seeks to establish and inform people of alternatives.

Mort Weisinger, *1001 VALUABLE THINGS YOU CAN GET FREE*, Bantam Books, New York, 1968; 163 pp.; 75¢. Lots of crap, but some good stuff. Worth getting.

FIGHT!

CHAPTER 1: TELL IT ALL, BROTHERS AND SISTERS

EVERY SOLDIER A SHITWORKER AND EVERY SHITWORKER A SOLDIER, ILS, 1925 Grove St., 16 pp.; 25¢. It covers basic office skills such as press releases, press conferences, preparing leaflets and posters, and developing working relations with the straight press.

HOW TO MANUAL: POSTERS, Agitprop Literature Programme, 160 N. Gower St., London, NW 1. $1.25. Silkscreening, how to start a workshop, paper, and all that's necessary to print good quality posters. Agitprop also puts out other How To Do It Manuals of excellent quality for a quarter each. Send for *STREET THEATRE, LOCAL JOURNAL, PRINTING, LEAFLETS, FILMS, PRESS PUBLICITY, POWER RESEARCH GUIDE*.

HOW TO START A COMMUNITY NEWSPAPER, HOW TO SUSTAIN A G.I. UNDERGROUND PAPER, Vocations for Social Change, Canyon, California 94516, 25¢ If you're thinking of starting a G.I. or a community newspaper, these articles offer information on the finances, distribution and printing.

HOW TO START A HIGH SCHOOL UNDERGROUND PAPER, CHIPS, 530 North Brainard St., Naperville, Ill. 60540; 25¢. Put out by high school students, it explains in clear detail how to put together an exciting paper.

HOW TO START AN UNDERGROUND PAPER, Underground Press Syndicate, Box 26, Village PO, New York, NY 10014. Send postage. Covers printing, distribution, layouts, and graphics.

J. Ben Liebeiman, *PRINTING AS A HOBBY*, Signet–New American Library, 1963; 128 pp.; 95¢ . A good book for beginners with little money.

CHAPTER 3: DEMONSTRATIONS

DEMONSTRATION GUIDELINES, New York Civil Liberties Union, 156 Fifth Ave., New York, NY 10010, 1970; 5¢ . A nice little booklet which goes in the legalities of picketing, leafleting, sound equipment, etc. in demonstrations.

CHAPTER 4: TRASHING
General Alberto Bayo, *150 QUESTIONS FOR A GUERRILLA*, Panther Publications, Box 369, Boulder, Colorado, 80302, 1963; 86pp.; $2.00*

Captain S.J. Cuthbert, *WE SHALL FIGHT IN THE STREETS*, Panther Publications, Box 369, Boulder, Colorado 80302, $2.00. Explains how to turn a city into a death trap. Subjects covered are demolition, training and arms equipment for fighting in cities.

Major H. von Dach Bern, *TOTAL RESISTANCE,* Panther Publications, Box 369, Boulder, Colorado, 80302, 1965; 173 pp.; $6.50. Highly readable while at the same time being very thorough. Has great illustrations and is well worth the bread.

Che Guevara, *GUERRILLA WARFARE,* Vintage Books, New York, 1961; 133 pp.; $1.65. A good manual, especially on the psychological aspect applied in warfare.

George Hunter, *HOW TO DEFEND YOURSELF, YOUR FAMILY AND YOUR HOME, A COMPLETE GUIDE TO SELF-PROTECTION,* David McKay Co., Inc., 1970; 307 pp.; $6.95. Although right-wingy in tone, this is an excellent guide to security systems, including home protection, unarmed and armed self-defense. Very worthwhile reading.

"Yank" Berk Levy, *GUERRILLA WARFARE,* Panther Publications, Box 369, Boulder, Colorado 80302, 1964; 119 pp.; $2.00. Written for the English Home Guard when England was threatened by Nazi invasion. An easy to read book that's very useful in urban situations.

Carlos Marighella, *MINIMANUAL OF THE URBAN GUERRILLA,* British-Tricontinental Organization, 15 Lawn Road, London NW 3, England, 1969, 40 pp.; $1.25. A great manual describing how to wage effective warfare in the large urban centers. Written by the famed Brazillian revolutionary.

RIOT AND DISASTER CONTROL (FM19-15), Normount Armament Co., Box 211, Forest Grove, Oregon 97116, 1967, 230 pp.; $3.00. Shows all the formations the pigs use in trying to prevent people from trashing.

*Panther Publications has changed its name to PALADIN PRESS to avoid confusion with radical groups.

CHAPTER 5: PEOPLE'S CHEMISTRY*

BOOBYTRAPS (FM 5-31), Army, 180 pp.; $3.50. Principles of construction, methods of use, detection, installation, removal, triggering.

DuPont, *BLASTERS HANDBOOK*, 1967; 524 pp.; $6.00. Complete details on mining, blasting, fuses, "Prima cord," black powder, electric firing, precautions.

EXPLOSIVES & DEMOLITION (FM 5-25), Army, 215 pp.; $4.00. Handling and use of all types of explosives.

Stoffel, *EXPLOSIVES & HOMEMADE BOMBS*, 92 pp.; $5.50. Methods of construction, triggering fusing, deactivation, evacuation.

All the above four books can be gotten by writing the Adobe Hacienda, Route 3, Box 517, Glendale, Arizona 85301.

BRITISH TEXTBOOK OF EXPLOSIVES, 42 pp.; $1.50. Clear and concise coverage of the basics of explosives.

DEMOLITION MATERIALS (TM-1946), 166 pp.; $3.50; A catalogue of U.S. demolition materials and devices, military and civilian.

*Most of these heavy books and equipment come from companies with neo-fascist mentality. For years they have been supplying their products not just to police departments and the armed forces, but also to right-wing organizations such as the Klu Klux Klan and the Minutemen. The government never paid any attention to their operations. Now that revolutionary violence has become commonplace, these firms have been under congressional attack. It would be advisable when writing for stuff, to use fictitious names and cool addresses. It also is not advisable to say you need the material for your Weatherman study group. Try and sound like a pig writing for information in order to have an understanding of what the radicals are learning so as to better combat them. That seems to be the successful approach. When you get a good book, make some copies and get it out to others. It will not be long before the government ends this traffic and we have to print all our own stuff. Be advised!

GUIDE TO VIETCONG BOOBYTRAPS & EXPLOSIVE DEVICES (DAPAM 381-11) 100 pp.; $2.50. Great illustrations and data on grenades, mines, fuses and firing devices.

MILITARY MATERIALS (TM-1910/TO 11A-1-34) 350 pp.; $6.00. An encyclopedia on the subject of explosives.

The above four books can be purchased by writing Normount Armament Co., Box 217, Forest Grove, Oregon, 97116. It's good to say you're a ROTC student when ordering.

THE CUTTING, PROCESSING AND CURING OF PORK, anonymous underground free publication 30-40 pp.; 1970. The most complete and reliable information available on bombing formulas, timing devices, how to rig a bomb to an automobile and other practical information. Good emphasis on safety factors. The most revolutionary work available.

SPECIAL FORCES DEMOLITION TECHNIQUES, Panther Publications, Box 369, Boulder, Colorado 80302, 67 pp.; $3.50. Gives the latest demo techniques.

UNCONVENTIONAL WARFARE DEVICES AND TECHNIQUES, Army Manual TM 31-200-1, Currently the government has stopped distribution of this hot item. Available only through Panther Publications, Boulder, Colorado, 234 pp.; $10.00. The most comprehensive and up-to-date manual on the subject. Especially good on homemade devices.

Catalogues

Bilton Products, PO Box 28, Riveredge, NJ 07661. (Books on pyrotechnics, formulas, fireworks casings, 2 shot motor barrels, professional tools, fuses and pro. fireworks kits.)

Estes Industries, Inc., PO Box 227, Penrose, Colorado 81240. (Free catalogue of rockets-max. thrust cap. 7 lbs. for 3 seconds.)

Arthur Kill Pub. Co., Staten Island, NY 10309. (Several books on tear gas formulas, grenades, thermite and explosives formulas. Free catalogue.)

Scientific Enterprises, PO Box 137, Pompton Lakes, NJ 07442. (Books on fireworks, explosives, formulas, etc. Catalog free.)

William H. Zeller, 1416 Kiel Highway, Audson, Mich. 49247. (Technical publications as well as fuses, exothermic ignition wire, and other equipment) Catalog sent for $1.

CHAPTER 6: FIRST AID FOR STREET FIGHTERS

H. Brainard, *CURRENT DIAGNOSIS AND TREATMENT*, Lange Medical Publications, Drawer L, Los Altos, Calif. 94022, $9.50. Describes treatment for hundreds of common injuries. Useful in the training of street medics and as a text in first aid classes for revolutionaries.

MEDICAL CADRE, ILS, 1925 Grove St., Berkeley, Calif., 25¢ . Explains basic first aid for demonstrations and how to go about setting up medical centers.

J.L. Wilson, *HANDBOOK OF SURGERY*, Lange Medical Publications, Drawer L, Los Altos, Calif. 94022, $6.00. Great for those that want to become good in handy medical care.

CHAPTER 7: HIP POCKET LAW

Allan Blackman, *FACE TO FACE WITH YOUR DRAFT BOARD*, World Without War Council, 1730 Grove St., Berkeley, Calif. 94709, 1969; 90 pp.; 95¢ . A guide to personal appearances, this book is designed for conscientious objectors and is valuable to all men facing a personal appearance before their draft board. It helps to clarify fundamental beliefs while assisting the reader in obtaining the classification he wants and deserves.

Kathy Boudin, Brian Glick, Eleanor Raskin, Gustin Reichbach, *THE BUST BOOK,* Grove Press, New York, 1970; 159 pp.; $1.25. A people's law book. Tells you how to handle yourself in all kinds of pig hassles.

THE DRAFT PHYSICAL, Brooklyn Bridge Press, PO Box 1894, Brooklyn, NY 11202, 1970; 12 pp.; $1.00. Lists all the physical and psychological defects that would disqualify you from the draft.

Tuli Kupferberg & Robert Bashlow, *1001 WAYS TO BEAT THE DRAFT,* Grove Press, New York, 1967;75¢. A book of the absurd, but then again, so is the Army.

Bob Lefcourt, ed. *LAW AGAINST THE PEOPLE: ESSAYS TO DEMYSTIFY LAW, ORDER AND THE COURTS,* Random House, Spring 1971 publication. The radical lawyers and some of their defendants attack the law and the legal system.

MANUAL FOR DRAFT-AGE IMMIGRANTS TO CANADA, Toronto Anti-Draft Program, PO Box 41, Station K, Toronto 315, Ontario, Canada. 1968; 105 pp.; $2.00. For those planning to split this book is a must.

MOVEMENT LEGAL DEFENSE, International Liberation School, 1925 Grove St., Berkeley, Calif., 50¢. Explains how the criminal process works so that people arrested for their political actions will be able to better plan their strategy and tactics.

Robert S. Rubin, *THE DRAFTEE'S GUIDE,* Grove Press, New York, 1970; 38 pp.; $1.75. Explains the legal rights of G.I.'s. Goes into detail on military law, court-martial, how to file a complaint, etc. Also includes lawyer referral services and counseling organizations.

David Suttler, *IV-F A GUIDE TO DRAFT EXEMPTION*, Grove Press, Inc., New York, NY, 1970; 171 pp.; $1.50. Explains how to obtain that ever lovin IV-F.

Arlo Tatum, *HANDBOOK FOR CONSCIENTIOUS OBJECTORS*, World Without War Council, 1730 Grove St., Berkeley, Calif. 94709. 110 pp.; 1968; $1.00. A guide to the legal means of becoming a conscientious objector under Selective Service Regulations.

CHAPTER 8: STEAL NOW, PAY NEVER

Alfred Alexander, Val Moolman, *STEALING*, Cornerstone Library, Inc., 630 5th Ave., New York, NY 10020., 1966; 128 pp.; $1.00. Learn how to cheat, rob, steal, hustle, by reading this book and learning the tricks of the trade.

Elihu Blotwick, "How to Counterfeit Credit Cards and Get Away With It," *SCANLON'S MAGAZINE,* Volume 1, Number 4, June 1970; pp. 21-28. Gives good tips but leaves out a few steps.

Mary O. Cameron, *BOOSTER AND THE SNITCH,* MacMillan Company, 866 3rd Ave., New York, NY 10032. 1964; $5.95. Techniques are described in an easily understood manner.

Sargent J. Curtis, *MODERN RETAIL SECURITY,* Thomas C.C. Publisher, 301-327 E. Laurence Ave., Springfield, Ill. 62707., 1960; $25.00. Describes electronic security devices used in stores.

Loren E. Edwards, *SHOPLIFTING AND SHRINKAGE, PROTECTION FOR STORES,* Thomas Publishing Co., 461 Eighth Ave., New York, NY 10001; 1958, $7.50. Great detail on how to stop fast sneaky hands, or if read backwards, how to get everything in a store without getting caught.

Lizzie Liftwell, *RIP-OFF*, Rat, 241 E. 14th St., New York, NY, 2/6/70; 26 pp.; 25¢ . Gives great tips for women shoplifters.

Pearl Paperhanger, *MORE RIP-OFF*, Rat, 241 E. 14th St., New York, NY, 3/21/70; 30 pp.; 25¢ . The ins and outs of credit cards and passing bad checks.

David W. Mauer, *WHIZ MOB*, College & University Press, 263 Chapel St., New Haven, Conn. 06513, 1964; $1.95. Deals with the art of pickpocketing.

Charles P. Rudnitsky, L.M. Wolff, *HOW TO STOP PILFERAGE IN BUSINESS AND INDUSTRY*, Pilot Books, Box 141, Grand Marais, Mich. 49839.; $2.00. For those workers who feel the boss owes him something.

Edwin H. Sutherland, *PROFESSIONAL THIEF*, University of Chicago Press, 5750 Ellis Ave., Chicago, Ill. 60637, 1956; $1.95. What a thief does on the job.

CHAPTER 10: PIECE NOW

BASIC PISTOL MARKSMANSHIP, BASIC RIFLE MARKSMANSHIP and *BASIC SHOTGUN MARKSMANSHIP*, all good booklets that can be gotten by writing the National Rifle Association, 1600 Rhode Island Ave. NW, Washington, D.C. 20036. They cost 25¢ each.

FIREARMS AND SELF DEFENSE, International Liberation School, 1925 Grove St., Berkeley, Calif., 1969; 40 pp.; 50¢ . A great book for beginners. All aspects of guns in an easy-to-understand fashion.

SGM Frank A. Mayer, *SPECIAL FORCES FOREIGN WEAPONS HANDBOOK*, Panther Publications, Box

369, Boulder, Colorado, 1970; 180 pp.; $12.95. A super glossary of different weapons used around the world.

SHOOTER'S BIBLE, Follett Publishing Co., 1010 W. Washington Blvd., Chicago 7, Ill., 1970; 576 pp.; $3.95. Gives complete presentation of new guns and ammo. Has hundreds of illustrations and some good articles on the use of weapons.

W.H.B. Smith, *THE BOOK OF PISTOLS AND REVOLVERS*, Stackpole Books, Cameron & Kelker Streets, Harrisburg, Pa. 17105. $14.95. A very comprehensive book that goes in great detail on hundreds of pistols and revolvers used throughout the world. $16.95.

W.H.B. Smith, *SMALL ARMS OF THE WORLD*, Stackpole Books, Cameron & Kelker Streets, Harrisburg, Pa. 17105. A good complete guide to all the small firearms of the world. $16.95.

L.R. Wallack, *THE ANATOMY OF FIREARMS*, Simon & Schuster, 630 5th Ave., New York, NY 10020. $6.95. With detailed illustrations, it goes into the complete breakdown of the more widely used firearms.

Other sources

There are also many small books dealing with one firearm, such as the M-1 Garand, and Carbine, Browning Hi-Power pistol, etc., which go into detailed field stripping, history, overhauling, etc. They are put out by publishing houses such as Panther Publications, Box 369, Boulder, Colorado 80302 or The Adobe Hacienda, Route 3, Box 517, Glendale, Arizona 85301.

Pulse Publications, Dept 6, P.O. Box 11211, Indianapolis, Ind., 46201. Wholesale gun directory and how to become a firearms dealer. 2nd edition contains names of wholesale gun dealers. Federal Firearms License application form and how to fill it out is included.

Harpers Ferry Ordinance, 180 N. Wacker Drive, Room 605, Chicago, Ill. 60606. An old friend, Clark Kissinger, runs this unique gun shop in Chicago and encourages radicals to write him or drop in.

CHAPTER 11: LIVING UNDERGROUND

Barbara Berk, *FIRST BOOK OF STAGE, COSTUME AND MAKE-UP*, Franklin Watis, Inc., Sub. of Grober, 575 Lexington Ave., New York, NY 10022, 1954; $1.95. Cosmetics, fake hair, costumes, are explained here to make it relevant to fish in the sea.

Richard Carson, *STAGE MAKEUP*, Meredith Press, 250 Park Ave., New York, NY 10017, $7.50. Explains in detail the use of theatrical make-up.

HOW TO AVOID ELECTRONIC EAVESDROPPING & PRIVACY INVASION, $2.98. Investigator Information Service, 806 Robertson Blvd., L.A. Calif. 90035. How to listen and detect those devices that Big Brother used to bug you.

LOCKSMITHING, Locksmithing Institute, Little Falls, NJ 07424. Everything you'll want to know about locks.

SUBMINIATURE ELECTRONIC DEVICES CATALOG, Ace Electronics, 11500 BN W. Seventh Ave., Miami, Fla. 33168.

SURVIVAL EVASION AND ESCAPE, Superintendent of Documents, U.S. Government Printing Office, Washington, D.C. 20402. For those who plan to jump bail or escape from jail.

Form Distributors, PO Box 893, League City, Texas 77573. Birth Certificates. . .etc. Customized forms printed—$15.00 first one, regular price after—1,400 standardized forms, 2 for $1.00.

International Police Equipment Co., 906 S. Robertson Blvd., L.A., Calif. 90035. Police badges, professional I.D. cards, tech, manuals, black light equipment, bug detectors, pin tumbler lock picking gun, police radio monitors, miniature cameras, recorders, etc.

The communications of the Weatherman Underground are all superb examples of how to get information that masses of young people can relate to above ground. Check your local underground newspapers and see if they regularly carry the communications.

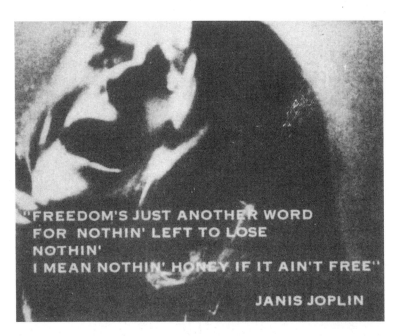

"FREEDOM'S JUST ANOTHER WORD
FOR NOTHIN' LEFT TO LOSE
NOTHIN'
I MEAN NOTHIN' HONEY IF IT AIN'T FREE"

JANIS JOPLIN

INDEX

books on printing, 297-98
Post office employment, as source of stolen credit cards, 208
Pot. See Grass; Dope
Power failures, creating, 212
Pregnancy tests, 62
Press conferences, 67-70; interviews when living underground 226
Press, underground. See Newspapers, underground
Pressure points, body, 166
Pricing, of underground papers, 120
Priest's garb. See Clergy, impersonating
Printing, community: in Chicago, 263; in San Francisco, 282
Printing workshop, starting, 113-16; books on, 297-98
Prophylactic, contraceptive, 61, 63
Prop room, 2, 6
Psychiatric care. See Mental health
Psychiatric deferment, 191-93
Plamondon, Pun, 221
Publicity, for demonstrations, 147-48
Public land. See Land, free
Public Welfare Directory, 86
Published Ordinaces: Firearms, U.S. government publication, 219

Radio Free People, 73
Radio Free New York, WBAI, 252
Radio, guerrilla, 73, 139-41
Radio Hanoi, 145
Radio shows, call-in, 70
Receipt switching, airline, 38
Recipes, 16-19; books, 288-89
Records, free, 84-85
Rector, James, 45
Regan, Ronald, 45
Rental agencies, 50
Restaurants, ripping-off, 2-5
Revolvers. See Handguns
Rhythm method of birth control, 61
Rifles, 216-17. See also Firearms

Rip-offs, various, 90-91; books on, 304-05. See also Shoplifting;Jobs and theft,
Rice and Cong Sauce, recipe, 18
Rides, local information, 32
Rifles, 216-17. See also Firearms
Riot gear, purchasing, 163
Roach-in-the-plate gambit, 3-4
Road Hog Crispies, recipe, 16
Rock concerts, 69-70, 221-22
Rubber tires, making sandals of, 22-23
Rudd, Mark, 221
Runaway houses, 47
Rural living, 51-54

Safe deposit box and dead fish, 211-12
Safety measures: in bomb handling, 170-79, passim; in gun handling, 218
Sailors, and free food, 6
Salvation Army and cheap clothing, 22
Sandals, how to make, 22-23
San Francisco, 275-283
"say-so" bust, 27-28
Schools, free. See Education, free
Searches, legal, 187, 189
Security, monetary, 106-07; when living underground, 223
Self-defense, 160, 163-68; books on, 299
Shock, symptoms and treatment, 182
Shoes; for demonstrations, 148; making sandals, 22-23; stealing from bowling alleys, 22
Shoplifting, 7-10, 199-205; books on, 304-05. See also Rip-offs
Shopping bags, dummy, 204
Shotguns, 217-218. See also Firearms
Shots, free, 59
Shrapnel bombs, 179
Signs: use in communication, 70; for hitch-hiking, 28-29; as weapons, 156
Silk screening, 115-16
Sinclair, John, 100
Skyjacking, 39
Slings, weapons, 161
Slingshots, 160-61